open water sport diver manual

ii

International Standard Book Number 0-88487-115-0

©Jeppesen Sanderson, Inc., 1975, 1976, 1978, 1984, 1986, 1989
All Rights Reserved

First Edition
First Printing May 1975
Second Printing July 1975
Third Printing January 1976
Fourth Printing April 1976

Second Edition
Fifth Printing October 1976
Sixth Printing May 1977

Third Edition
Seventh Printing May 1978
Eighth Printing May 1979
Ninth Printing August 1981

Fourth Edition
Tenth Printing June 1984
Eleventh Printing December 1986
Twelfth Printing January 1989

55 Inverness Drive East
Englewood, Colorado U.S.A. 80112-5498

foreword

Welcome to the exciting and spectacular world of underwater diving. You are going to see and do things that go far beyond your dreams and expectations. Diving is never adequately described; it must be experienced.

Divers are penetrating what could prove to be man's last frontier on earth. Three-fourths of our planet's surface is covered with water, and most of it is not only unexplored, but has not even been seen by man. This thrilling realm is open to every certified diver in the world. Becoming a certified diver permits you to join an international diving community that explores, collects, photographs, works, and does research in both salt water and fresh water.

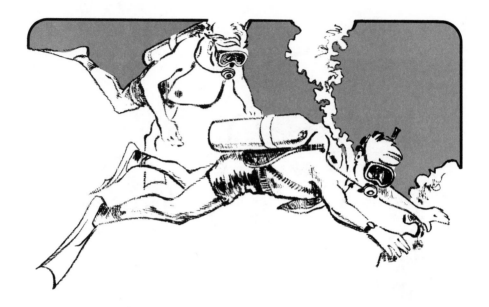

Diving is not limited to a few "uniquely trained specialists." Anyone with ordinary swimming ability and normal physical fitness can gain certification with adequate instruction. Today's certified diver is educated and highly trained in the classroom, pool, and open water.

A certified *skin diver* is competent in the use of the mask, fins, snorkel, and buoyancy compensator during breath-hold dives. The certified *scuba diver,* in addition, has the knowledge and skill of using underwater breathing equipment. (Scuba is a word coined from the first letters of **S**elf-**C**ontained **U**nderwater **B**reathing **A**pparatus.) Dive shops and air stations will not sell air or rent equipment to divers who cannot show proof of certification. In addition, some dive shops and charter boat operators require divers to present a diver logbook to document currency and experience level.

There are several recognized agencies and instructor organizations that issue certification. They issue a "C" card when a student has passed an examination and has completed the required hours of combined classroom and water training.

This Manual and its supporting Workbook are designed to supplement, under the guidance of a qualified instructor, classroom instruction and water training. Together these components form a *multimedia instructional program* with the goal of attaining certification as a Sport Diver.

This approach uses a *variety* of teaching tools and media forms to help you learn. The media chosen may vary and include — but not be limited to — such things as: textbooks, models, slides, audio tapes, video tapes, blackboard illustrations, and lectures.

To better understand how it works, let's follow a skill such as normal ascents, through a multimedia sequence. First, the Manual explains ordinary ascent procedures. The artist's rendition of the skill, combined with the workbook exercises, serves to reinforce the text. In class, the instructor goes over the skill again when the Workbook exercises are graded. Underwater photography in the audiovisual presentations shows the same skill with a new visual image and explanation. Review questions following the film reinforce the audiovisual message. Lectures and class discussions show another perspective. Finally, the instructor covers the skill once more during the briefing before the water training session, followed by student performance; first in the pool, then in open water.

An important feature of multimedia learning is the reinforcement of the material through *meaningful repetition.* A particular skill or concept is presented several times throughout the instructional program. Each repetition varies from the previous presentation and continually presents a new slant, or different perspective, on the same subject.

Combining the above tools and techniques results in a *systems approach* which is the heart of the Jeppesen Sport Diver Learning System. When this method is used, multimedia and other teaching tools work together to achieve a specific learning objective. Each component in the system is constructed to match, support, and complement the other parts of the system.

The system approach plays an important part in the *learning rhythm.* After information is received through various media, a skill is performed based on that input. It is a passive and active sequence. You passively read, see, or hear about a skill, then actively perform it.

The objective is to produce competent, knowledgeable open water divers. The audiovisual presentations, reading the manual, instructor lectures, workbook exercises, and homework assignments are all designed to work together. Basic skills are taught in an order that is most useful. The result is a meaningful learning sequence supported by system components which reinforce what has been learned.

Basic Sport Diver information is provided in the Manual in a manner designed to interest the novice and "old timer" alike. Its emphasis is on teaching how to perform in real-life diving situations. You will find that it will be an excellent reference text throughout your diving career.

A look at the Manual's table of contents will quickly define the sections. They are carefully sequenced in a logical order; however, they can be studied independently or in conjunction with other sections. For example, in one study session, the section on *equipment* used for underwater breathing might be combined with the section on the *science* of breathing underwater.

Although basic skills are discussed in the Manual, specific instruction techniques and the "how to do" are left up to the instructor. The Manual is divided into four parts:

PART I — THE EQUIPMENT

Skin and scuba diving equipment is presented in the order in which the student learns its use. The skills and techniques needed by the student to select, maintain, and use the equipment also are included in this part.

PART II — THE DIVER

The diver's mind and body are discussed in Part II. Physics, physiology, and safety procedures are introduced to give a thorough understanding of what the diver can expect underwater and what must be done to safely enjoy this sport.

PART III — THE ENVIRONMENT

The diver is introduced to his surroundings in this part. It builds appreciation for how fresh waters and salt waters were formed, how and why water moves, and water's effect on the diver. A discussion of underwater animals and how man affects their environment also is presented in this part.

PART IV — DIVE ACTIVITIES

The spectrum of skin and scuba diving activities is covered. Dive planning, photography, and advanced wreck and commercial diving are addressed along with a preview of other professional diving careers.

Becoming a qualified diver is easy and enjoyable and is the key to a lifetime of exciting adventure. So let's get started. Good diving!

table of contents

PART I   the equipment

PART II   the diver

PART III   the environment

PART IV   dive activities

PART I the equipment

introduction

With the proper equipment, people can safely and comfortably enter and enjoy a different environment. The right equipment lets people see, move, and breathe easily in water — transforming an alien, sometimes hostile world into a delightful new home.

The waters of the world have always fascinated people, but until recently, only the most highly trained and equipped experts regularly ventured into the sea. Before the 1950s, skin and scuba diving were known to only a few people, for one reason — no equipment. Diving below the surface meant entering a blurry, confusing, and cold place for only a short time. The evolution of sport diving, then, has been primarily dependent on the development of diving equipment. Advances in underwater equipment and technology, once begun, continue to increase so rapidly every year that it is often hard to keep up with the changes.

The diving pioneers, who experimented and invented diving equipment, were curious and brave people who encountered obstacles that demanded solutions. Overcoming each problem required a unique piece of equipment or a special procedure. Through progressive effort and change, sport diving has become established as an exciting, comfortable, and safe sport.

Now that you are beginning sport diver training, it is important that you study each piece of diving equipment. The knowledge gained will allow you to select and use this specialized equipment safely and efficiently.

SKIN DIVING EQUIPMENT

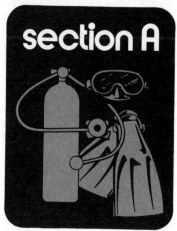

section A

seeing and swimming

- MASK
- FINS
- SNORKEL
- ENTRIES
- SURFACE DIVES

MASK, FINS, SNORKEL, ENTRIES, AND SURFACE DIVES

The major challenges that faced early divers were basic ones of seeing and moving under water. To accomplish this, the basic equipment of the skin diver—the mask, fins, and snorkel—was developed to restore crystal clear vision and to increase the mobility of the swimmer.

MASKS

Try to remember the first time you opened your eyes under water. Everything was blurry, out of focus, and confining. The human eye, especially designed for seeing through the light density of air, does not work well in the heavy medium of water. Surrounding the eyes with air was found to be the simplest solution for attaining underwater visibility. Early divers wore goggles with polished, tortoise-shell lenses, similar to those pictured in figure 1-1. The lenses provided air spaces in front of the eyes which restored vision.

Fig. 1-1 Early Tortoise-Shell Swimming Goggles

Swimming goggles are still available with tempered glass lenses and rubber straps, but these are of no use to today's skin or scuba divers. Goggles can be used safely by surface swimmers to protect their eyes from chlorine and irritants. But when a diver descends even a few feet, the increasing water pressure tends to squeeze the air spaces in the goggles. This is painful and can cause injury at greater depths.

The first goggles solved the vision problem, but they also created a pressure problem that was not solved until about 1865 when the first modern mask was invented. Instead of two small lenses with two airtight spaces, one big lens that covered the eyes and nose in one common air space was used. (See figure 1-2.)

Fig. 1-2 Early Single-Lens Mask

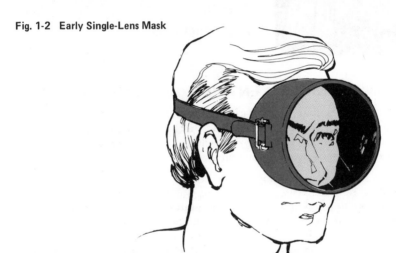

The single-lens mask allows the diver to exhale through the nose to increase the air pressure inside the mask so it equals the water pressure outside the mask. The basic design of this early mask has changed very little.

SELECTING A MASK

There are many types of masks in use today. To help clarify the main differences and to better discuss them, we will create three general classifications: low volume, wide-angle, and a general-use mask. See figure 1-3 for a typical example of each mask.

Low-volume masks are designed to keep the air space inside the mask as small as possible. The lens fits close to your face and has a pocket for your nose. Both skin and scuba divers favor this type of mask, because it is easy to clear water from inside the mask and to equalize pressure.

The wide-angle mask usually has a larger internal volume, which requires more air to clear the mask and to equalize pressure than a low-volume mask. For this reason, it is more commonly used by scuba divers than skin

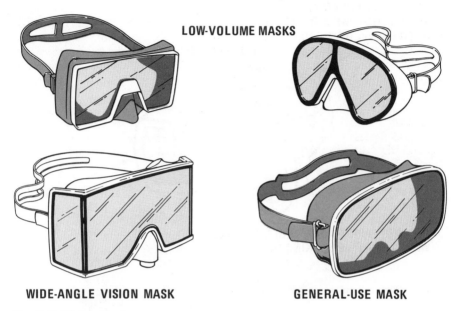

LOW-VOLUME MASKS

WIDE-ANGLE VISION MASK   **GENERAL-USE MASK**

Fig. 1-3 Diving Masks

divers. The advantage of a wide-angle mask is the increase in peripheral vision provided by the two small plates on the sides of the mask. A good compromise between volume and visibility is the general-use mask, shown in figure 1-3. It can be used for both skin and scuba diving.

Clear silicone and black rubber are the common materials used to construct mask skirts and straps. Silicone remains flexible throughout most temperature ranges and allows more light to filter into the mask than with other types. It is hypoallergenic, resistant to ozone deterioration, and requires little care other than rinsing in clear fresh water and an occasional washing with mild soap. Black rubber is durable and provides good service when cared for properly.

WHAT TO LOOK FOR IN A MASK

Once you have decided on a type of mask, look for the following features: (See fig. 1-4.)

1. Make sure the lens is tempered or safety glass. The word "tempered" or "safety" should be printed directly on the lens.
2. The band that holds the lens in place should be made of some type of noncorrosive material, such as hard plastic or stainless steel, and it should be removable in case you need to replace the lens.
3. The mask strap should be easily adjustable with strong buckles and a positive locking device. The strap should also be split to fit over both the upper and lower parts of the back of your head. A one-piece strap slips up or down too easily.

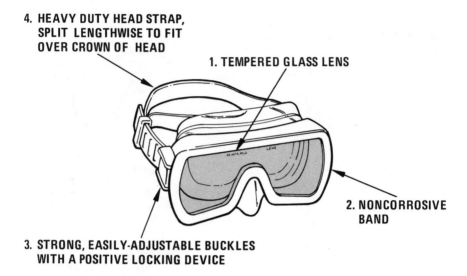

4. HEAVY DUTY HEAD STRAP,
   SPLIT LENGTHWISE TO FIT
   OVER CROWN OF HEAD

1. TEMPERED GLASS LENS

2. NONCORROSIVE
   BAND

3. STRONG, EASILY-ADJUSTABLE BUCKLES
   WITH A POSITIVE LOCKING DEVICE

Fig. 1-4 What to Look for in a Mask

MASK FEATURES

As you descend, water pressure increases. The pressure in the air spaces inside your head must be equalized with the surrounding pressure; otherwise, you will feel pain in your ears or sinuses. Some people can equalize by yawning or swallowing, but many have to hold their nose, close their mouth, and blow lightly. Because of this, all masks have a built-in finger or nose pocket so you can seal off your nostrils to equalize; note figure 1-5. Equalization is discussed in detail in Part II, Section C.

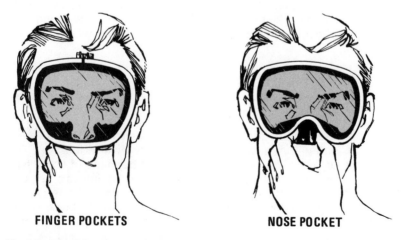

FINGER POCKETS   NOSE POCKET

Fig. 1-5 Equalizing Features for Masks

Masks do not stay perfectly dry inside. Small amounts of water leak in and must be cleared regularly. The purge valve, as shown in figure 1-6, is a feature that helps remove water. It is a one-way valve that lets air and water out of the mask when you exhale, but does not let water enter the mask. The larger the purge valve, the quicker it will clear the mask completely, even if the mask is full of water.

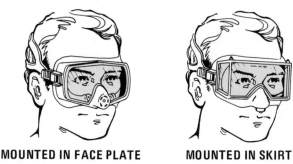

MOUNTED IN FACE PLATE   **MOUNTED IN SKIRT**

Fig. 1-6 Purge Valves

The diver who wears prescription glasses or contact lenses has several options. Many divers prefer masks with built-in corrective lenses. These are available through dive stores and optical companies that specialize in prescription diving masks. Figure 1-7 shows some of the different ways corrective lenses can be used under water. There is no reason why contacts cannot be worn while diving if certain precautions are followed. As in any active sport, losing a lens is always possible, especially if a mask is suddenly flooded. Hard contact lenses are more easily displaced than soft contacts. The buildup and elimination of gas bubbles is another problem associated with contact lenses. Generally, soft contacts and gas permeable lenses minimize the problem. If you are considering contact lenses, check with an ophthalmologist who is familiar with diving considerations.

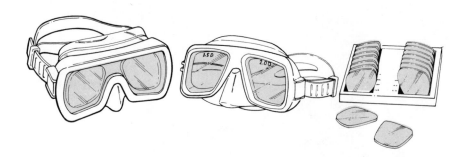

Fig. 1-7 Masks with Corrective Lenses

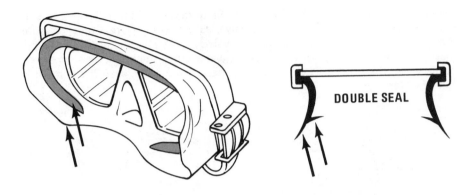

Fig. 1-8 Mask Seal

To keep water from leaking into the mask, the skirt must form a good seal with your face. Most masks incorporate a double seal, as shown in figure 1-8. The seal extends around most of the mask with the exception of just under the nose pocket.

MASK FIT

One of the most important things in selecting the right mask is finding one that fits the size and general shape of your face. The soft rubber skirt of the mask should conform to your face without pinching or pressing harder in one place than another. To make sure a mask fits properly, hold it lightly in place without using the strap. The sealing edge should touch your face everywhere, with no air leaks, gaps, or pressure points. Inhale gently. This should pull the mask close to your face without letting air leak into it. If the fit is good, you will be able to hold it in place with light air pressure alone, as illustrated in figure 1-9. It will feel secure and comfortable. Try this test with several different models until you find the best possible fit.

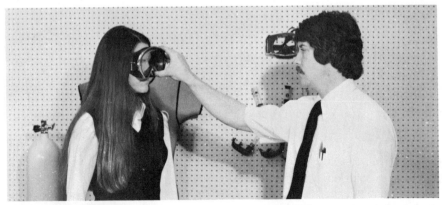

Fig. 1-9 Testing Mask Fit

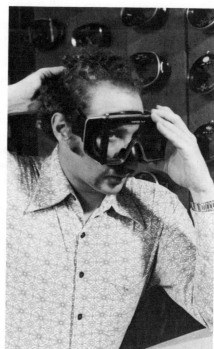

Fig. 1-10 Putting a Mask in Place

MASK USE

A diving mask should have sturdy, easily adjustable strap fasteners attached to both sides. The best and most effective way to put on the mask is to put the mask in place on your face first, and then pull the strap back. (See figure 1-10.) The strap should be worn tightly enough to keep the mask firmly and comfortably in place. A loose strap means the mask will leak and a strap worn too tightly causes headaches.

The position of the strap is very important. The mask may press against your face unevenly if the strap is too low or too high, which could cause leakage. On some masks, it is a good idea to use electrician's tape to hold the strap ends in place after you have it adjusted. This will ensure that your mask will fit immediately when you put it on with no further adjustments needed. When putting the mask on under water, exhale slightly through your nose to avoid the feeling of water being forced into your nostrils.

Before getting the mask wet, be sure to coat the inside of the lens with an anti-fogging solution. Otherwise, the warm humid air inside the mask will condense and fog the lens which is cooled by the surrounding water. Some chemical solutions prevent water droplets and fog from forming in the mask lens. Such things as liquid dishwashing detergent and saliva also work, but usually are not as effective as chemical wetting agents. If the lens fogs over during a dive, let a little water inside the mask to rinse it away.

One skill you must master in order to use a mask effectively is mask clearing—removing all the water from the mask and replacing it with air while under water. This skill is easier than it sounds, even when the mask is completely flooded. By pushing the top part of the mask against your forehead and exhaling quickly and forcefully through your nose, you create a greater pressure inside the mask than out. This forces the air and water out of the bottom of the mask or through a purge valve, as shown in figure 1-11. Exhaled air replaces the water that escapes from inside the mask.

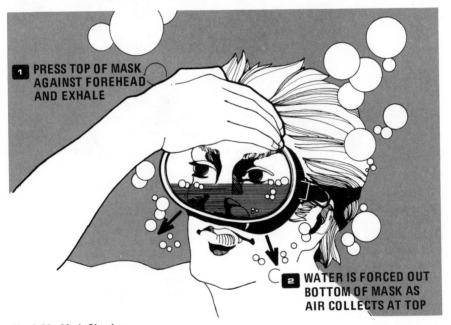

Fig. 1-11 Mask Clearing

When clearing a mask with a large purge valve, the valve should be as low as possible. Large purge valves let all the water drain out, while small purge valves are used for clearing water that seeps in around the nose. Masks with small purge valves should be cleared the normal way. Masks without purge valves can be cleared in almost any position as long as the highest part of the mask is firmly sealed against the face during exhalation. Figure 1-12, for example, shows a diver clearing his mask from the side.

As you descend, you should equalize the pressure inside the mask and inside your ears. To equalize the mask, gently breathe air into it through your nose; otherwise, the increasing water pressure will tend to squeeze the mask against

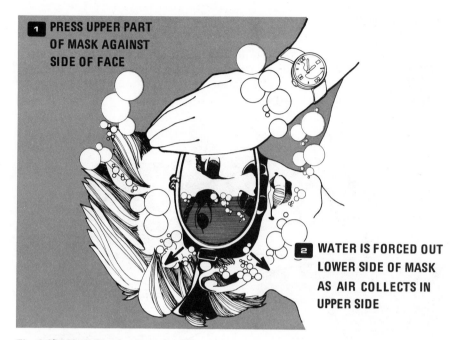

Fig. 1-12 Mask Clearing from the Side

your face. A severe mask squeeze can be painful but is extremely uncommon with trained divers.

To avoid an ear squeeze, use the equalizer pockets in the mask to seal your nose, then blow gently. You can also wiggle your jaw from side to side, swallow, or yawn. Whatever method or combination of methods you use, be careful not to blow too hard—this can damage your ears. Just blow until you feel a fullness in your ears or until any discomfort disappears.

Always equalize before the dive to flex the eustachian tube and prepare it for equalization in the water. If you have problems equalizing your ears in the water, stop periodically or ascend a few feet until the pain disappears or subsides. In any case, do not ignore any discomfort that might develop in your ears. For a closer look at equalizing, see Part II, Section C.

FINS AND FOOTWEAR

Under water, a good swimmer can move fairly well for short periods of time without equipment. But prolonged swimming, even for a highly trained athlete, demands an extraordinary amount of strength and endurance. The advent of rubber foot fins in the 1930's was an important breakthrough because of the increased mobility it gave to skin and scuba divers. Fins substantially increase the power of the naked foot. They enable the diver to swim greater distances for longer periods of time without tiring.

SELECTING FINS

Fins fall into two general categories: the full-foot and the open-heel types, as shown in figure 1-13. Full-foot fins are built like rubber shoes with blades attached. They come in many different shoe sizes, from ½ to size 14. Open-heel fins usually come in four different sizes: small, medium, large, and extra-large.

FULL-FOOT FIN

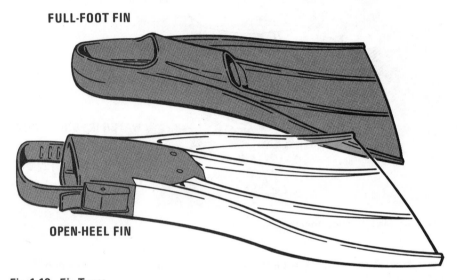

OPEN-HEEL FIN

Fig. 1-13   Fin Types

WHAT TO LOOK FOR IN FINS

Fins with large blades generally are more powerful than those with small, more flexible blades, but you need strong legs to use them for long periods of time. As in selecting the proper mask, it is necessary to know what features to look for when choosing the right fins for your feet. The essential features to consider are as follows:

Materials. Notice the quality of the material and manner of construction. Fin blade material can be black rubber, graphite, polyurethane, thermoplastic, or a composite material. All types are durable and provide good service when cared for properly. Polyurethane and thermoplastic are not as susceptable to ultraviolet and ozone deterioration as black rubber. Thermoplastic blades may warp when exposed to high heat. Fin pockets normally are made of soft, flexible material to increase comfort.

Buoyancy. Some fins sink, some float, and some are neutrally buoyant (neither sink nor float). If you plan to dive in relatively deep water with limited visibility, fins that float might be better since you won't lose them as easily. On the other hand, when diving in clear water, it might be easier to keep track of fins that sink.

Fit. Adjustable heel strap fins have obvious advantages in achieving a perfect fit over fins that are not adjustable. A fin that is too tight can restrict circulation and cause cramps, while a loose-fitting fin can rub, chafe, fall off, or cause cramps from trying to keep it on your foot.

The vented fin blade, pictured in figure 1-14, is another fin design feature worth considering. Vented fins have several slots, or vents, located along the blade to effectively redirect the flow of water through and along the fin. This provides for less tiring leg strokes and gives maximum power. Vented fins are purported to produce more thrust with less effort than fins without vents.

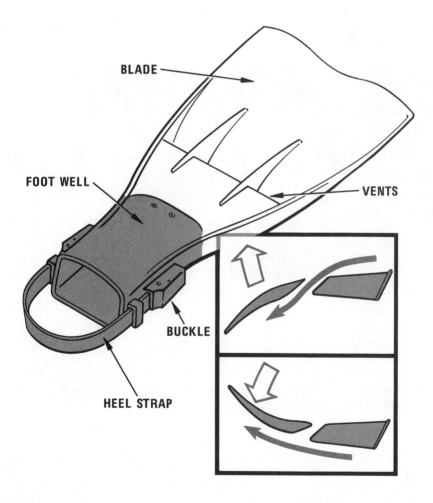

Fig. 1-14   Water Flow through Vented Fins

FIN FIT

When selecting open heel fins, try them on over a pair of wet suit boots. Adjust the straps so the fins are firmly in place, and then try to kick them off, as shown in figure 1-15. They should feel secure without binding, cramping, or pinching. Remember, fins will slip more in the water. If possible, experiment with the fins in water before making a final decision.

Selecting fins that fit properly over boots depends on the size of the foot pocket and the strap. Boots are made out of wet suit material and are necessary for warmth during cold water diving. (See figure 1-16.) Warm water divers also use boots for protection from rocks and coral. The foam neoprene serves as a good cushion between the foot and the fin pocket, and minimizes the possibility of blisters. Tennis shoes and socks are poor substitutes for boots even though both are sometimes used by divers. They do not protect against cramps and cold, and they do not stop sand and other abrasives from causing blisters.

Fig. 1-15 Testing Fin Fit

Fig. 1-16 Wet Suit Boots

FIN USE

There are a few tricks to putting on fins. See figures 1-17 and 1-18 for illustrated examples. Make sure your feet, boots, and fins are wet so the fins will slip on easily. If you are using full-foot fins, fold the heel back to form a "handle" to pull on the fins. With open-heel fins, work the fin over the foot as far as possible and then slip the strap up over your heel.

Few things feel as clumsy as trying to walk with fins on your feet. In fact, walking forward while wearing fins is nearly impossible, as well as being very dangerous. Walking backward in fins on a pool deck, beach, or in shallow water is much easier and safer. Climbing boat or pool ladders should be avoided when wearing fins. The safest approach is to remove them in the water and throw them into the boat or up on the pool deck. If you prefer, hold the fins in your hand, or slip the straps over your wrist when climbing up the ladder.

Fig. 1-17 Putting on Full-Foot Fins

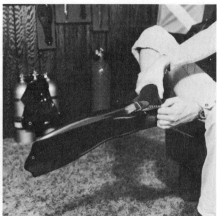
Fig. 1-18 Putting on Open-Heel Fins

When you enter the water, fins become graceful and powerful extensions of your own body. In fact, fins are so effective that your arms and hands are not used when swimming with fins. Instead, you can let your arms hang naturally at your sides, or use your hands for other functions such as exploring or carrying extra equipment.

Kicking

The flutter kick, pictured in figure 1-19, is the most widely used kick in diving. It is a slow, steady kick that moves a lot of water with each stroke. Legs are kept as straight as practical and ankles swing back and forth like hinges. There is no reason to swim fast—doubling your speed in water takes four times the effort. When doing the flutter kick at the surface, be sure to keep your legs and fins well under water.

Fig. 1-19 Flutter Kick

The scissors kick is sometimes used for variation. The first stroke is almost identical to the flutter kick. Notice the similarity in figure 1-20. The power stroke, however, stops when your feet come together. After gliding for two to three seconds, repeat the first stroke with the same leg coming forward and the same one going back. Because of the glide feature in the scissors kick, it is a relaxing, restful stroke for any distance.

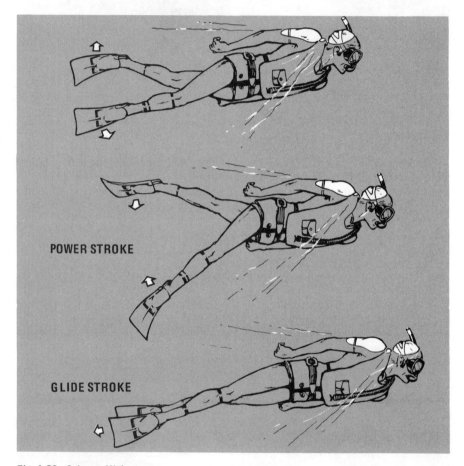

POWER STROKE

GLIDE STROKE

Fig. 1-20 Scissors Kick

The frog kick is not commonly used in diving, but it is a good powerful stroke with a relatively long and restful glide. Variation in kicks is important, especially for long surface swims. Occasionally changing to the frog kick, for example, requires using different muscles than in either the flutter or scissors kicks. As a result, your legs won't tire as easily and will be less likely to cramp. The frog kick begins with a slow separation of your legs, as shown in figure 1-21. The power stroke brings your legs together forcefully and ends in a long easy glide which lasts until you lose most of your forward momentum.

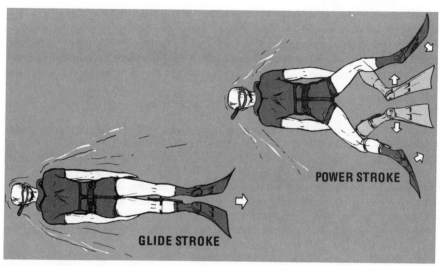

Fig. 1-21 Frog Kick

The dolphin kick is a useful variation underwater. As seen in figure 1-22, both legs stay together and work with the upper part of the body. Begin the dolphin kick in a horizontal position. Bring your fins up by bending your legs at the knees; then, bring your legs down in a power stroke by straightening your legs and bending slightly at the waist. The next step is to bring your fins up again by bending at the knees slightly and, at the same time, straightening your body at the waist and arching your back. As you gain speed, your body moves forward in a wave-like motion in the same way that a dolphin or whale swims.

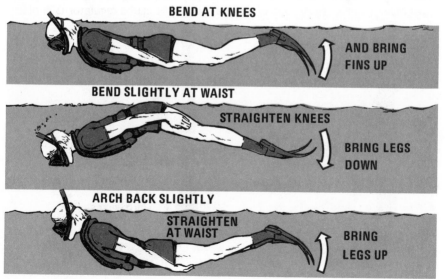

Fig. 1-22 Dolphin Kick

What happens if you accidently lose a fin while diving? The flutter, scissors, and frog kicks all depend on two fins moving in opposite directions. The fins balance each other and convert side motion into forward motion. With only one fin, this balance is missing. The dolphin kick does not depend on two legs and two fins balancing each other. It is the only kick that works well with one fin.

SNORKEL

Breathing tubes of one kind or another have probably been used for over 2,000 years, but it wasn't until the snorkel joined with the modern mask and fins that man was able to swim and relax effortlessly on the surface. The snorkel, with its curved tube and mouthpiece, enables you to swim on the surface without constantly lifting your face above the water to breathe. Your face can remain submerged as long as desired with the aid of a snorkel. With your head down and body relaxed, you have maximum buoyancy and can remain comfortable for hours. You can hang motionless at the surface and breathe through the snorkel without expending any effort to stay afloat.

The snorkel is both a skin and scuba diving tool. The scuba diver uses it to conserve air while swimming on the surface, to and from the dive sites, and while surveying a dive area.

SELECTING A SNORKEL

For discussion, we are going to establish two general classes of snorkels: skin diving snorkels and scuba diving snorkels. Figure 1-23 shows both types of snorkels. The skin diving snorkel generally has a large internal bore for easy breathing, so the air supply is not reduced even when the diver is working hard. The scuba diving snorkel is usually more flexible than the skin diving snorkel. This snorkel often has an accordion shaped curve that permits the mouthpiece to drop easily out of the way when the scuba regulator is in place.

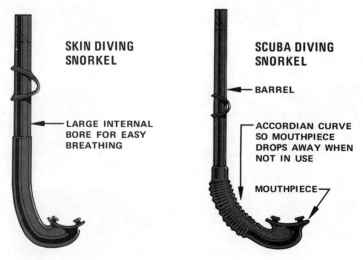

SKIN DIVING SNORKEL

LARGE INTERNAL BORE FOR EASY BREATHING

SCUBA DIVING SNORKEL

BARREL

ACCORDIAN CURVE SO MOUTHPIECE DROPS AWAY WHEN NOT IN USE

MOUTHPIECE

Fig. 1-23 Skin and Scuba Snorkels

WHAT TO LOOK FOR IN A SNORKEL

Two major things to consider when selecting a snorkel are breathing resistance and comfort. An easy breathing snorkel has a large bore and clean, simple lines with gentle curves. Do not use snorkels with nonreturn valves at the top of the tube. These increase air resistance and can stick in an open or closed position creating an unsafe condition. A snorkel does not have to be long to work well. Excessive length, in fact, increases breathing resistance and dead-air space. Breathing resistance also is increased when the snorkel has sharp curves, a reduction in bore size, or corrugations inside the snorkel tube.

Some snorkels have a one-way purge or self-draining valve near the mouthpiece, as shown in figure 1-24. When you surface, the water in the upper part of the tube drains out through the submerged valve, as gravity forces it to seek the level of the surrounding water. The remaining water is easily removed with a small, forceful exhalation.

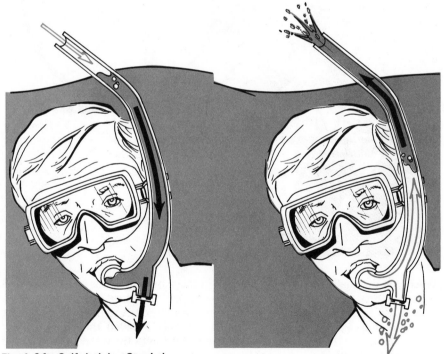

Fig. 1-24   Self-draining Snorkel

A mouthpiece that does not fit can be extremely uncomfortable. Be sure to test the mouthpiece before selecting a snorkel. Mouthpieces come in many different sizes, shapes, textures, and degrees of flexibility. Some can even be molded for a personalized fit. Try a number of different snorkels until you find one that feels comfortable and meets your needs.

SNORKEL USE

As shown in figure 1-25, the snorkel is always worn on the left side to avoid confusion with the scuba regulator hose and mouthpiece which are routed over the right shoulder. The snorkel is attached to the mask strap with the help of a small rubber snorkel keeper. Adjust the position of the snorkel keeper on the snorkel and along the mask strap until the mouthpiece feels comfortable and the snorkel itself is nearly vertical when you are swimming on the surface with your face in the water.

Fig. 1-25   Position and Location of the Snorkel

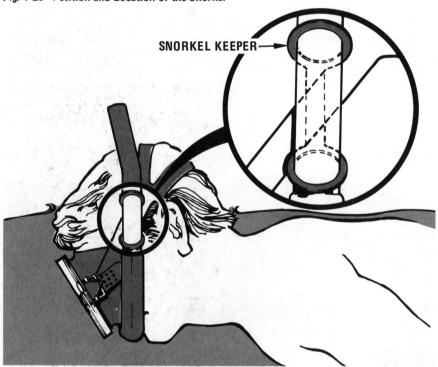

SNORKEL KEEPER

When you dive below the surface, the air in the snorkel bubbles out the top and water fills the tube. There are two different ways to get rid of this water when you return to the surface. The most common method is to blow hard and fast into the snorkel, as shown in figure 1-26. This is called the "popping" or "blasting" method of snorkel clearing because it forces the water up and out of the tube very quickly. Be careful not to blow around the mouthpiece. After clearing the snorkel, your first breath should be slow and shallow to keep from inhaling any water that may remain in the tube.

When swimming at the surface, it is not uncommon for water to spill into the snorkel. When it does, simply clear it. This soon becomes second nature and you will automatically clear your snorkel regularly.

Fig. 1-26 Popping Method of Snorkel Clearing

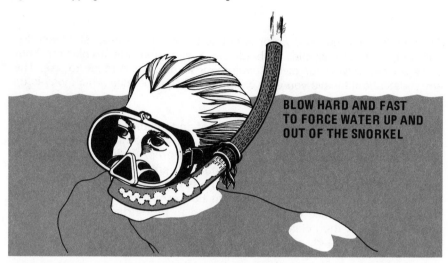

BLOW HARD AND FAST
TO FORCE WATER UP AND
OUT OF THE SNORKEL

The expansion or displacement method of snorkel clearing can be used when returning to the surface. As you ascend, look up toward the surface. This points your snorkel down. (See figure 1-27.) As you approach the surface, exhale lightly into your snorkel. The air expands naturally and clears the snorkel automatically. This method is easier than popping the snorkel clear, but it only works on ascent.

Fig. 1-27 Snorkel Expansion Method

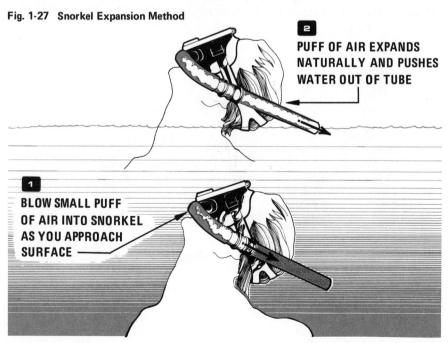

2
PUFF OF AIR EXPANDS
NATURALLY AND PUSHES
WATER OUT OF TUBE

1
BLOW SMALL PUFF
OF AIR INTO SNORKEL
AS YOU APPROACH
SURFACE

USING THE MASK, FINS, AND SNORKEL TOGETHER

ENTRIES

The best way to enter the water is to use the easiest, safest, and least disorienting method possible. It should be a transition, not a collision. Your entry should leave your diving equipment in place and ready to use. The entry also should leave you well oriented with a good idea which way is up and which way is down.

Before every dive, evaluate your entry point and the dive site. Make sure the water is deep enough for the entry and there are no hidden hazards. You also should be aware of any currents in the area. Perform a final buddy check to make sure both of you are ready to enter the water. If you are entering before your buddy, make sure he is ready and knows that you are going first. Grip your mask and weight belt firmly to keep them in place during the entry. Once in the water, come to the surface, let your buddy know you're OK, then clear the entry area. Watch while your buddy makes his entry and be ready to assist, if needed.

BOAT, DOCK, AND POOL DECK ENTRIES

Feet-first entries generally work well when you are entering from a firm surface such as a large boat, pool, or dock. They keep you in an upright position so you can maintain orientation throughout the entry. Figure 1-28 shows three different techniques for making feet-first entries. They include walking or stepping off the edge, jumping with feet together, and the giant-stride position. The idea of the giant-stride is to keep your legs spread and

WALKING   JUMPING   GIANT-STRIDE

Fig. 1-28 Feet-First Entries

arms extended until you touch the water. At that point, bring your legs together and your arms down forcefully against the water to slow your speed and to keep your head above the surface. The giant-stride entry can cause injury from great heights; but from lower entry points, it is a good technique to use if the water is shallow or if you want to stay near the surface.

The back roll entry, shown in figure 1-29, is often used when diving from a small boat or rubber raft. It is very useful to keep the boat from rocking; however, it can leave you disoriented and offers no protection against objects under the surface. Front roll entries should not be used because of the increased chance of injury and the disorientation after you enter the water.

Fig. 1-29 Back Roll Entry

The controlled seated entry is an excellent entry to use from a low pool deck or boat. Sit on the side with your feet in the water. Hold on to the side of the boat or pool, then turn and slip gracefully into the water, as shown in figure 1-30. This is a completely controlled entry because you stay in contact with the boat or pool deck at all times, and there is hardly any impact with the water. You remain oriented and in full control of the situation.

Fig. 1-30 Controlled Seated Entry

SHORE ENTRIES

When making an entry from a shore, put your regulator in your mouth and make sure your mask and weight belt are in place. You will have to decide whether or not to wear your fins. If you have to climb over rocks or through mud, it may be safer and easier to carry your fins into the water until it is deep enough to support your weight. Then, put on your fins and dive.

When making an ocean beach entry through surf breaking near the shore, put on your fins, walk backward into the water until it is deep enough to swim, then turn around and swim out through the surf. If the surf is breaking far out from the shore, carry your fins out to knee-deep water and put them on there. This will help keep sand out of your fins. Remember, do not try to walk forward with fins on your feet. Walk backward and shuffle your feet to help keep your balance. Part III, Section B gives further information on shore entries.

SURFACE DIVES

There are two basic kinds of surface dives: the head-first and feet-first. The purpose of both types is to lift as much of your body out of the water as you can so your body's weight can push you down into the water. If done properly, the head-first dive will drop you 15 to 20 feet below the surface without kicking.

The head-first surface dive, pictured in figure 1-31, starts from a face-down floating position with your legs near the surface. The first step is to bend your body at the waist to force the top half of your body straight down. Then, lift your legs up completely out of the water. This is the key to the head-first surface dive. The higher you can get your legs out of the water and over you, the more downward force the wieght of your legs will create.

1 BEND AT THE WAIST, FIRST

2 THEN LIFT YOUR LEGS UP COMPLETELY OUT OF THE WATER

3 LET THE WEIGHT OF YOUR LEGS FORCE YOU DOWN

Fig. 1-31   Head-First Surface Dive

The feet-first surface dive, while skin diving, is used primarily in kelp where there is not enough room to swim or float horizontally at the surface. It lets you begin in a floating, vertical position. (See figure 1-32.) The objective is to lift yourself as far out of the water as possible. Start by separating your legs and bringing your arms up; then, kick hard and bring your arms down quickly. As you shoot up and out of the water, keep your arms against your sides and drop straight down beneath the surface. When below the surface, raise your arms to help force you down. When you stop descending tuck into a ball, turn your head down, and swim toward the bottom. Your buddy should surface dive immediately after you.

SEEING AND SWIMMING UNDERWATER

The mask, fins, and snorkel are basic, not only to skin diving, but also to scuba diving. They may feel awkward and clumsy at first, but they add so much to your ability to see, move, and breathe underwater, that you will

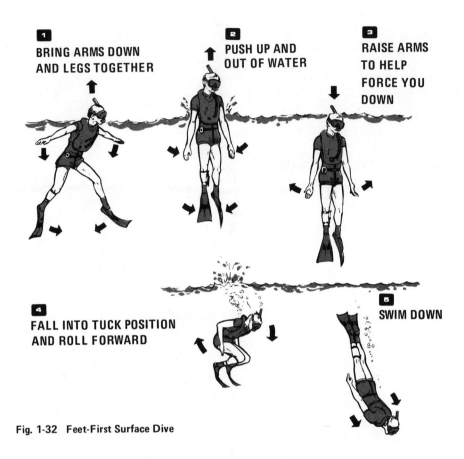

1 BRING ARMS DOWN AND LEGS TOGETHER

2 PUSH UP AND OUT OF WATER

3 RAISE ARMS TO HELP FORCE YOU DOWN

4 FALL INTO TUCK POSITION AND ROLL FORWARD

5 SWIM DOWN

Fig. 1-32 Feet-First Surface Dive

soon feel practically immobile without them. You will also learn to appreciate the importance of good, comfortable, and reliable equipment no matter what the cost. The most expensive mask, for example, may not be the best for you. The best mask is the one that meets your needs, fits your face, and feels comfortable, regardless of the price.

ASCENDING AND SURFACING

Prior to beginning your ascent, check your buddy. As you ascend, extend your arm as protection from obstructions above. Turn as you ascend. Look up and listen for boats or other objects which may be in your path. Upon surfacing, clear your snorkel, then rest. Leave your mask in place and breathe through your snorkel. Keep your head and face in the water. Relax and take advantage of your natural buoyancy. Positive buoyancy can be increased by keeping your lungs full between breaths. If you intend to stay on the surface for some time, inflate your buoyancy control device. Throughout your ascent and rest at the surface, you should always be aware of your buddy's whereabouts and condition.

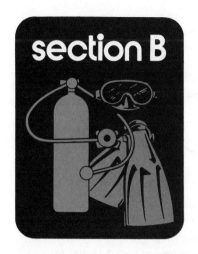

section B

warmth and buoyancy

- ● WET SUIT
- ● WEIGHT BELT
- ● BUOYANCY COMPENSATOR

WET SUIT, WEIGHT BELT, AND BUOYANCY COMPENSATOR

The mask, fins, and snorkel solved the problems of seeing and swimming under water, but they also led to a new problem: cold. It is tempting to prolong diving time when wearing basic skin diving equipment. But skin divers lack the whale's protective blubber or the otter's thick, oily fur to insulate them. Divers must wear protective suits to retain body heat.

The wet suit satisfactorily solves one problem, but creates a conflict in another area—the wet suit's material increases buoyancy. For a diver, excessive floating is just as bad as excessive sinking. The simplest way to counteract the buoyancy of the wet suit is by adding a weight belt. The puzzle of maintaining warmth and controlling buoyancy was solved by a three-part system, consisting of the wet suit, weight belt, and buoyancy compensator (sometimes called a vest).

WET SUIT

Water absorbs body heat 25 times faster than air. Because of this, a temperature that might be uncomfortably warm in air could be uncomfortably cold in water. A resting diver, for example, chills in one to two hours when the water temperature is between 75° and 80°F (approximately 25°C). Cold water, however, is not only uncomfortable, but also is dangerous. People have died in an hour in 40°F (4° - 5°C) water.

During the first attempts to solve the problem, divers wore long underwear covered with a waterproof rubber dry suit, as shown in figure 1-33. The smallest

Fig. 1-33
Early Dry Suit

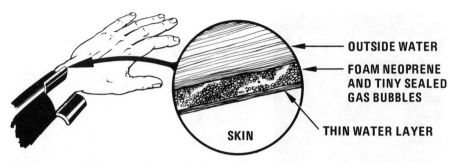

Fig. 1-34 Cross-Section of Foam Neoprene

leak or tear in the dry suit, however, ruined everything: divers quickly found soggy underwear and thin rubber suits were undependable insulators.

Divers finally discovered that they did not have to be bone dry to stay warm. Preventing body heat from escaping required an insulating material to stop it from passing into the water. A wet suit made of foam neoprene, three-sixteenths to one-fourth inch thick, proved to be an effective insulator.

Foam neoprene is synthetic rubber filled with tiny bubbles, as shown in figure 1-34. It is widely believed that the wet suit warms the body by allowing a thin layer of water to enter between the neoprene and the skin, which is then warmed and actually insulates the body. However, this is not altogether desirable, because if there is room for the water to enter in the first place, there is room for the water to circulate. If the water circulates, it must be continually rewarmed, which pulls body heat away. It is better to have a suit that fits snugly enough that it stops all water circulation into, inside, or out of the suit. No water circulation lets you stay warmer than even very little circulation.

Thicker foam neoprene provides increased insulation but also increases buoyancy and tends to restrict movement. Whatever the thickness, as a diver descends increased pressure compresses the material. Consequently, its buoyancy and insulation are diminished.

Nothing is more important to diving comfort than a good wet suit. This is especially true in water temperatures below 75°F (24°C), where most sport diving takes place. In many areas, the wet suit extends the diving season from a few summer months to all year. The wet suit also protects against the sun and almost anything else that could irritate, bruise, chafe, or harm delicate human skin. The wet suit also provides reserve buoyancy.

SELECTING A WET SUIT

Sport divers commonly dive in water between 40° to 75°F (4° —24°C). In this temperature range, you must cover your entire body with a full wet suit, including hood, gloves, and boots.

In warmer water, you may only need a one-eighth inch thick jacket. In cooler water, a hooded vest and high-top pants, sometimes referred to as "Farmer Johns," will help keep your torso warm. Figure 1-35 portrays three types of wet suit protection.

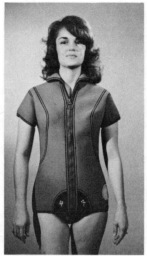

Fig. 1-35 Scuba Diving Suits

The extent of body coverage and thickness of necessary wet suit protection depends on many things. Thin divers, for example, need more protection than heavy divers. Extremely active divers need less protection because they produce more body heat. All divers require extra protection when diving in deep water, since temperature drops as depth increases.

When selecting a wet suit, you can choose between a standard-size or a custom-made suit. The correct fit is extremely important for maintaining warmth. A suit that is too tight can keep you warm, but it also restricts breathing, circulation, and freedom of movement. Custom-made suits ensure a perfect fit, but stock sizes are acceptable if they fit snugly and feel comfortable. A complete discussion of how to select a custom wet suit is included in the Advanced Manual.

WHAT TO LOOK FOR IN A WET SUIT

After deciding on the type of wet suit protection you need, study the neoprene material and see how it is made. Wet suits lined inside and out with four-way stretch nylon fabric are the most durable. The inside lining makes it easier to climb into; it works like a dry lubricant. The external lining slightly reduces the flexibility of the suit, but the increase in strength and suit life is worth this small disadvantage. Suits without nylon, or only on one side, are equally warm, and more flexible than those of two-sided nylon construction. However, they are more difficult to put on and take off.

WET SUIT FEATURES

Zippers at the ankles and wrists are not necessary, but they make dressing and undressing easier. Usually an extra strip of neoprene under zippers restricts water leakage. (See figure 1-36.) If you plan to dive in extremely cold water, avoid wet suits with zippers since some water seeps through them.

Fig. 1-36 Wet Suit Zippers   Fig. 1-37 Wet Suit Features and Options

Wet suit jackets are available with a spine pad, which is an extra strip of foam neoprene that fits into the depression along your spine. The spine pad prevents cold water from entering into this area. Pockets, reinforcing patches, knee and elbow pads, and special knife or tool holders also can be built into wet suits, as shown in figure 1-37. Neoprene socks or boots are available with hard rubber or felt soles to protect both boots and feet when walking over sharp rocks or coral.

The one wet suit feature that is *not* optional is a good fit. A suit should feel snug all over your body without binding or pinching. There should be no gaps or spaces under the arms, at the neck, or in the crotch. The ankles, waist, wrist, and neck openings should be tight enough to keep water from sloshing in and out, but loose enough to allow free body circulation. In short, your wet suit should fit like a second skin.

WET SUIT USE

Using a wet suit is easy. Once you have it on, you can forget about it and enjoy its warmth. Getting it on and taking it off is the challenging part. Dressing can be frustrating, time consuming, and exhausting for the new diver. To avoid any confusion, follow these steps when preparing for entry on your first dive, especially when you don't own the equipment. Normally all equipment would be adjusted prior to leaving for the dive site.

1.   **Pants.** Pants go on first. Fold the pants down over the knees as though you were turning them inside out. This insures a good fit from the ankle to the knee. Once the pants are on up to the knees, simply roll them up your legs checking that the crotch fits snugly. (Fig. 1-38)

2. **Boots.** Roll the tops of the boots down, and inside out, just past the heel. Then work the foot into the boot as far as you can before pulling it over your heel and ankle. Zippers in pant legs are helpful because the boots *must* tuck under the wet suit pants. (Fig. 1-39)

3. **Fins.** Get your fins and boots wet and put the fins on over your boots to make proper adjustments. Then, lay them near the water so they will be handy when you make your entry. Have all the equipment you need near the entry point before putting on your wet suit. You can become overheated if you delay entry while wearing a wet suit. (Fig. 1-40)

4. **Jacket.** Pull the wet suit jacket on like any ordinary shirt or jacket, one arm at a time. Make sure the sleeves are up all the way to your arm pits so there are no gaps under your arms. Jacket arms that are not up all the way will pull and bind at your shoulder. This is uncomfortable and limits arm movement. Before zipping the jacket, fasten the crotch strap to help hold the flaps together. (Fig. 1-41)

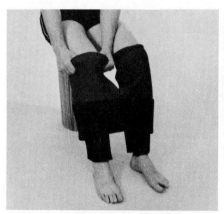

Fig. 1-38 Wet Suit Dressing: Pants

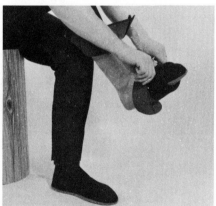

Fig. 1-39 Wet Suit Dressing: Boots

Fig. 1-40 Wet Suit Dressing: Fins

Fig. 1-41 Wet Suit Dressing: Jacket

Fig. 1-42 Wet Suit Dressing: Vest

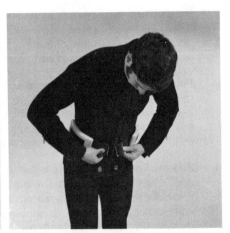

Fig. 1-43 Wet Suit Dressing: Weight Belt

Fig. 1-44 Wet Suit Dressing: Hood

Fig. 1-45 Wet Suit Dressing: Mask

5. **Buoyancy Compensator or Vest.** Inflate the buoyancy vest completely (if you fasten a deflated vest, it will be too tight after inflation). Adjust and tighten the waist strap first and then the crotch strap. Deflate the vest, and position the buckle on the right side so it will not be confused with the weight belt and backpack buckles. Then, take vest off. (Fig 1-42)

6. **Weight Belt.** The weight belt goes on after the scuba tanks and before the fins. It should be put on so that when you remove it in an emergency, it is not held in place by other equipment. The weight belt should be adjusted now so it will be ready to go when you are. Make sure the weights are evenly balanced somewhere near the front of the belt. Also, the belt should not be too long. If it sticks out of the buckle more than eight inches, cut it off and burn the end (if made out of nylon) to keep it from unraveling. Take the belt off and put it next to your other equipment. (Fig. 1-43)

7. **Hood.** Put the hood on next. Pull it from the front of your forehead down and toward the back of your head so it will pull your hair out of the way. The lower skirt of the hood should be tucked under the collar of the wet suit jacket. (Fig 1-44)

8. **Mask.** Put the mask on to make sure it is adjusted properly. The mask skirt should be sealed firmly against your face underneath the hood. After adjusting both mask and snorkel, lay them next to your other equipment. (Fig 1-45)

9. **Gloves.** Gloves are the last thing to put on. Wet suit gloves go on like ordinary gloves, but diving gloves must be pulled on completely. A glove only half on is clumsy and tiring. Your buddy can help in tucking the gloves under your sleeves at the wrist. (Fig. 1-46)

Fig. 1-46 Wet Suit Dressing: Gloves

Fig. 1-47 Wet Suit Drying and Storage

WET SUIT CARE AND MAINTENANCE

After the dive, remove your equipment and wet suit in the reverse order that you put it on. Rinse the wet suit inside and out in clean, fresh water. Hang it on wide wooden or plastic hangers in an open, shaded area to dry, as shown in figure 1-47.

For permanent storage, do not fold the suit. Folds and creases in neoprene compress and weaken the material. Excessive heat and direct sunlight also are harmful.

Use neoprene cement to mend small tears. Lubricate metal fittings and zippers with silicone spray, candle wax, or a bar of soap to keep them working smoothly. Occasionally, wash the wet suit with a mild detergent in lukewarm water. Many divers use the bathtub for washing and the shower-head for rinsing. Open all snaps and zippers and push the suit up and down in the tub water for about five minutes.

Heat and sunlight damage foam neoprene and so does ozone, a chemical contained in smog. If you live in a smog-filled city, store your suit in an airtight plastic bag. Otherwise, hang it on two-inch wide hangers or lay it flat to help distribute the weight evenly. A good wet suit will last indefinitely with proper care and maintenance.

WEIGHT BELT

A diver in the water wearing only a full wet suit floats very well. So well, in fact, it is impossible for him to dive below the surface for any length of time. A medium-size, one-fourth inch thick wet suit at the surface of fresh water has about 18 pounds of buoyancy. It is like wearing a thin life jacket all over your body. The diver wearing a wet suit will be warm and comfortable, but without a weight belt to counteract the buoyancy of foam neoprene, he is trapped at the surface. The lead weight belt is the solution to the buoyancy problem caused by the wet suit.

SELECTING A WEIGHT BELT

How heavy should a weight belt be? Each diver must experiment to find out for himself. Your goal is to be either neutrally buoyant at the surface or neutrally buoyant at a given depth. To achieve neutral buoyancy at the surface while wearing a wet suit, you need about 10 to 20 pounds of weight. To determine the exact amount, put on all the equipment you wear during a dive. Get in the water and start adding and subtracting weight until you sink slightly after you exhale and rise slightly when you completely inhale, as shown in figure 1-48. Inflate your buoyancy control device in case you put on too much weight. Release the air from your buoyancy control device until you can determine your weight requirements.

To achieve neutral buoyancy at depth, you need less weight. For example, if you plan to scuba dive to between 30 and 50 feet, you might want to be neutrally buoyant at about 33 feet. To achieve neutral buoyancy at 33 feet, divide the pounds you need for neutral surface buoyancy by the number of atmospheres at 33 feet. For instance, if you need 12 pounds at the surface, you will need about six pounds at 33 feet for neutral buoyancy, about eight pounds at 16.5 feet, and so forth.

Fig. 1-48 Neutral Buoyancy

Some divers regularly weight themselves for neutral buoyancy at 15 to 20 feet. This forces you to descend against a slight positive buoyancy, but it has the advantage of giving you positive buoyancy at the surface at all times without ditching equipment or inflating the buoyancy compensator. Whether you choose to be neutrally buoyant at the surface or at depth, never wear more weight than is necessary.

Since you are somewhat more buoyant in salt water than fresh, remember to add between two and five pounds of lead when going from fresh to salt water. These are only general guidelines. Weight needs are individual, and often change depending on the age and condition of a wet suit, body type, experience, and equipment. Even the food you eat before the dive has an effect. Usually, you are more buoyant after a meal because digestive gases are present in your stomach and intestines.

Fig. 1-49   Weight Belts

WHAT TO LOOK FOR IN A WEIGHT BELT

Figure 1-49 shows the two basic types of materials used for weight belts—nylon web and rubber. Nylon is the most common and durable. Rubber will not last as long, but it stretches, which is an advantage to the descending diver. When pressure increases, the gas cells in the foam neoprene are compressed, which makes the wet suit thinner. If the diver is wearing a nylon belt, it will become loose as he descends. A rubber belt, on the other hand, pulls into the space vacated by the suit, compressing with the increasing depth, and stays tight around the diver's waist. A nylon belt equipped with a depth-compensating device is shown in figure 1-50.

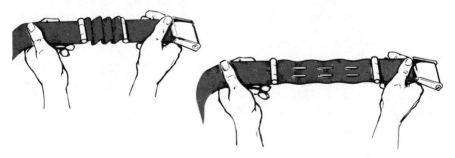

Fig. 1-50   Depth-Compensating Nylon Weight Belt

The weight belt buckle must be easily distinguishable from other equipment buckles and be a quick-release type, as shown in figure 1-51. You should be able to release it immediately with either gloved hand. The clasp-type quick-release buckle may have a prominent notch in the buckle to help reduce confusion with other buckles. The wire buckle is especially useful because it is unlike any other scuba equipment buckle and, therefore, prevents confusion with the buoyancy compensator or backpack buckles.

Fig. 1-51 Quick-Release Weight Belt Buckle

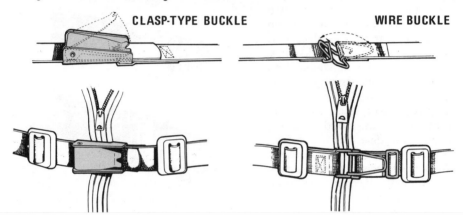

There are different kinds and sizes of lead weights as shown in figure 1-52. Some have slits so they can be donned or taken off without unbuckling the belt. Hip weights are available in 6 to 10 pound sizes and should be used as pairs and worn to balance each other. Some weights are vinyl coated to help protect boat and pool decks. Vinyl coated weights are available in a variety of colors.

The shot-filled weight belt, pictured in figure 1-53, does not use ordinary lead weights. It uses a mass of tiny lead balls, or shot, contained in a vinyl compartment. Shot is added or removed to adjust for difference in buoyancy. This is more complicated than changing lead weights and the vinyl compartment is more bulky—but it is a comfortable belt because the shot conforms to the body.

Fig. 1-52 Weights

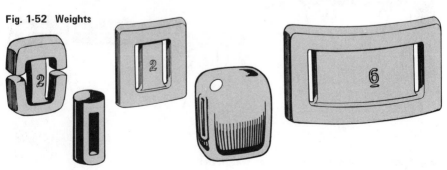

USING THE WEIGHT BELT

The wet suit-weight belt combination is a dynamic safety pair. They keep you warm and let you achieve instant buoyancy whenever you want or need it. The weight belt lets you approach neutral buoyancy at the surface. It is also extremely important as a safety device because it gives you buoyancy the instant you take it off. This does not mean you ascend rapidly from depth when you drop the weight belt, but shedding it does make it easier for you to swim up faster. *The weight belt must not be held in place by other straps or equipment.*

A quick-release buckle enables you to ditch the belt immediately in an emergency. Simply unfastening the buckle is not enough. You must pull the belt completely away from your waist as far as you can to let it drop freely and clearly, as shown in figure 1-54. Otherwise, it could get hung up on other straps, a knife handle, or even a fin.

In an emergency, common sense should tell you to drop anything that impedes your ascent to the surface, such as full game bags, treasures, or even the tank. Some divers even take the weight belt off and hold it if they feel a tense situation developing. In the case of possible panic then, it would be dropped naturally.

Ditching the weight belt when you don't have free access to the surface does not always help you in an emergency. The situation could be worsened because you reduce buoyancy control. But if you should run into a problem while diving in areas where you have free access to the surface, do not hesitate to drop the belt. You can always go back down and get it and, even if you cannot find it, the cost of a weight belt is a small price to pay for the security of almost instant buoyancy. (See also Part II, Section C for a discussion of emergency ascents.)

Fig. 1-53
Shot-Filled Weight Belt

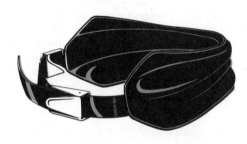

Fig. 1-54
Ditching the Weight Belt

BUOYANCY COMPENSATOR

At this point, complete buoyancy control is not yet solved. The weight belt adequately counteracts the buoyancy of the wet suit at the surface, but buoyancy changes when you descend because of wet suit compression. If a medium size wet suit has 18 pounds of buoyancy at the surface, for example, the same suit will have an extreme loss of buoyancy at a depth of 100 feet. The diver who wears 18 pounds of lead to achieve neutral buoyancy at the surface may find himself as much as 10 pounds too heavy at 100 feet. The bouyancy compensator, or BC, was designed to help you counteract these changes in buoyancy.

SELECTING A BUOYANCY COMPENSATOR

There is a wide variety of buoyancy compensators. The ones shown in figure 1-55 are commonly referred to as "horse collar" BCs. They were the original buoyancy compensators designed for diving and still are the ones primarily used by skin divers. A skin diving BC should be equipped with an over-expansion relief valve that automatically releases air when the BC is over inflated. Another important feature is an oral inflation/deflation tube to manually increase or decrease the volume of air inside the BC. Skin diving BCs also should be equipped with a CO_2 inflation device that can be activated to achieve positive buoyancy.

The low-profile BC, shown in figure 1-56, is designed primarily for scuba diving. The majority of the buoyancy is located around the waist and under the arms. This provides added lift at the surface, because the actual volume of air remains underwater. During a dive, the buoyancy is located around your natural center of gravity near the weight belt. A wide cummerbund also helps to reduce the tendency for the BC to ride up. Adjustable shoulder straps ensure a comfortable fit and makes it easier to put on or take off. Like

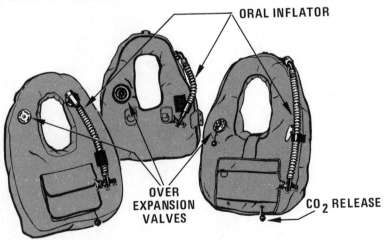

ORAL INFLATOR

OVER EXPANSION VALVES

CO_2 RELEASE

Fig. 1-55   Horse-Collar Buoyancy Compensator

all BCs used for scuba, it should be equipped with an over-expansion relief valve and an oral inflation/deflation tube. Almost all BCs include a connector for a low pressure mechanical inflator. This device allows you to inflate the compensator using air from the scuba cylinder. A dump valve also is included on most buoyancy compensators. It allows air to be rapidly expelled for descent or to control your rate of ascent. The valve can be activated by pulling a string, lever, or the inflator hose.

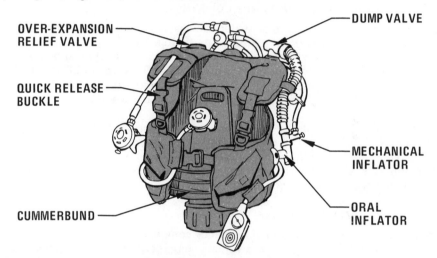

Fig. 1-56 Low-Profile Buoyancy Compensator

The buoyancy control jacket, shown in figure 1-57, is another kind of buoyancy compensator. It has a large, three-dimensional shape with the buoyancy located around the waist and over the shoulders. The buoyancy control jacket normally is equipped with the same features as other scuba BCs. On some compensators, the mechanical inflator may incorporate a scuba regulator for emergency breathing.

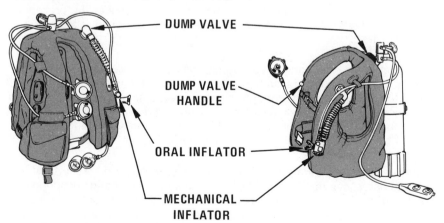

Fig. 1-57 Buoyancy Control Jacket

The buoyancy control pack, shown in figure 1-58, is another alternative. It is usually a horseshoe-shaped unit that is attached to the tank backpack. This configuration places the buoyancy behind you, which removes some of the straps and bulkiness in front of you and makes it easy to rest or snorkel in a horizontal position. Some manufacturers integrate a system of weights into the pack.

WHAT TO LOOK FOR IN A BUOYANCY COMPENSATOR

The construction of the compensator usually falls into one of two broad categories: double bag or single bag. The double bag design has an inner bladder protected by a strong outer fabric shell. With a single bag buoyancy compensator, the shell itself serves as the bladder. This type of BC is usually referred to as a bladderless design. Double bags are normally easier to repair if damaged, while single bags offer reduced bulk and lower drag.

The inflator hose should be large and attached high on the collar for easy inflation and deflation. The mechanical and oral inflator buttons should be easy to operate with and without gloves. They also should be easy to recognize. Pockets and hose retainers should be conveniently located to help secure and organize your equipment.

BUOYANCY COMPENSATOR USE

Never dive without some form of buoyancy compensation device. It is one of the most useful diving tools. It is a valuable emergency device. Keep your BC at least partially inflated while on the surface. Using energy to stay at the surface is unnecessary; let the buoyancy compensator do the work.

Filling a BC with a mechanical inflator is easy, but you also should learn to fill it orally in case of an equipment failure. The bobbing technique is one of the easiest and safest methods. Simply kick to the surface, take a deep breath, press the button on the oral inflator, and exhale into the BC. You will sink slightly during the exhalation, but when you have finished, just kick back to the surface for another big breath of air and repeat the procedure. (See figure 1-59.) You will establish good positive buoyancy after two or three breaths.

The technique for deflating the buoyancy compensator varies according to its design. On compensators without dump valves, the inflator hose is held above the BC and the deflator button is depressed, as shown in figure 1-60. This allows air to easily escape. On BCs that incorporate a dump valve, the deflation mechanism is pulled. Since the valve is usually located at the highest point on the compensator, air escapes easily.

When underwater, inflate your BC either mechanically or orally until you begin to rise above the bottom. Then, deflate it until you hang suspended, as shown in figure 1-61. Using this technique together with controlling air in your lungs, enables you to maintain a state of neutral buoyancy throughout any dive at any depth. When you are ready to ascend, inflate the BC just

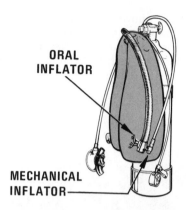

ORAL
INFLATOR

MECHANICAL
INFLATOR

Fig. 1-58   Buoyancy Control Pack

Fig. 1-59   Inflating the BC at the Surface (Bobbing Technique)

enough to begin the ascent. You must vent air out of the BC as you ascend to maintain a controlled rate of ascent that does not exceed between 30 and 60 feet per minute.

CARE AND MAINTENANCE OF THE BUOYANCY COMPENSATOR

After every dive, fill the buoyancy compensator about one-third full with fresh water, inflate it with air, and slosh the water around, as shown in figure 1-62. Hold the inflator hose down and open the oral inflator valve to let the water run out. Just before it is completely empty, taste the water and make sure it is clean. If it tastes salty, repeat the rinsing procedure. If the BC has a CO_2 cartridge, remove it and let the water flow through the opening of the mechanism. Again, taste the water to make certain all salt has been flushed.

Fig. 1-60   Releasing Air from the BC

Fig. 1-61   Buoyancy Control

After the inside is clean, rinse the outside of the buoyancy compensator, taking special care to clean push-button valves, inflation mechanisms, and other parts. Lubricate the CO_2 cartridge threads and puncture disc with white all-purpose grease or some other kind of waterproof material to prevent corrosion.

Test for leaks by inflating the BC and submerging it in the bathtub or sink. Look for tiny air bubbles. Repair any leaks before the next dive. When you store the BC, leave it half full of air to keep the insides from sticking together.

With proper care, your buoyancy compensator, weight belt, and wet suit will work together as a warmth-and-buoyancy control team for many years. Take care of it and it will take care of you.

Fig. 1-62   Rinsing the Buoyancy Compensator

SCUBA DIVING EQUIPMENT

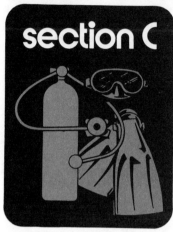

section C

breathing underwater

- TANK
- REGULATOR
- BUDDY BREATHING
- BUDDY SYSTEM

TANK, REGULATOR, BUDDY BREATHING, AND BUDDY SYSTEM

No matter how comfortable the skin diver is underwater, time reminds him that he is not a fish. After what seems like only seconds, the skin diver must return to the surface to breathe. The problem of staying underwater for a matter of hours instead of minutes was solved long before skin diving became a sport.

Diving bells, hoods, underwater boats, and deep sea hard hats, as illustrated in figure 1-63, were used, or at least thought of, for centuries. But these contraptions limit the one thing always dear to the sport diver's heart: freedom of movement. You cannot swim in a hard hat rig. With the air hose and lifeline attached, the diver may feel like a fish, all right—but a fish caught on a hook.

Fig. 1-63   Early Underwater Breathing Apparatuses

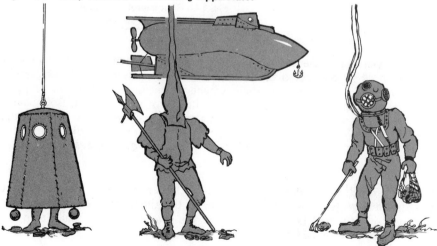

The sport diver needed a *self-contained* air supply to give him both time and freedom of underwater movement. He needed two things—a large amount of air in a small container and a way to control the release of air so he could breathe. Amazingly, these two things existed almost 80 years before a true self-contained underwater breathing apparatus (SCUBA) unit was invented.

In 1825, W. H. James, an Englishman, invented a self-contained diving suit with a supply of compressed air. (Note figure 1-64.) But no one was particularly impressed or interested in the outfit.

Fig. 1-64
James' Self-Contained Diving Suit

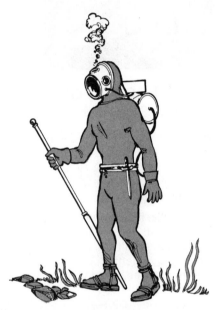

Fig. 1-65 Rouquayrol's Apparatus in
20,000 Leagues Under The Sea

Some 41 years later, Benoist Rouquayrol of France patented the first *demand regulator*. When connected to a supply of high pressure air, Rouquayrol's regulator delivered air to the diver whenever he inhaled. When he stopped inhaling, the regulator stopped letting air flow. For some reason, Rouquayrol did not bother to attach his regulator to a container of compressed air like the one James had used. Jules Verne, the only person who did make this connection, used it in his book, *20,000 Leagues Under the Sea*, as shown in figure 1-65.

In 1925, Frenchman le Prieur took a tank of high pressure air and attached it to a diving mask, as shown in figure 1-66. By this time, however, Rouquayrol's demand regulator had been forgotten, so the diver had to manually turn the air on and off, wasting a lot of the limited air supply.

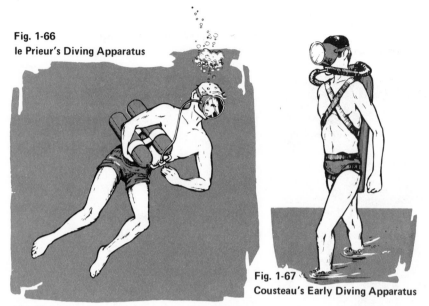

Fig. 1-66
le Prieur's Diving Apparatus

Fig. 1-67
Cousteau's Early Diving Apparatus

Finally, in 1943, Jacques Cousteau of France and Emile Gagnan, an engineer from Canada, put everything together. They had been skin diving for several years with masks and fins. They wanted the freedom of skin diving along with the extended time that a compressed air supply would offer. One June afternoon in the south of France, Cousteau attached a demand regulator to a high pressure tank and tested the world's first fully automatic compressed air diving apparatus, shown in figure 1-67. It worked. Diving was revolutionized.

Never before had man carried this much air on his back — air that was supplied to him automatically, whenever he inhaled. It also delivered air at the correct depth pressure. Cousteau called it the passport to the underwater world, and that is exactly what it was.

TANK

The scuba tank used by sport divers has changed little since Cousteau made the first scuba dive. It is a simple device—a seamless metal container with threads at the neck for a valve. But the manufacture of this and all other high pressure containers is a carefully controlled process. From the time it comes from the factory, until it is retired, the tank is regularly tested and inspected. It would be difficult to find, let alone buy, a new scuba tank that is not good. You should, however, understand tanks well enough to select, use, and take care of one intelligently.

SELECTING A TANK

The first two decisions to make when selecting a tank concern size and materials. Tank sizes are measured by how much air they contain at a certain maximum pressure. They run from 15 cubic feet to 94.6 cubic feet. The tanks used most often are shown in figure 1-68. The 71.2-cubic-foot tank is the most common size tank used by sport divers. Smaller tanks are lighter and easier to handle for young or lightweight divers, but larger tanks have a greater air capacity.

1 50 CU. FT.
ALUMINUM OR STEEL

2 71.2 CU. FT.
ALUMINUM OR STEEL

3 80 CU. FT.
ALUMINUM

Fig. 1-68   Different Size Tanks

The *seventy-one*, however, is a good compromise between weight and air capacity. It weights about 28 to 35 pounds depending on whether it is empty or full. It is a little over two feet long, six to eight inches wide, and is designed to hold air at a maximum of 2250 to 3000 pounds per square inch (psi) of pressure depending on design.

A full *seventy-one* contains about the same amount of air as a telephone booth. How long does the air last? This is a common question that has no correct answer. It depends on depth, lung capacity, activity level, water temperatures, and other factors that will be discussed in Part II, Section C.

Until 1970, all sport diving tanks were made out of steel. Since that time, they also have been made out of an aluminum alloy. The main difference between steel and aluminum is the way the two metals corrode—rust forms on steel, and aluminum oxide forms on aluminum.

When a metal corrodes, oxygen combines with it to form a new substance, usually the original ore. Rust resembles the ore used initially in making steel. It is much softer than steel, so it crumbles and flakes off. (See figure 1-69.)

This oxidation process happens faster when water or water vapor is present; salt water increases it even more. With enough oxygen, water, and salt rust can gradually eat through a steel tank wall.

Rust does not form on all metals. A gray coating called aluminum oxide forms on aluminum when it is combined with oxygen. As illustrated in figure 1-70, aluminum oxide is hard and clings tightly to the metal underneath. It

Fig. 1-69 Rust: Oxidation Process of Steel   Fig. 1-70 Aluminum Oxide

clings so well, that it actually prevents more oxygen from coming in contact with the aluminum. Without oxygen, corrosion cannot take place, so the aluminum oxide protects the metal it covers.

For all practical purposes, aluminum scuba tanks will not corrode as long as the protective aluminum oxide coating stays in place. Steel tanks corrode if water and salt leak into the tank, but steel is just as durable as aluminum if the tank is kept clean and dry, inside and out.

Warning: Aluminum cylinders exposed to fire or heated to temperatures in excess of 350° Fahrenheit should be condemned. If refinishing, do not use catalyst paint strippers. Cylinders which have been refinished and/or subjected to high temperatures should be hydrostatically tested before filling. Do not modify or alter a cylinder in any way. Failure to heed this warning may result in the cylinder rupturing causing serious injury or loss of life.

WHAT TO LOOK FOR IN A TANK
Coatings

There are a number of inside and outside coatings for scuba tanks which protect them and make them more attractive. All steel tanks should be galvanized to protect outside surfaces from moisture and air—two things necessary for rust. Vinyl and epoxy coatings are sometimes painted over the zinc coating for color and additional protection, but if any of these coatings are punctured or scratched, rust forms underneath. Ordinary paint is not durable enough to either protect or beautify a steel tank for any length of time. Aluminum tanks do not need any coatings or undercoatings, but they are available with vinyl or epoxy coatings to add color.

Steel tanks are not coated with zinc inside since zinc can be toxic in heavy doses. Only the outside of the tank is galvanized. Epoxy paint is sometimes used to coat the inside of steel tanks. It protects the bare metal from corrosive effects of air and water, but the coating works only if the epoxy maintains a perfect seal over the steel. Moisture can penetrate underneath the epoxy even through a tiny hole. When this happens, rust forms *under* the coating where you cannot see it.

Tank Markings

Like all high pressure containers, scuba tanks must conform to regulations set by the Canadian Transport Commission (CTC) and the U.S. Department of Transportation (DOT). The manufacturing, transporting, and testing of scuba tanks is a carefully controlled process. All tanks manufactured in the United States must have CTC/DOT stamped on the neck, along with a series of other markings The numbers, letters, and symbols stamped on the tank describe and identify the tank and also provide a record of testing validations. The meanings of these markings are shown in figure 1-71.

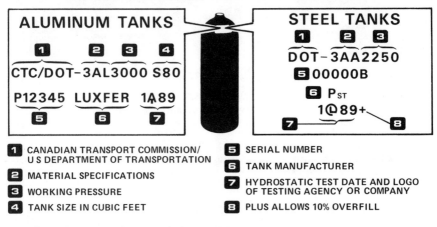

Fig. 1-71 Tank Markings

Without correct markings, a tank is illegal. Reputable dive stores will not fill illegal tanks. You should understand the meaning of tank markings so you can recognize an illegal tank. This is especially important when buying old or used equipment.

Tank Valves

Tanks have one of two kinds of valves at the top to turn the air on or off. The body of the valve is threaded and screws into the tank neck. The tank valve stays in place continuously, except for tank inspections. The nonreserve, or "K" valve, as it is usually called, is a simple on-and-off valve. The "J" or constant reserve valve, has an extra lever connected to the special spring-loaded reserve mechanism. It serves as a warning device to prevent the diver from accidentally running out of air. The reserve valve allows air to flow until the pressure inside the tank gets down to about 300 psi. Then the spring pressure shuts off the air flow. Pulling down the reserve lever opens the valve manually so the diver can use the remaining 300 psi of air for the ascent. "J" and "K" valves have a number of safety, or convenience features, as shown in figures 1-72 and 1-73. The small "O" ring that surrounds the air outlet forms the seal between the tank valve and the regulator yoke. Without the "O" ring, a tank valve is useless, so always carry an extra. (Divers often carry extra "O" rings between the wing screw and the yoke on the regulator.)

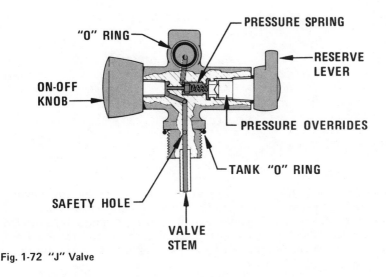

Fig. 1-72 "J" Valve

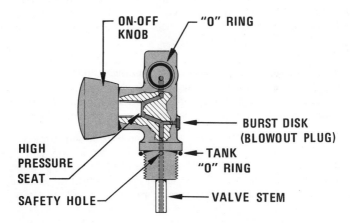

Fig. 1-73 "K" Valve

The *burst disk assembly* or *blowout plug* is an important safety feature, especially against overfilling. Air expands when heated. If a full scuba tank is heated as a result of being left in the sun, in the trunk of a car, or in some other similar area, the air can expand greatly. If it were not for the blowout plug, an over-heated tank could explode. Instead, the thin metal disk ruptures and lets the expanded air escape harmlessly. The burst disk, illustrated in figure 1-73, is designed to give way somewhere between 125 and 166 percent of the tank's stamped working pressure. Valves without a blowout plug are *illegal*.

Fig. 1-74   Tank Boots

Fig. 1-75   Self-Draining Tank Boot

Before you remove a tank valve, be sure to release all of the air. Unscrewing the valve with high pressure air behind it could be dangerous. Because of this, some valves have a small safety hole, as shown in figure 1-73, drilled into the threads. This lets any pressurized air escape before you have unscrewed the valve more than a few turns. This should never be done except by professional repairmen.

The valve stem extends into the tank and helps keep water, rust, or other impurities (that should not be in your tank), out of your regulator. Even if you turn a tank upside down and turn on the valve, water will stay in the tank because it cannot get past the two inch valve stem. (See figure 1-73.)

Tank Boots

An upright tank is unstable and might fall over unless someone is holding onto it. Tank boots, like those in figure 1-74, were designed to protect the tank, floor, deck, foot—anything an unbalanced tank might fall on. Most boots let the tank stand upright by itself, but this is obviously not their primary purpose.

Some tank boots are designed like a large rounded cup that encloses the bottom of the tank. This design also traps water and can lead to serious corrosion. Other boots, like the one shown in figure 1-75, are designed to let water flow out the bottom. If possible, boots should be removed and washed occasionally. This is especially true of non-galvanized steel tanks coated with vinyl or epoxy.

Backpack

The purpose of the backpack is to securely attach the scuba tank to your back. They can be either an integral part of the buoyancy compensator or a separate unit, as shown in figure 1-76. Separate backpacks should have quick release buckles at the waist and on at least one shoulder strap.

When you select a backpack, make sure everything on the pack is made out of noncorrosive materials. The tank retaining band holds the tank on the backpack. The retaining bands can have either adjustable buckles or velcro straps. Most adjustable tank bands are designed to fit any size of tank. (See figure 1-77.)

Fig. 1-76 Tank Backpacks

Make sure the tank band is tight before each dive. Bands made of nylon webbing should be wet before the tank is secured. Adjust the backpack so that your head does not hit the tank valve when you lean back. After securing the backpack, lay the tank on its side until you are ready to put it on. Tanks left standing can fall over and cause damage to a boat or pool deck and injury to nearby people.

There are many different ways to put on a scuba tank. Your buddy can hold it for you while you slip your arms through the shoulder straps, fasten the shoulder and waist buckles, and adjust the straps. (See figure 1-78.) Another method of donning jacket and low-profile scuba units is shown in figure

Fig. 1-77 Tank Retaining Band   Fig. 1-78 Putting on the Scuba Tank (1)

Fig. 1-79 Putting on the Scuba Tank (2)

1-79. While resting at the surface, position the tank and BC assembly with the front facing toward you. Leave the shoulder straps buckled, but loose. Then, slip your right arm through the shoulder strap and slip the assembly on like you would a jacket. Make sure the hoses and straps are not entangled before you secure the cummerbund and tighten the shoulder straps.

CARE AND MAINTENANCE OF THE TANK

Scuba tank care, for the most part, means keeping out moisture. Like all diving equipment, the exterior should be rinsed thoroughly with fresh water after each dive and washed with mild soap and water when it gets dirty. To keep water out of the valve and tank, keep approximately 100 pounds of air pressure in the tank.

When carrying the tank in a car, either lay it sideways on the floor or lengthwise in the trunk, with the valve toward the rear. Wrap the valve in thick cloth, such as a beach towel, and lash it down or block it so it cannot move.

If you are traveling by air in either commercial airlines or light planes, slowly release all the air from the tank and leave the valve open. This is required by the U.S. Department of Transportation.

Rust will form inside a warm tank full of high pressure air where the oxygen from the air is concentrated. Steel tanks, therefore, should be stored in cool areas with no more than 100 psi of air inside. The metal in the tank is thicker at the bottom than around the side, so it is better to store it standing up than lying down. Aluminum tanks and perfectly dry steel tanks can be stored in any position. Whenever you store your tank, tie it down and keep it away from children.

Visual Inspections (Internal and External)

There is only one way to make sure that a tank is clean, safe, and rust-free. Thorough visual inspection at least once a year by a professional inspector is not required by law, unless there is obvious visual damage or an odor in the air, but it is highly recommended by most equipment dealers. Aluminum tanks do not rust, but they should be inspected to be sure there are no contaminants or pitting inside. Most dive shops will not fill a tank without evidence that it has had an annual inspection.

It is easier to prevent the problem of a contaminated tank than to solve it. Never release *all* the tank air. If you release it accidentally, shut the valve immediately to keep water from entering the tank. When you push the regulator purge valve with the tank valve open and the tank empty, there is a direct and open route into the tank. This increases the possibility of contamination.

Water can also get inside the tank if air is released too quickly. For example, suppose you want to store a full tank for several months. If you open the valve far enough, most of the air will escape in a matter of minutes. But, since gases cool when they expand (refrigerators and air conditioners are based on this principle), the air, and the tank itself, will become very cool. As a result, water vapor will condense on the inside of the tank. To prevent this, take a few hours to let all the air out of the tank. You can also put it in water to keep the tank's temperature from dropping too much.

When filling a tank or when attaching the regulator, make sure all fittings, openings, and "O" rings on or attached to the tank valve are clean and dry. Filling a tank with a wet valve is a sure way to introduce water into the tank.

Between annual visual inspections, look, smell, and listen to your tank for hints of water inside.

1. **Look.** Turn the valve on and check the air coming out. Damp air is white. Dry air is clear and you cannot see it.

2. **Smell.** Pure, clean air does not smell. If the air coming out of your tank smells damp and metallic, there could be water, oil, or rust inside.

3. **Listen.** Put your ear next to the tank. Turn the tank upside down so that anything inside will fall to the other end. You should not be able to hear a sound.

If you have cause for suspicion, take it in for a visual inspection. Otherwise, take it in once a year. A full-service dive store is usually equipped to inspect and test tanks. Hydrotesting firms specialize in servicing all kinds of high pressure cylinders.

The visual inspection begins when the inspector examines the tank's exterior after removing the tank band and boot. He looks for any dents, scratches, or corrosion. Then, he slowly lets all the air escape and removes the tank valve. He uses a special light or series of lights to see inside.

Rust, water, salt, flaked epoxy linings, and especially pits or rough and scaley surfaces must be cleaned. The inspector fills the tank half full with some kind of abrasive materials, such as carbide or aluminum oxide chips. After capping the tank, he lays it down on two rotating rollers to tumble, as shown in figure 1-80. The abrasive chips scrape the inside of the tank clean so the inspector can see clearly how much damage has been done. Some hydro-testing firms use a rotating chain or sandblasting machine to clean the inside, but these methods are neither thorough nor complete. *Never* let a hydrotester use chemicals inside the tank—fumes can be toxic. After tumbling, the inspector looks inside again to see if corrosion was only on the surface, or if it was more serious.

Fig. 1-80   Tank Tumbling

Hydrostatic Testing

Every five years, you must have your tank hydrostatically tested. The Department of Transportation sets testing standards and governs interstate transportation. The Bureau of Explosives investigates testing violations. Illegal hydrostatic testing operations do exist, so ask your diving instructor or dive store to suggest a reputable hydrotester. He must be licensed and authorized by the Bureau of Explosives and he should have a current letter of authorization.

After a complete visual inspection, the hydrotest begins. It is designed to measure the elasticity of the metal within the tank. A good strong tank will stretch and then return to within 10 percent of its original size with very little, if any, permanent expansion.

The tank is filled with water, connected to a high pressure water pump, and submerged in a sealed container that is also filled with water. (See figure 1-81.) Water is forced into the tank at five-thirds of its working pressure which makes the tank expand. The expanding tank forces the surrounding water in the sealed testing chamber through a tube and up into a thin glass measuring tube called a burette.

The testing pressure is held for 30 seconds and then released to let the expanded tank return to normal. To pass the test, the tank's permanent expansion cannot be more than 10 percent of the total expansion.

If the examiner feels the tank is in good enough condition to be filled 10 percent over its working pressure, he will stamp a plus sign after the new hydro date. However, this is not always done. The tank must have this 10 percent overfill to actually hold 71.2 cubic feet; otherwise, it only holds about 65 cubic feet. A tank is eligible for a plus if it has a high "K" factor. This is a number determined by measuring the thickness of the tank wall, its expansion, elasticity, and several other things. If the "K" factor is too low, your tank will not get a plus. The examiner can simply refuse to give a plus sign; it is his choice whether to use it or not. Aluminum tanks never have plus signs because the pressure stamped on them is their full rated pressure.

What happens if the tank ruptures during the hydrostatic test? Nothing much. Unlike a tank filled with air, a water-filled tank is not explosive. If the tank should break, it relieves the water pressure almost immediately without much expansion.

After the hydrotest, the tank must be thoroughly dried with hot air from the inside. Usually, hot air is blown into the tank through a tube. Heating the tank from the outside does not work—it causes steam to form which later condenses in the tank when it cools.

Hydrotesting is safe, reliable, and cheap, especially when you consider the insurance it provides. It is comforting to know your tank will hold almost twice the amount of internal pressure you will ever put into it. Feel free to hydrotest your tank more often but it must be hydrotested at least every five years.

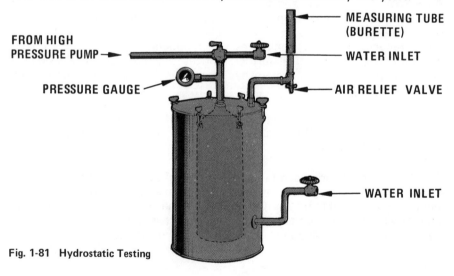

Fig. 1-81 Hydrostatic Testing

THE REGULATOR

Squeezing air into a cylinder at over 150 times its normal pressure is easy, compared to making that air usable for the diver. An ordinary on-and-off valve on top of the tank lets the air escape, but the diver using that air does not need it all the time. When he does, he needs only a small amount of air at just the right pressure. Regulating the air flow becomes pretty complicated for a simple valve; even if the diver could manually control the air flow, he would have to devote all his time and concentration on it.

This is why the demand regulator was so important to the growth of diving. Without it, a diver would have to turn the air on and leave it on—wasting most of his limited supply in a hurry. With the regulator, the diver gets just the right amount of air, at the right pressure, and at the right time.

SELECTING A REGULATOR

Regulators are finely adjusted, precise pieces of equipment designed for reliability and durability. Some regulators, however, breathe easier and more smoothly than others. A regulator that is difficult to inhale from or exhale into has *breathing resistance*. This is annoying at best and extremely tiring at worst.

Breathing resistance is caused by a number of things. Hard work and cold water make you breathe much harder. Most regulators have very little breathing resistance at the water surface. The real test occurs near the end of a long hard dive, in deep water, when the tank pressure is low. Here, heavy breathing, increased water pressure, and decreasing air pressure inside the tank all tend to increase breathing resistance.

What makes one regulator easier to breathe through than another? To understand the answer, and to know what to look for in a regulator, you must have a basic understanding of regulator operation. Modern regulators reduce the tank pressure to a breathable pressure in two stages. The first stage reduces the high tank pressure to about 140 psi over ambient pressure. The second stage further reduces that pressure to a workable breathing pressure. This system has proven itself to be very smooth and reliable.

The single hose, two-stage regulator, shown in figure 1-82, provides a consistent delivery of air. The single hose regulator puts the second stage next to the mouthpiece.

There are two designs used in the first stage of the single hose, two-stage regulator: the diaphragm and the piston. The first stage diaphragm, shown in figure 1-83, is flexible rubber. On one side of the diaphragm is a spring that pushes about 140 pounds of pressure against it. On the other side is a spring with about 140 pounds to counteract the first spring.

Fig. 1-82 Single Hose, Two-Stage Regulator

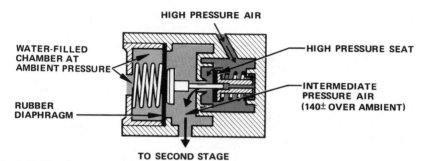

Fig. 1-83 First-Stage Diaphragm

When you inhale, you lower the pressure which overrides the springs. This opens the high pressure seat and allows air to flow into the collecting chamber. When you descend, water pressure pushes against the diaphragm and helps the outer spring maintain the 140 pound balance over ambient pressure.

The piston's first stage is similar to the diaphragm, but a piston, instead of a diaphragm controls the airflow, as shown in figure 1-84.

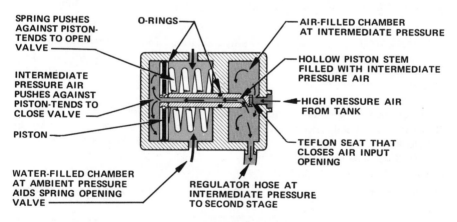

Fig. 1-84 First-Stage Piston

Either type of first stage can be "unbalanced" or "balanced." Since, in the two preceding illustrations, only one side of the first stage valve is exposed to tank pressure, the valve is unbalanced. In this case, as tank pressure varies so does the pressure provided to the second stage. This causes breathing resistance to increase as the tank pressure decreases. Therefore, more inhalation effort is required to open the first stage valve at the end of a dive when the tank pressure is low.

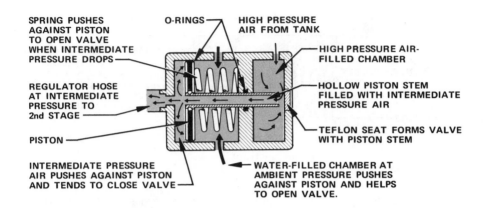

SPRING PUSHES AGAINST PISTON TO OPEN VALVE WHEN INTERMEDIATE PRESSURE DROPS

O-RINGS

HIGH PRESSURE AIR FROM TANK

HIGH PRESSURE AIR-FILLED CHAMBER

REGULATOR HOSE AT INTERMEDIATE PRESSURE TO 2nd STAGE

HOLLOW PISTON STEM FILLED WITH INTERMEDIATE PRESSURE AIR

PISTON

TEFLON SEAT FORMS VALVE WITH PISTON STEM

INTERMEDIATE PRESSURE AIR PUSHES AGAINST PISTON AND TENDS TO CLOSE VALVE

WATER-FILLED CHAMBER AT AMBIENT PRESSURE PUSHES AGAINST PISTON AND HELPS TO OPEN VALVE.

Fig. 1-85 Balanced Piston First-Stage

To achieve a balanced condition both sides of the first stage valve are exposed to the identical pressure. As shown in figure 1-85, this is achieved by venting or porting air to both sides of the first stage valve. In this condition, the first stage delivers air to the second stage at a relatively constant pressure which is controlled by spring tension. With this design, changing tank pressure does not affect breathing resistance and the second stage can be better tuned to the constant pressure provided by the first stage.

The pressure to the second stage stays at about 140 psi over the ambient pressure. This intermediate pressure is further broken down to ambient levels by the second stage at the mouthpiece.

Early one hose regulators used a *tilt valve* in the second stage. As the term implies, the tilt valve opens by tipping to one side when you inhale, as shown in figure 1-86. But this constant tipping tends to deform the valve seat and causes leakage.

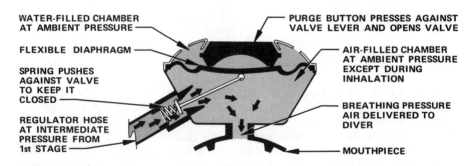

WATER-FILLED CHAMBER AT AMBIENT PRESSURE

PURGE BUTTON PRESSES AGAINST VALVE LEVER AND OPENS VALVE

FLEXIBLE DIAPHRAGM

AIR-FILLED CHAMBER AT AMBIENT PRESSURE EXCEPT DURING INHALATION

SPRING PUSHES AGAINST VALVE TO KEEP IT CLOSED

BREATHING PRESSURE AIR DELIVERED TO DIVER

REGULATOR HOSE AT INTERMEDIATE PRESSURE FROM 1st STAGE

MOUTHPIECE

Fig. 1-86 Single Hose Upstream Regulator

The downstream lever action valve solved the problem of the tilt valve deforming the valve seat. *Downstream* refers to a valve that opens *away* from the pressure and with the airflow. The *upstream* valve opens *toward* the pressure and against the flow of air. High pressure air tends to push the downstream valve open, so this type opens very easily and smoothly. The downstream valve is flat and sits directly against a flanged seat. When it opens, the lever simply pulls the valve away and allows the air to flow into the second stage without deforming the valve seat. (See figure 1-87.) If the valve fails to close it will "free flow." When a regulator free flows, air is rapidly lost. However, you can still breathe from the regulator. This is a safety feature that allows you to get to the surface safely.

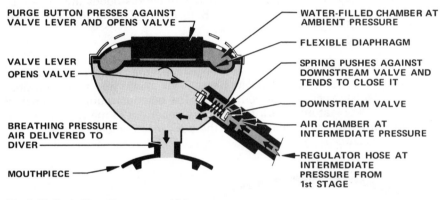

PURGE BUTTON PRESSES AGAINST VALVE LEVER AND OPENS VALVE

WATER-FILLED CHAMBER AT AMBIENT PRESSURE

FLEXIBLE DIAPHRAGM

VALVE LEVER OPENS VALVE

SPRING PUSHES AGAINST DOWNSTREAM VALVE AND TENDS TO CLOSE IT

DOWNSTREAM VALVE

BREATHING PRESSURE AIR DELIVERED TO DIVER

AIR CHAMBER AT INTERMEDIATE PRESSURE

REGULATOR HOSE AT INTERMEDIATE PRESSURE FROM 1st STAGE

MOUTHPIECE

Fig. 1-87 Single Hose Downstream Valve

All one hose demand regulators have a large rubber diaphragm in the second stage. As water pressure increases, it presses against the rubber diaphragm which puts pressure against the lever inside the second stage. The water pressure acting directly on the diaphragm and lever aids the diver in compensating for the ambient water pressure surrounding his chest and lungs. Because of this, the second stage valve opens with an absolute minimum of effort. In fact, most high quality regulators manufactured today almost breathe for you; they require very little breathing effort.

A high quality regulator is important. The regulator is the lifeline to your complete system; without it, nothing else works. While most regulators manufactured today are good, there are important differences between the low cost and the more expensive models.

The differences are in durability and dependability. Most low cost regulators have chrome-plated brass inside, while most expensive regulators are machined stainless steel. You find higher quality parts in the more expensive regulators and the method for reducing air pressure is more sophisticated and dependable than in the lower cost models.

RESERVE OPTIONS

Octopus Regulator

Beginning about 1965, single hose regulators became available with a second hose and mouthpiece. This double, or "octopus," regulator is shown in figure 1-88. The second mouthpiece and hose are attached to an extra low-pressure port on the regulator's first stage.

The octopus regulator has two valuable safety features. It provides a safety backup system to the primary regulator in case of failure. It also provides an independent mouthpiece for emergency buddy breathing. If one member of a buddy team loses his air supply, he simply notifies his buddy and breathes from his buddy's octopus mouthpiece. Both divers ascend to the surface while sharing air from the same tank.

The octopus regulator hose is usually longer than the primary hose, so it is important not to let it hang loosely. Secure it in some way to keep it protected but readily available for your buddy. The octopus regulator is such a significant safety feature, that it has become important to many sport divers as a standard piece of equipment like the buoyancy compensator and submersible pressure gauge.

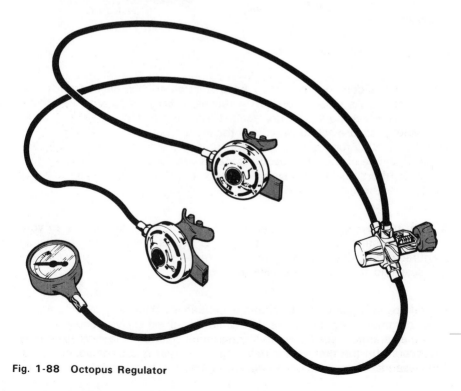

Fig. 1-88 Octopus Regulator

First Stage Reserves

The diver who runs out of air underwater has no excuse. With proper dive planning, you can easily finish every dive with the minimum 500 psi left in your tank. The "J" valve is a common first stage reserve that warns you when your air supply reaches approximately 300 to 600 psi. To work, however, the "J" valve lever must be in the up position until you pull it down to use the reserve air. If it accidentally gets knocked down, or if you forget to set it before the dive, it will not work. A conscientious diver, though, should not have to wait to be warned before surfacing. The more air you have in your tank at the end of the dive means the more air you will have to cope with unforeseen problems at the surface.

One solution to the problem of a nonworking lever is to omit it altogether so it cannot be accidentally knocked down. The audible, or sound, reserve is built into the first stage of some regulators. It is automatic. When your air supply gets down to the warning level, the audible alarm buzzes or clicks every time you inhale. When this happens, both you and your buddy know you are breathing reserve air and that it is time to ascend.

Both the "J" valve and the audible alarm warn you, but they do not give information about your air supply. The submersible pressure gauge, shown in figure 1-89, tells you exactly how much air you have left in your tank at any time. It is a standard piece of equipment for scuba divers and should be considered mandatory. The pressure gauge is like a fuel gauge in a car — it does no good unless you look at it. Check your pressure gauge regularly during the dive. It's a very important piece of equipment—don't ever dive without one. (See also Part I, Section D.)

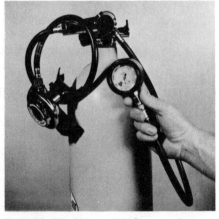

Fig. 1-89 The Submersible Pressure Gauge

Pressure gauges are connected to the first stage of the regulator at the high pressure port. Together with a "J" valve or audible alarm, the pressure gauge lets you monitor your air supply throughout the dive, while the warning device works as a backup system to warn you when you go on reserve.

USING THE REGULATOR

The outside of the regulator is a rugged metal container. The inside is more delicate and should be kept as clean as possible. Protect the mouthpiece from sand and dirt, and always keep a plastic dust cap firmly in the first

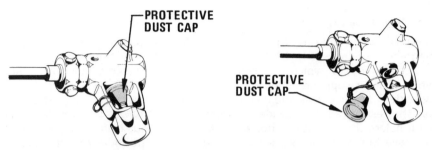

Fig. 1-90 Protective Dust Cap

stage regulator yoke, as shown in figure 1-90. Never move or store a regulator that is attached to the tank valve. Remove it as soon as you finish diving.

Assembly

Attaching the first stage to the tank is a critical operation. Check that the opening in the tank valve is clean and dry. Then follow the steps illustrated in figure 1-92, when you attach the regulator to your tank.

1. Begin with the tank in front of you and the backpack on the opposite side. Momentarily open the tank valve to blow out any dust or moisture which may have accumulated. Stay clear of the opening while blowing it out.

2. Check the "O" rig in the valve. If it is nicked or broken — replace it.

3. Hold the second stage of the regulator in your right hand, the first stage in your left and put the yoke over the tank valve. (The air hose always comes over your right shoulder.)

4. Turn the regulator yoke screw until it is two-finger tight. If you tighten it too much, it will be hard to remove and will damage the "O" ring. Check the exhaust valve by attempting to inhale through the regulator. If you cannot inhale, the valve is functioning properly.

5. Turn the valve knob counterclockwise to turn on the air. Always hold the pressure gauge down and away from your face in case it ruptures. Carefully open the valve all the way turning it very gently. When the valve is all the way open, close it about one-quarter turn. Listen for leaks. If you hear one, turn the valve off and locate the source of the leak.

6. Press the purge valve. You should hear air flowing freely. Then, place the mouthpiece in your mouth, inhale and exhale to make sure it is working. If the exhaust is stuck shut, place the second stage in water for a few moments, then blow hard into the mouthpiece.

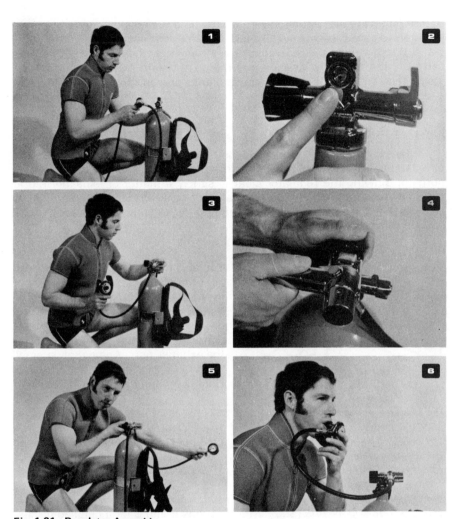

Fig. 1-91   Regulator Assembly

REGULATOR CARE AND MAINTENANCE

If clean fresh water is nearby, rinse the regulator and tank before taking them apart. Flush water into the mouthpiece and through the exhaust ports, as shown in figure 1-92. Be careful not to ever press the purge button while rinsing the second stage inside, however it is alright while rinsing the outside. This will keep water from entering the air hose which should always stay clean and dry.

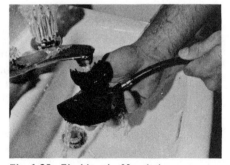

Fig. 1-92   Flushing the Mouthpiece

Before removing the regulator, turn off the air and press the purge button to let intermediate pressure air escape. Dry the dust cap before putting it in place. When storing the regulator, do not hang it by the regulator yoke. This can bend the hose and weaken it at the point where it attaches to the first stage. Instead, store it in a protective bag to prevent dust and abuse from shortening the regulator's life.

REGULATOR CLEARING

If you take the regulator out of your mouth underwater, the mouthpiece and air chamber will fill with water. There are two ways to clear it: blowing or purging. Blowing the regulator clear is simply a matter of exhaling into it. Unlike clearing a snorkel, only a small puff of air is needed to completely clear it. If you feel you do not have enough air in your lungs to exhale, try coughing a couple of times.

You also may clear the regulator with air from the tank. With the regulator in your mouth, just push the purge button momentarily as shown in figure 1-93. Air coming into the regulator will force the water out through the exhaust port. Again, only a small amount of air is needed to completely clear the regulator.

Fig. 1-93 Clearing the Regulator Using the Purge Button

After clearing the regulator, inhale cautiously. There may still be water in the regulator air chamber. If there is, clear again. When using a regulator underwater, breathe deeply and regularly. Do not breathe at a faster than normal rate and do not breathe slower in order to save air. *Remember, never hold your breath underwater while using scuba. Always keep breathing, especially during ascent.* (See Part II, Sections B and C for a detailed discussion of breathing.)

REGULATOR RECOVERY

How do you find a lost mouthpiece? One sure way is to reach back with your right hand to where the regulator is attached to the tank, as shown in figure 1-94. (This may be easier if, with your left hand, you lift the bottom of the tank and tilt the top toward your right shoulder.) When you find the attachment point move your hand down the hose until it runs into the mouthpiece.

Another method is to simply dip your right shoulder down and to the right. The mouthpiece should swing around and hang in front of you, as shown in figure 1-95.

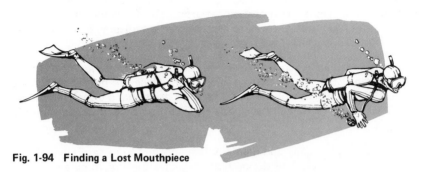

Fig. 1-94   Finding a Lost Mouthpiece

Either of these two methods will work in or out of the water. Normally, if the mouthpiece is not in your mouth, it will be draped over your shoulder or hanging along the right side of the tank.

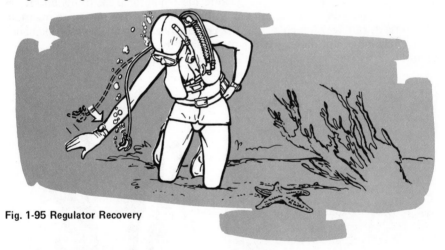

Fig. 1-95 Regulator Recovery

BUDDY BREATHING

With good equipment care and dive planning, there is little chance you will ever lose your air supply. But you cannot eliminate the possibility of equipment breakdowns and diver mistakes. Buddy breathing is one method of returning to the surface safely, but it is recommended that you use octopus regulators whenever possible to avoid any problems or confusion that often accompany the need to share air. Two additional techniques, emergency swimming ascents and emergency buoyant ascents, are discussed in Part II, Section C.

Buddy breathing is a process in which two divers share one air supply. It has been taught for years as an emergency ascent method for any diver who runs out of air or experiences equipment failure. It has been an especially important technique for emergency use whenever obstructions, such as caves, wrecks, heavy kelp, or ice, have come between the diver and the surface.

Recent advances in equipment design and diving techniques, however, have given the diver important alternative ascent procedures for emergencies. Buddy breathing is no longer the *only* way to ascend in an emergency, but it is still an important sport diving skill.

Buddy breathing begins when the diver who needs air, the *needer*, notifies the diver who has air, the *donor*, that he needs help. Once the needer recognizes the problem and gains control, he uses the appropriate hand signals, as shown on pages 2-10 and 2-11, to tell his buddy he is out of air and wants to buddy breathe.

Since the needer is physically and mentally handicapped from "air hunger," the donor must take control. The donor must regulate the breathing and ascent rates.

The buddy team should quickly establish a breathing rhythm with each diver taking one or two breaths before passing the regulator back to his buddy, as shown in figure 1-96. The donor should be in front of the needer to maintain eye contact, but far enough to the right of the needer to enable easy exchange of the regulator mouthpiece without bending the regulator hose. The divers should hold each other's equipment straps with their free hands.

Fig. 1-96
Buddy Breathing with Single Hose Regulator

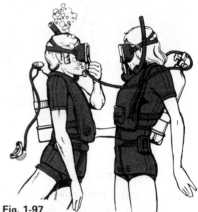

Fig. 1-97
Buddy Breathing with Octopus Regulator

Once the buddy team establishes a breathing rhythm, stable position, and neutral or slightly positive buoyancy, they should ascend by kicking slowly and exhaling carefully between inhalations. Each diver should try to blow the regulator clear on each exchange, but should be ready to use the purge button if necessary.

If you need buoyancy, exhale into the oral inflator on the buoyancy compensator while your buddy breathes from the regulator. Too much buoyancy will make you rise too rapidly, but too little buoyancy will force you to swim too hard, so try to establish neutral or slightly positive buoyancy before ascending.

Buddy breathing with an octopus regulator is, of course, much easier, as shown in figure 1-97. Once the needer has the octopus mouthpiece in place, the two divers can ascend simply and safely. In all buddy breathing situations, however, it is likely that if one diver is out of air, the other diver will also be low on air. As a result, you should be prepared to stop buddy breathing at any time during the ascent and switch to an emergency swimming or buoyant ascent.

Buddy breathing requires coordination between buddies; you also need a lot of concentration. It is easy to lose track of your rate of ascent, and it is especially tempting to hold your breath when the regulator is not in your mouth. *Again, never hold your breath when using scuba gear. When buddy breathing, make sure both you and your buddy exhale continuously when not inhaling.*

Buddy breathing in a pool or on a training dive is a complex skill that needs repeated practice and drill for it to work smoothly in an emergency. *Don't forget to exhale continuously. When the mouthpiece is not in your mouth, your first instinct is to hold your breath. Don't. Make a point to blow a stream of bubbles out of your mouth at all times and make sure your buddy does the same. If he does not, stop your ascent until he starts exhaling.*

BUDDY SYSTEM
Buddy breathing is only one small part of a broader technique that should be practiced on every dive you make — the buddy system. In fact, with the buddy system as an essential part of your diving skills— the need for buddy breathing will be minimized. Both you and your buddy will have agreed upon time and depth limits *before the dive* to ensure there will be ample air left for both of you to ascend.

There are other pre-dive pointers that are crucial for the buddy system to operate smoothly:

1. Know your buddy's gear as well as your own. This includes knowing where all your buddy's equipment is located so you can find it at a moment's notice. It is especially important to know how each buckle works and how to inflate the buoyancy compensator. (See figure 1-98.)

2. Know what you want to accomplish during your dive. Both you and your buddy should collectively prepare a dive plan. As shown in figure 1-99, the plan should be reviewed prior to entering the water. this allows you to coordinate how you will use equipment and stay together to carry out the common goal.

3. Determine how you will stay together, what signals to use, and what to do if you should become separated, or in case of an emergency.

4. Know your entry and exit points and what diving conditions to consider, for example, weather, current, and bottom configuration. (See also Part III, Section A.)

Fig. 1-98 Equipment Check

Once in the water you should stick with your dive plan and maintain visual or physical contact so you will be able to render aid the moment it is needed. (For a discussion of first aid techniques, see Part II, Section B.)

The self-contained breathing apparatus was little more than a recurring dream for over 2,000 years. Almost suddenly, science fiction became scientific fact in the middle of this century. A complete understanding of this "breathing machine" and how to use it with the buddy system, gives you uncomplicated, free access to the underwater realm.

Fig. 1-99 Review the Dive Plan

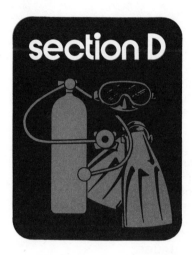

section D underwater information

- PRESSURE GAUGE
- WATCH
- DIVE TIMER
- DEPTH GAUGE
- DIVE COMPUTER
- COMPASS
- NATURAL NAVIGATION

PRESSURE, TIME, AND DIRECTION DEVICES

Living on land is a relatively flat, two-dimensional experience. The position of the sun, countless clocks, convenient roads, and other landmarks help determine time and direction. Terrestrial air supply is normally unlimited.

The underwater realm, however, is an uncharted, three-dimensional place. The regular time indicators disappear. Ordinary direction markers are obscured, making all directions indistinguishable. A diver's air supply is definitely limited.

This, of course, is part of what gives the diving environment its magic. But without correct information, it can lead to disorientation. The diver needs equipment to inform him of exactly how much air remains in his tank, where he is, and how long he has been there. Like all diving gear, this equipment has one primary purpose—safety.

SUBMERSIBLE PRESSURE GAUGE

At one time, the submersible pressure gauge was a fancy option. Now it is a standard piece of a diver's equipment. It is the *only* way to assess accurately how much time you can continue to dive. Diving without a submersible pressure gauge is like driving a car without a fuel gauge.

SELECTING A PRESSURE GAUGE

The submersible pressure gauge attaches to a high pressure port on the first stage regulator. The gauge should be built to withstand rugged abuse and shock. Durable metal housings, rubber protective cases, and consoles all help to protect the gauge. A swivel head, large markings, and scratch resistant glass make the gauge more usable underwater.

USING THE PRESSURE GAUGE

Figure 1-100 illustrates the proper technique for turning on the air and reading the tank pressure. When you turn on the tank valve, hold the pressure gauge by the hose or console; do not hold onto the gauge itself. Never point the gauge at yourself or your buddy while turning on the air, in case the glass accidentally shatters.

While submerged, make sure the pressure gauge is secure and does not hang loose. Some buoyancy compensators have velcro straps that are specifically designed to hold the pressure gauge. You also can attach the pressure gauge to a tank strap or tuck it under your BC. Whatever you do, don't forget to use it. Develop the habit of regularly monitoring your gauge, air consumption, and remaining air supply.

CARE AND MAINTENANCE OF THE PRESSURE GAUGE

Rinse the pressure gauge thoroughly after every dive, being careful not to let water enter the high pressure hose. This could introduce contaminants into the gauge and tank regulator. When storing the gauge, do not crimp the hose. Keep it straight or in a gentle curve.

DIVING WATCH

It is almost impossible to correctly estimate the passage of time underwater, because the sun is difficult to see and your attention is usually focused intensely on other things. Diving is an extremely active sport, requiring concentration on your buddy, the equipment, the environment, and yourself. With so much happening, time passes quickly. Below 30 feet, the time factor becomes critical. Your time on the bottom must stay within certain limits to avoid decompression problems. (See Part II, Section D.) A diving watch, like the one in figure 1-101, is a necessary piece of equipment.

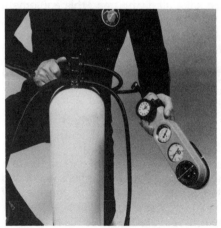

Fig. 1-100 Submersible Pressure Gauge

Fig. 1-101 Diving Watch

SELECTING A DIVING WATCH

Not all water-resistant or waterproof watches can withstand increased underwater pressure. A diving watch should be labeled and pressure tested to at least 220 feet (660 feet preferred). It should have a solid stainless steel machined case.

The movable bezel, surrounding the watch face, marks elapsed time. Notice this part in figure 1-101. It should have a positive hold to eliminate any accidental movements. A large, serrated edge makes the bezel easier to set, especially when you are wearing gloves. Some watches incorporate a liquid crystal display (LCD) stop watch that simplifies the reading of elapsed time. The new electronic watches that are specifically designed for sport diving are inexpensive and reliable.

DIVE TIMERS

Keeping track of your bottom time is made simple through the use of timers like the one in figure 1-102. Several styles are available with either LCD readout or sweep hands. Bottom timers are basically stopwatches that are activated by pressure when the descent begins, and stopped when you return to shallow water. Some models can even keep track of your surface interval time and number of dives.

DEPTH GAUGE

You should always have a way of monitoring your depth. When you dive below 30 feet, you must know exactly how deep you are diving to estimate the rate of air consumption and to avoid problems with decompression. (See Part II, Sections D and E.) Because of this, a depth gauge is considered standard equipment.

SELECTING A DEPTH GAUGE

There are three kinds of depth gauges: the capillary, bourdon tube, and diaphragm gauge. Depth gauges are not always accurate and, in fact, can become inaccurate with normal use. Therefore, you should have your depth gauge tested periodically.

The capillary gauge is the simplest and least expensive. It has no moving parts and is extremely accurate down to about 60 feet. "Capillary" refers to the thin plastic tube shown in figure 1-103. It has one open end, so when the diver descends, increased water pressure compresses the air and allows water to enter the tube. At 33 feet, for example, the air in the tube is compressed to half its original volume; at 66 feet, it is compressed to one-third; at 99 feet, one-fourth; and so on. The depth reading is the point on the dial where air and water in the tube meet.

The tube should be removed from the dial and cleaned occasionally. This is especially true in salt water. Salt crystals can form inside the tube. If this happens, use a pipe cleaner to remove the crystals.

Fig. 1-102 Dive Timer

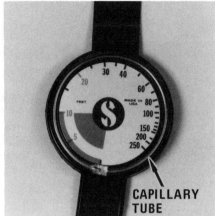

Fig. 1-103 Capillary Depth Gauge

The bourdon tube and diaphragm depth gauges are more expensive than the capillary gauge, but they are more accurate and easier to read below 30 feet. (See figure 1-104.) As you descend, ambient pressure is transmitted to an internal mechanism that, in turn, moves the indicator on the face of the gauge. Some depth gauges have a small opening in the case that allows water and, therefore, ambient pressure to act directly on the mechanism. This type of gauge should be rinsed in warm, fresh water after every dive. Before storing it, soak the gauge in water to help keep salt crystals from forming inside the case.

The depth gauge in figure 1-105 incorporates a maximum depth indicator. As you descend, both needles move to show your actual depth. When you ascend, the maximum depth needle remains at the deepest depth attained, while the other needle continues to register your present depth. This gauge eliminates the guesswork of determining your maximum depth after a dive.

Fig. 1-104 Depth Gauge

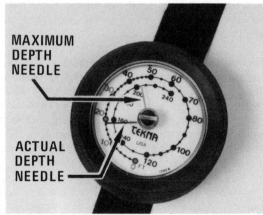

Fig. 1-105 Maximum Depth Gauge

Fig. 1-106 Dive Computers

DIVE COMPUTERS

The growth of microprocessor and computer technology has brought significant changes to the diving community in recent years. The introduction of dive computers like the ones shown in figure 1-106, could revolutionize the way divers monitor and plan their dives. Before you use one of these devices, you should research and understand its limitations, as well as how the information is derived and displayed. The dive computer tells you what is happening during the dive and provides a historical record of how the dive turned out. It does not eliminate the need to preplan the dive and to plan repetitive dives with the use of the dive tables. Always use the dive tables to plan depths, times, and surface intervals. It is also advisable to cross-check the computer with your watch, submersible pressure gauge, and depth gauge until you feel comfortable that the dive computer is providing the information you want.

COMPASS

The compass is important for both safety and convenience. A compass is the only way to maintain a sense of direction in murky or turbid water where visibility is poor. Night diving requires a compass for both underwater and surface orientation. In some coastal waters, it is not uncommon to descend under blue skies and surface in a thick fog. The compass indicates the way to shore and is a valuable navigation tool even when visibility is excellent. It is the only way to avoid repeated trips to the surface to check direction.

SELECTING A COMPASS

The simple watchband compass shown in figure 1-107, is the least expensive. It gives general direction but is not very accurate. The larger side-reading wrist compass in figure 1-108, is more accurate and gives good directional and navigational information.

Fig. 1-107 Watchband Compass   Fig. 1-108 Side-Reading Compass

Probably the most common underwater compass is the top-reading navigation type shown in figure 1-109. It is designed for complete underwater navigation and has a movable face marked with desired course bracket lines
that can be set for a specific course. The lubber line helps maintain course
by providing a sighting line. The movable face should be ratcheted, or
notched, so it will not move accidently during a dive.

USING THE COMPASS

To use a compass you must first understand basic direction. A compass
displays direction in terms of a 360° circle; where 0° is north, 90° is east,
180° is south, and 270° is west. To navigate underwater, take the hand that
has the compass and grasp the opposite arm at the elbow. Your opposite
arm should be pointing in the direction you plan to swim, as shown in figure
1-110.

If you want to swim a westerly course, set the movable bracket lines on the
face of the compass opposite 270° on the bezel. Then, move until the com-

Fig. 1-109 Top-Reading Navigation Compass

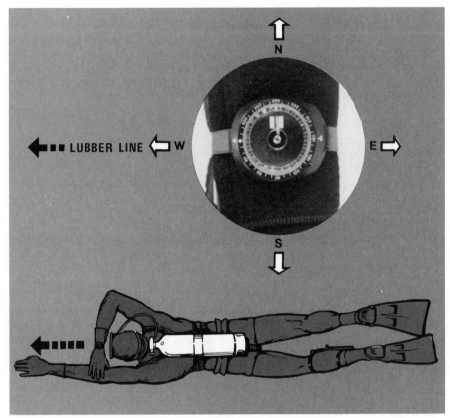

Fig. 1-110 Using the Compass

pass needle is between the brackets. To maintain the heading, simply keep the compass needle between the bracket lines and sight along the lubber line.

Hold the compass level. When tilted too far, the compass card will no longer move freely and will drag on the compass body, preventing accurate direction control.

RECIPROCAL DIVE COURSES

Before you can compute a reciprocal dive course, (coming back on the same course line you went out on) you must first determine the compass heading for the outbound course. For example, assume the outbound course is 290°. The return, reciprocal, or inbound course is 180° from the outbound course. In this case, it would be 110°, (290° - 180° = 110°). Because the outbound course is 290° it is easiest to subtract 180°. If the outbound course is less than 180°, the proper procedure would be to add 180°.

NATURAL NAVIGATION

Although the compass is a valuable piece of equipment, you should also use the natural aids available to you to help in underwater navigation. Maintaining your direction and orientation underwater can challenge your senses. Underwater your senses of touch, hearing, and seeing are severely handicapped, especially when wearing a wet suit with hood and gloves. However, your sense of direction and orientation can be greatly enhanced if you learn to use the numerous natural navigation aids.

Before entering the water study the diving area from a vantage point. The underwater environment is normally an extension of the shoreline. The land contours above water can be indicative of land contours beneath the water. Note the relative location of any kelp beds, shallow reefs, rocks, and other features which can be used later to help maintain your direction. The speed and direction of any currents is also relevant information. The tidal condition should be considered and verified with appropriate charts or tables. Notice the position of the sun or moon and the direction the light rays enter the water. Anticipate the movement of the sun or moon during your planned dive.

As you descend, maintain your orientation by facing in the direction of your initial heading. Pay attention to your surroundings. Check the direction and strength of the current. Normally, it is wise to begin your dive into the current and then take advantage of it as you return to the starting point. Above all, avoid having to fight the current toward the end of your dive. On the bottom, note any features that can be used as landmarks. Check the bottom contour and the depth. Normally, they are indicators of the distance and direction from shore. The ambient light level and presence of various colors are also natural depth indicators.

Throughout the dive look for features that were observed during your initial overview of the dive area. In addition, use any natural directional indicators that are available. Ripple marks on a sandy bottom generally run parallel to the shoreline. Sand dollars, standing on end, also parallel the shoreline. Surge always moves in and out in relation to the shoreline. The surge movement toward the shore is always stronger than the movement away from it. Sometimes a constant sound or noise can be used as a direction indicator. The intensity of the sound may be used as an indication of your distance from the source.

Natural navigation requires a keen awareness of the environment. This instinct will develop as you continue to experience the underwater environment and exercise your powers of observation. For a complete discussion of underwater navigation techniques, see the Advanced Manual.

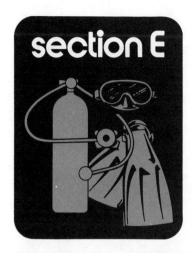

section E

tools and accessories

- FLOAT/FLAG, WHISTLE, AND FLARE
- KNIFE
- LIGHT
- LOGBOOK, THERMOMETER, AND DIVE TABLE
- GEAR BAG

SPECIAL EQUIPMENT AND TOOLS

People need special tools for most sports and jobs. A tool may be as simple as a baseball glove or as complicated as a computer, but whatever it is, it makes the task easier and safer. After skin diving and scuba diving began to grow in the 1950's, it didn't take long to develop waterproof and corrosion resistant tools. Now, the diver has tools to notify others of his location, to perform underwater tasks, to gather and record information, and to repair and protect equipment. Once you have fully adapted to the underwater environment, using tools becomes a big part of diving.

FLOAT AND FLAG

A boater on the surface cannot see an underwater diver. Even when buddy teams are at the surface, they are difficult to see from a fast-moving boat. This is why the diver's flag is an important safety tool. It protects the dive team by warning boats to stay clear. It means that divers are in the area—stay away.

Figure 1-111 shows the two flags in common use. The sport diver's flag is red and white with a white diagonal stripe. It means, "there are free-swimming sport divers below; keep well clear at slow speed." The diver's flag should be flown only when sport divers are actually in the water. This is the primary flag used for sport divers and is governed by tradition and some state regulations. The "alpha" flag is white and blue with a "v" cut into one edge. It is primarily a boaters flag that means, "this vessel has divers below and maneuverability is

Fig. 1-111 Diver's Flags

restricted." It is generally used when divers are tethered to the vessel by hoses or lines, such as during commercial diving operations. The use of the alpha flag is governed by U.S. Coast Guard regulations and applies only to international and inland navigable waterways.

The diver's flag hangs from a pole that can be attached to either a small buoy, inner tube, surfmat, surfboard, or small boat. (See figure 1-112.) Floats can be resting stations during the dive, and larger floats are good places to store equipment. In emergencies, the floats quickly become helpful pieces of rescue equipment.

Fig. 1-112   Diving Floats

WHISTLE (Surface Signal)

Your buddy is your constant under-water companion; you should never leave your buddy, and the two of you should not stray far from the dive float or beach. A whistle effectively reunites divers who have strayed or separated accidentally. A simple whistle made out of plastic or some other noncorrosive material should be tied to the oral inflation tube on your buoyancy compensator. (See figure 1-113.) A whistle is easier to hear over wind and waves and is less tiring than shouting or yelling.

Fig. 1-113   Emergency Diving Whistle

FLARE

A special day and night diving flare, pictured in figure 1-114, has a red smoke flare at one end and a red light at the other, for either day or night use. It should be taped to a belt or knife sheath. Even though the flare is waterproof, it will not ignite while submerged. Although available, flares are expensive and not in common use.

Fig. 1-114 Day and Night Flare

Fig. 1-115 Chemical Glow Light

For night diving, the chemical glow light, shown in figure 1-115, is an excellent safety device. It is a small glass container surrounded by a sealed plastic tube. To light the flare, simply bend the tube and break the glass container. When the two chemicals mix, they create a light-green glow that is extremely visible underwater at night. Both buddies should activate their glow lights at the beginning of a night dive for easy location. A common practice is to tie the glow light to the tank valve. In this position it will float up and not interfere with night vision.

DIVE KNIFE

A knife is one of the most useful diving tools. The knife might be called the diver's primary tool. It is a hammer, saw, screwdriver, lever, pry bar, ruler, probe, and cutting tool. A primary purpose of a knife in fresh water is to cut fishing line if entangled. It is rarely, if ever, used as a weapon against underwater life. Trying to fight off a shark with a knife is not only ridiculous, it could also aggravate the situation.

The dive knife and dive tool, shown in figure 1-116, should be made out of high-quality, noncorrosive steel that is strong enough for prying and hard enough to hold a sharp edge. The blade should extend all the way through an unbreakable handle. Divers pound with the hard steel butt at the end of the handle.

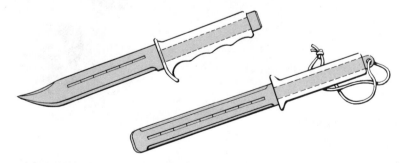

Fig. 1-116 Dive Knife and Tool

The knife sheath should have long, stretchable leg straps, strong buckles and a strong positive retainer to keep the knife in place.

For accessibility with both hands and to avoid snagging anything on the handle, wear the knife on the inside of the calf. Rinse and dry both knife and sheath after every dive.

UNDERWATER LIGHT

The underwater light makes night diving possible. It also adds a new dimension to daytime diving. Most colors are absorbed by water below 60 feet. The diving light restores vivid reds and yellows that would be lost without light.

There are three types of diving lights, as shown in figure 1-117. The first is basically a waterproof flashlight. The second light is much brighter. It uses more powerful dry cell batteries and sealed beam lamps. The sealed beam is like a waterproof automobile headlight with a built-in reflector and lens. The third type of underwater light uses a rechargeable battery. It comes with a separate charger and usually lasts from one to three hours before it needs recharging. Nonrechargeable battery lights often have a lower initial cost, but in the long run, they can be more expensive than rechargeable lights.

Fig. 1-117 Diving Lights

The diving light must, of course, be waterproof and pressure proof. If the battery fits into a plastic or metal case, be sure to store it separately from the housing and make sure everything is clean and dry before storing it. For a complete discussion of night diving and underwater lights, see the Advanced Manual.

LOGBOOK, THERMOMETER, AND DIVE TABLE

One of your most important tools is information. It helps you understand your diving experiences and enables you to plan future dives intelligently. The logbook provides a record of good diving spots, depths, visibility, diving times, and total diving hours. Recording temperatures, for example, helps you anticipate wet suit needs for the next dive. Diving ability improves with experience, so the more information you can gather and record, the more experience you can bring to the next dive.

The logbook, thermometer, and dive table, all shown in figure 1-118, help you gather and record information. Like all diving instruments, the thermometer should be waterproof, pressure proof, and easy to read. The dive table is an essential piece of equipment that enables you to plan your dive. An underwater slate can be used to record times, depths, temperatures, and other observations that you will want to transfer to the logbook later. You can also use it to communicate with your buddy during the dive.

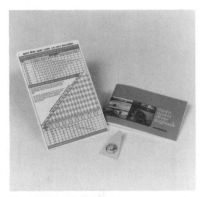

Fig. 1-118 Logbook, Thermometer, and Slate

SPARE PARTS AND REPAIR KIT

You may not realize the importance of each piece of diving equipment until you lose something as simple as a fin strap and are forced to bring the day's diving to an end. A simple repair kit with tools and spare parts is an excellent way to keep your gear working and you diving. Here are a few spare parts to take along:

1. Fin strap and buckle
2. Mask strap and buckle
3. "O" rings for tank valve
4. CO_2 cartridges
5. Snorkel-keeper
6. Regulator high pressure plug
7. Nylon line
8. Batteries
9. Silicone spray
10. Wet suit cement
11. Needle and thread
12. Mask lens
13. Silicone grease
14. Anti-fog solution
15. Waterproof plastic tape

Along with the spare parts, you should also have tools such as pliers, adjustable wrench, and screwdriver.

GEAR BAG

There are a number of different gear bags, packs, and containers to hold your gear and keep it organized, as shown in figure 1-119. Make certain it is large enough to hold all your gear except the tank and weight belt. Seams, handles, and zippers should be heavy duty and noncorrosive. Heavy cotton or nylon canvas, reinforced vinyl, or plastic are often used for gear bags.

When packing your gear bag, put the fins and other nonbreakable items on the bottom. Pack delicate instruments such as regulators, meters, gauges, compasses, and cameras in separate, rigid containers. Tanks are usually carried separately. Do not store anything in your gear bag unless it is perfectly clean and dry. The gear bag is both convenient and important when it comes to protecting equipment. Be sure it is strong enough to *withstand rough handling.*

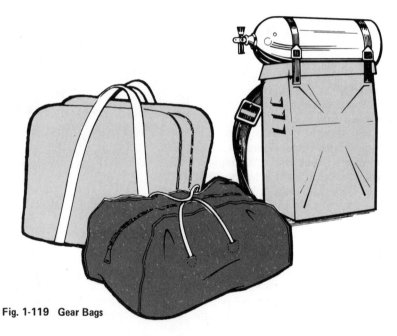

Fig. 1-119 Gear Bags

The amazing growth of diving as a sport depended almost entirely on the development of diving equipment. It has enabled thousands of swimmers to experience the underwater world with comfort and freedom. Continuing advances in diving equipment are enabling divers to become more and more like fish. Someday, perhaps, your air supply will be unlimited and decompression will no longer be a concern, because artificial gills will let you exchange oxygen and carbon dioxide directly with the surrounding water.

The future of diving will be exciting, but so is the present. Diving equipment developed in the last two decades solved dozens of problems humans encountered when entering the underwater world. The diver who has the right equipment, knowledge, and skills can easily adapt.

PART II

the diver

introduction

Creatures that live on land and breathe air have always looked at water with mixed feelings. No one can deny the attraction of streams, waterfalls, ponds, and oceans. Everything from small summer cabins to giant cities seems to prefer locations near water.

Maybe this attraction to water is not so unusual. After all, living things and water have been together since the beginning. Approximately 70 percent of the human body is water; most of it is similar to ocean water. For years, scientists have found blood, sweat, and seawater to contain remarkably similar amounts of calcium, potassium, and sodium.

But man and seawater are not compatible in many ways. For example, man cannot drink seawater, he cannot water his crops with it, and he can drown in as little as a teaspoonful. He is attracted to water, but he is also threatened by it.

We are not, however, the only air-breathing mammals to challenge the sea. The otter and the sea lion have adapted amazingly well. Like man, they must *learn* how to swim and dive, but they don't have the advantage of higher understanding and technology that humans have. The sport diver, with equipment and knowledge, can easily adapt to water. More importantly, the diver can thoroughly understand this adaptation.

Knowing how your body and mind work below the surface, and understanding how water affects your body and mind, is a must for safe and enjoyable diving. With this understanding, you will come to know that water is a different, but very rewarding environment for the intelligent sport diver.

sensations

- **FLOATING**
- **SEEING**
- **HEARING**
- **EXPOSURE**

FLOATING, SEEING, HEARING, AND EXPOSURE

To jump into even shallow water is to be bombarded by new sensations. You see, hear, smell, taste, and feel differently in water than in air. To really grasp these differences, you need to know what water is and how it differs from air. This knowledge will help explain the various sensations and what you must do to adapt to them.

FLOATING

The feeling of buoyancy, or floating in water, is perhaps the most relaxing and pleasant of all the underwater sensations. Water gives most of us the only relief we will ever know from the constant pull of gravity. It is this weightlessness that gives divers almost complete freedom of movement in all three dimensions.

"Weightless" is a good word for floating, for most people, if they were to stand on a scale under water, would weigh next to nothing. Figure 2-1 is a graphic example. They may not float like a cork, but they don't sink like a rock either. The reason for this is that approximately 70 percent of the human body is water. Substances either slightly heavier or lighter than water make up the rest of the body. Fat, for example, isn't as heavy as muscle. So, to put a person into water is like placing a container of water into water—either one sinks very slowly or not at all.

Fig. 2-1 Underwater Buoyancy

BUOYANCY

The question of floating, or buoyancy, is an important one for divers. We know that most people float easily; that is, they have *positive buoyancy*. This is shown in figure 2-2. A very few are *negatively buoyant:* they tend to sink. Others are *neutrally buoyant*: they tend to neither float or sink. Here is the reason. People whose bodies are heavier than the same amount, or volume, of water displaced by them sink. People whose bodies are lighter than the same volume of water float.

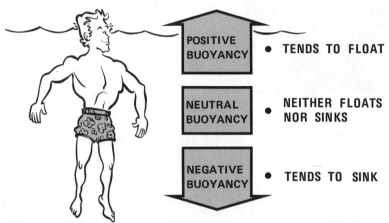

Fig. 2-2 Degrees of Buoyancy

No matter what it is, it sinks if it's heavier than water and floats if it isn't. A gallon of water, as shown in figure 2-3, weighs about eight pounds. A gallon of air is much lighter; it only weighs one-sixth of an ounce, so it floats. Similar volumes of wood and foam neoprene are also lighter than water and are positively buoyant. But similar volumes of lead, aluminum, and steel are heavier than water. They sink.

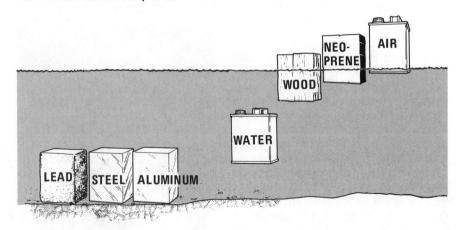

Fig. 2-3 Positive and Negative Buoyancy

Controlling Buoyancy

Fortunately for divers and swimmers, the human body has a built-in buoyancy mechanism that lets you adjust and control buoyancy in the water. The lungs hold about 1-1/2 gallons (five—six liters) of air when you inhale completely. This gives your body an extra 12 pounds of *buoyant force* in the water. In other words, 1-1/2 gallons of air will support 12 pounds above the surface of the water. When you inhale completely, your body has more than enough buoyancy to lift your face out of the water, as shown in figure 2-4.

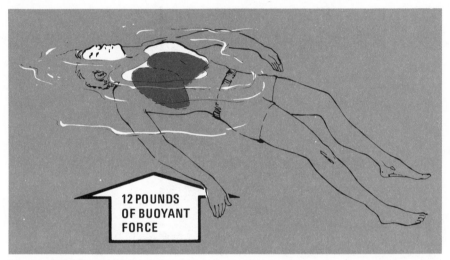

12 POUNDS OF BUOYANT FORCE

Fig. 2-4 Lung Buoyancy Force

By controlling the amount of air in your lungs, you can stay buoyant and relaxed at the surface without getting at all tired. It is important to remember, though, that the normal buoyancy of your body will only support a limited amount of weight above water. When resting on the surface, do not try to lift your head, shoulders, and arms out of the water. Stay as low as possible and keep your lungs as full as possible for maximum buoyancy.

Some people, depending on their body build, composition, and lung size, are more buoyant than others. Fat is not as heavy as muscle and bone, so obese people usually float better than thin people. However, even the skinniest diver can float with proper techniques, including inhaling as much air as possible and staying low in the water.

Changes In Buoyancy

Another thing that affects buoyancy is the weight, or density of water. Salt water, for example, is heavier than fresh water because it contains dissolved salts. The heavier the liquid, the greater the weight it will support. This is why it is easier to float in salt water than in fresh water. You will also be more buoyant in cold water than in warm. Cold water is more dense. The water molecules are closer together which makes the water heavier, or more dense, and more buoyant than warm water.

The laws of buoyancy were discovered by Archimedes. (See Appendix, Archimedes Principle.) He found that the amount of buoyancy an object has depends on how much water it *displaces*, or pushes away. To illustrate: if you put a box into water that displaces 64 pounds of water, then the box will be buoyed up with a force of 64 pounds, as shown in figure 2-5. The more water you displace, the more you will float. This is why wet suits and buoyancy compensators give buoyancy. They add very little weight to your body, but they cause you to displace much more water.

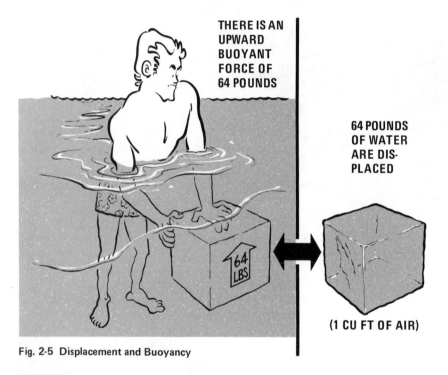

THERE IS AN UPWARD BUOYANT FORCE OF 64 POUNDS

64 POUNDS OF WATER ARE DIS-PLACED

64 LBS

(1 CU FT OF AIR)

Fig. 2-5 Displacement and Buoyancy

SEEING

The first time you opened your eyes under water without a mask was not only uncomfortable but also disappointing. The feeling of cold water directly touching the delicate tissues of your eyes was unexpected and unpleasant, especially if the water contained chlorine or salt. Everything was blurry and out of focus. Most of us can get used to the feeling of water, but the blurriness remains because of the way light travels in water.

LIGHT

The outer covering of the eye, surrounded by air, bends the light striking it at the exact angle necessary to focus it clearly on the back of the eye. Light meeting the eye directly from water must be bent at a greater angle to focus at the correct point. Both concepts are described in figure 2-6. Unfortunately, the eye is unable to adapt to this need, but the solution is fairly simple.

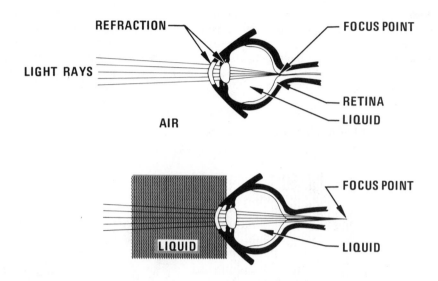

Fig. 2-6 Seeing on Land and Under Water

SEEING WITH A MASK

In theory, a special set of eyeglasses with the right lenses could correct the visual problem, but the face mask is a much more practical solution. The mask restores the necessary air space and also protects the eyes. Surprisingly, vision is one sense that, with the help of the face mask, actually improves under water. Figure 2-7 shows three underwater pictures of the same squirrel fish. The first shows what the fish looks like with water in direct contact with the eye: it is out of focus. The second picture shows what the fish looks like when seen through a mask. The third is the actual size of the fish.

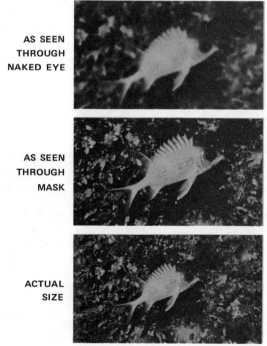

Fig. 2-7 Underwater Vision

Notice that the squirrel fish seems about 25 percent bigger and 25 percent closer as seen through the mask. The reason for the magnifying effect of the mask is shown in figure 2-8. Light travels from the water, through the glass in the face mask, into the air space of the mask, and finally into the eye. Water, glass, and air all bend light to different degrees, so the light is refracted, or bent, twice instead of only once. It is this double bending of the light that causes magnification and actually improves vision.

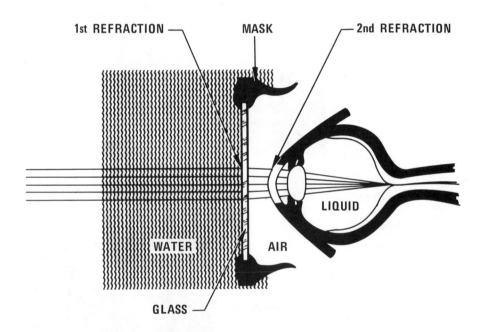

Fig. 2-8 Mask Magnification Underwater

Fig. 2-9 Turbid Water

TURBIDITY

Even though your underwater vision improves somewhat, light does not move as well as it does in air. Light from the sun or from artificial lights is scattered or absorbed by particles suspended in the water, as shown in figure 2-9. Water that contains suspended particles is said to be *turbid*. Extremely turbid water can almost eliminate visibility.

COLOR

Even if the water is very clear and clean, however, it still absorbs light. Sunlight is a mixture of all colors. Water absorbs different colors at different rates. The chart in figure 2-10 illustrates this. Reds and oranges are absorbed in the first 30 feet. Yellows and greens disappear at about 60 feet, so below this depth, everything goes from a bluish color to completely gray. Artificial lights used for vision or photography will restore all natural colors no matter what the depth. Part IV, Section C gives information on this concept.

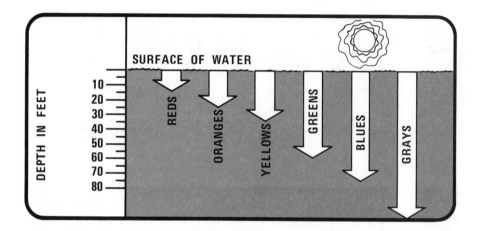

Fig. 2-10 Underwater Color

HEARING AND SPEAKING

Sound moves about four times faster under water than in air, but this does not improve your hearing. Ordinary speech is all but impossible below the surface, and it's very difficult to judge the direction of underwater sounds. In spite of this, the underwater world can be a noisy place. You can hear equipment clanking together, motorboats buzzing at the surface, bubbles leaving regulators, marine life, movement of rocks, and churning water.

The reason you cannot hear voices under water is that sound does not travel well from air into water, or from water into air. You can speak under water, but almost all the sound energy stays in your neck and mouth.

Judging the direction of sounds depends on a slight delay. For example, a noise made at your right side sends sound waves, as shown in figure 2-11. The sound hits your right ear first and your left ear a fraction of a second later which tells you from what direction the sound is coming. But because sound moves so much faster in water, this time delay is almost eliminated; the sound seems to be coming from every direction.

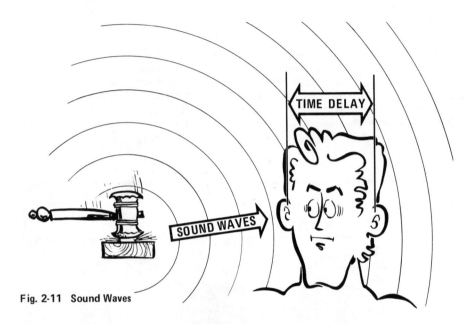

Fig. 2-11   Sound Waves

HAND SIGNALS

Underwater communication, especially between buddies, is extremely important. The diving community has developed a system of hand signals to meet
this need. There are several different signaling systems, but the hand signals
described in figure 2-12 are the most basic. Whatever system you use, make
sure you and your buddy agree on the meanings to avoid confusion.

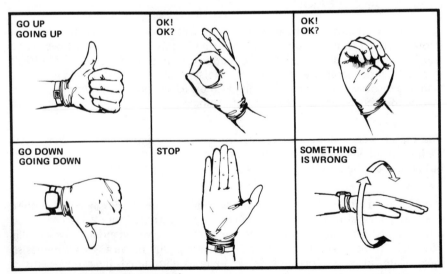

Fig. 2-12   Hand Signals (Page 1 of 2)

Fig. 2-12 Hand Signals (Page 2 of 2)

EXPOSURE

Most of us would agree that cold water produces an unpleasant sensation when you jump into it. The colder the water, the more unpleasant the sensation. Very cold water is not only unpleasant, it is also downright dangerous. It can cause unconsciousness and even death in extreme cases. (See Appendix for Water Temperature Protection Chart.)

MAINTAINING BODY TEMPERATURE

On land, the human body has an amazing ability to maintain a core temperature of 98.6° F. It cannot vary more than a few degrees without serious problems. The body can be thought of as a living heat machine. It generates heat constantly and controls its own temperature by regulating how much heat escapes into the surrounding air. The body's cooling systems, however, are designed for body heat passing into air, not water. Because of this, maintaining a constant body temperature in water is more difficult.

Conduction And Evaporation

Heat leaves your body in several different ways, but the two most important are *conduction* and *evaporation*. Conduction refers to heat passing from one thing into something else in direct contact with it. This is depicted in figure 2-13. When you put a pan of water on a flame, for example, the heat from the fire is conducted directly into the pan and from the pan directly into the water.

HEAT CONDUCTED
DIRECTLY FROM
FLAME, TO PAN,
TO WATER

Fig. 2-13 Heat Conduction

Evaporation occurs when a liquid changes into a gas. When this happens, the liquid absorbs heat as it changes into gas, as shown in figure 2-14. When you sweat, for example, perspiration absorbs heat as it evaporates. This is why it cools your body.

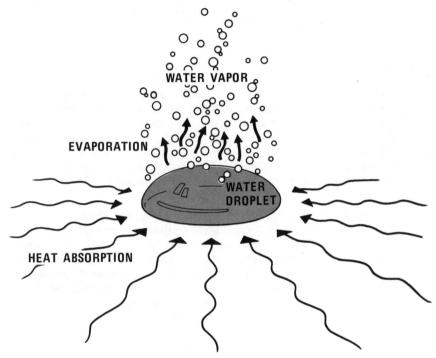

Fig. 2-14 Evaporation

When you jump into water, evaporation no longer works. Conduction is the main method of cooling the body in water but water conducts heat away from the body almost 25 times faster than air. This is why even relatively warm water feels cold when you first jump into it.

Maintaining Warmth

Your body, however, doesn't give up all that heat without a fight. Swimmers often talk about diving into "cold" water and then "getting used to it". What really happens when you get used to the cold is that certain changes take place in your body to prevent too much heat from passing into the water. The tiny blood vessels on the surface of the skin constrict automatically when plunged into colder temperatures. This reduces the amount of warm blood that flows to the cold surface of the body. As a result, less heat is conducted from the skin into the cold water.

If the reduced blood flow to the skin fails to keep the body warm, and if the skin temperature gets down to a certain level, then the body starts *shivering*. It takes muscular effort to shiver and this causes an increase in the body's production of heat. With a wet suit on, an extremely active diver stays warmer than a diver at rest for the same reason; the rate of heat loss may be the same, but the active diver produces enough to prevent a net heat loss. Physical activity can produce so much heat, in fact, that a diver in water warmer than 86°F (30°C) may have problems with *over*heating. Cold, however, is a much more common problem.

Effects of Cold Water

The wet suit, by surrounding the body in a layer of air or gas bubbles, reduces the rate at which heat passes from the body into the water. But even with wet suit protection, heat loss still occurs, especially through the head, hands, and feet. When heat loss is extreme, it can cause a loss of strength, difficulty in handling equipment, muscle cramps, and a decrease in problem-solving ability. When the water temperature is close to freezing, a diver's lips can become too numb to inflate the buoyancy compensator orally and the fingers can become too clumsy to activate mechanical inflators.

If you ever start shivering underwater, stop diving. Your body is telling you that its core temperature has dropped. When the body core temperature has dropped to about 95°F (35°C), a condition known as *systemic hypothermia* arises. At this temperature, breathing is rapid and deep, and shivering becomes vigorous and sustained. If the core temperature drops to about 90°F (32°C), reasoning fails rapidly, shivering diminishes, and the muscles become rigid. Any further drop in temperature can be considered life threatening.

Sunburn

Full wet suits protect you from both cold-water and sun exposure. If you snorkel at the surface in warm water without a wet suit, on the other hand, you become especially vulnerable to the sun's ultraviolet rays. Cool water washing over your back and legs makes you unaware that you are actually becoming severely sunburned.

Sunburn can cause first- and second-degree burns, and in extreme cases, may require hospitalization. Be careful to limit your exposure to the sun. If you do a lot of snorkeling at the surface of water too warm for wet suits, wear a T-shirt and pants or long shorts.

No other environment has a more profound effect on the body's five senses than the underwater environment. It changes your perceptions in every way. It creates a totally different set of experiences. Some sensations are enjoyable, others require adjustment by special techniques or equipment. In any case, there is no reason for underwater sensations to be unpleasant or uncomfortable. If they are unpleasant, you either need better equipment or more training.

section B

breathing

- **RESPIRATION**
- **PANIC AND EXHAUSTION**
- **ARTIFICIAL RESPIRATION**
- **CLEAN AIR**

RESPIRATION, PANIC AND EXHAUSTION, ARTIFICIAL RESPIRATION, CLEAN AIR

Breathing is one of those things we ignore most of the time. We ordinarily breathe constantly, day and night, without giving it a thought. Swimming or diving under water, however, changes all this; the beginning swimmer quickly realizes that he cannot "breathe water." Since diving can change, stop, slow down, or speed up the breathing process, you should have a good understanding of what is going on in your body and mind when you breathe, both on land and in the water.

THE RESPIRATION PROCESS

Respiration refers not only to the simple act of inhaling and exhaling air, but also to the more complex processes of exchanging gases, making energy, and eliminating waste in order to keep the cells of all living creatures alive. Respiration, then, is the primary life process, a process that involves more than the lungs. The circulatory system, including the heart, blood, and vessels, and every living cell in the body are intimately connected with respiration.

LUNGS

Human lungs are built something like a spongy, upside down tree, as shown in figure 2-15. The trunk of the lung tree is the windpipe, a hollow tube about 4-1/2 inches long and one inch wide. The windpipe divides into two smaller branches called the *bronchi*, which continue to subdivide into smaller and smaller branches. The smallest twigs, or ducts, end in tiny clusters of air sacs called *alveoli*. Each cluster looks like a tiny bunch of grapes.

The alveoli are the leaves of the tree. They are extremely thin membranes where oxygen, carbon dioxide, and other gases pass into and out of the

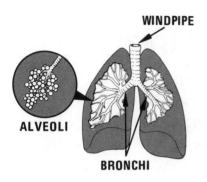

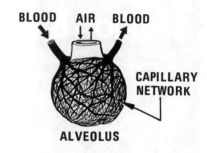

Fig. 2-15 Lungs

Fig. 2-16 Alveolus and Capillaries

bloodstream. The lungs contain about 300 million tiny alveoli. All of them make up an *alveolar* membrane with a surface area of about 775 square feet, or about the surface area of a tennis court. Each *alveolus* is surrounded by a network of tiny blood vessels, or capillaries. (See figure 2-16.)

The lungs are protected above and around the side by the rib cage. The diaphragm underneath is a powerful sheet of muscle. Figure 2-17 is an illustration of the diaphragm. When the diaphragm is flexed, it moves downward while the muscles around the rib cage lift the ribs up and out. Together, the action of the diaphragm and rib cage increases the size of the chest cavity. This is what pulls air down and into the lungs when you inhale.

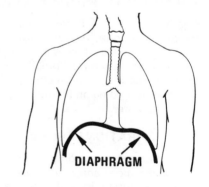

Fig. 2-17 Diaphragm

The alveolar membrane is elastic, so the air sacs have a tendency to contract and push air out of the lungs. When the diaphragm and muscles around the rib cage relax, air leaves the lungs. Ordinarily, this alternating contraction and relaxation of the muscles that control breathing is automatic. An average adult breathes between 12 and 20 times a minute. Small people and children usually breathe more often.

LUNG VOLUMES

An average pair of lungs can hold a total volume of 1.7 gallons (6.5 liters) of air. At rest, however, you only inhale and exhale a small fraction of this amount—a little over a pint (0.5 liters). This is called the *tidal volume*, as shown in figure 2-18.

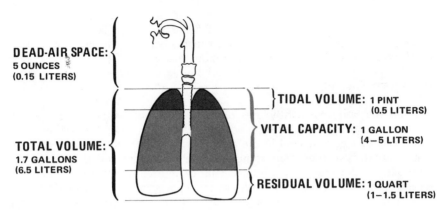

Fig. 2-18 Lung Volumes

Exchanging the relatively small tidal volume of air is enough for a person sitting quietly in a chair reading a book, but the long-distance runner or the hard-working diver may need much more air. For example, after inhaling a pint of air during an ordinary breath, you can continue to inhale between two and three quarts (2.5 liters). After you exhale the pint of air in an ordinary breath, you can continue exhaling almost three-fourths of a quart (0.7 liters).

When you breathe as hard as you possibly can, you can exchange over a gallon (four — five liters) of air on any one breath. This amount is the *vital capacity* and it varies a great deal depending on the size and physical condition of the person. A small woman may have a vital capacity of only three quarts (2.8 liters) and a trained male athlete could have one larger than six quarts (6.5 liters).

No matter how hard you exhale, however, you still cannot force all the air out of your lungs. Over a quart (1.2 liters) of *residual* air remains in the lungs all the time. This is called the *residual volume*.

All the air you inhale, even during a very large breath, does not find its way to the lungs. Some of it, about five ounces (0.15 liters), fills up the windpipe, throat, and nose and is exhaled without ever touching the inside of an alveolus. This area is called the *dead-air space* because no gas exchange takes place inside it.

GAS EXCHANGE

The air you inhale is a mixture of about 78 percent nitrogen, 21 percent oxygen, 0.03 percent carbon dioxide, and small amounts of other gases. Nitrogen has very little effect on ordinary respiration. It is an inert (chemically inactive) gas that does not support life, but has an intoxicating effect under pressure. (See Part II, Section D.) Oxygen and carbon dioxide are the two gases that are exchanged during respiration.

The air you exhale has about the same amount of nitrogen, but the percentage of oxygen decreases from 21 to 16 percent, and the percentage of carbon dioxide increases from 0.03 percent to 5.6 percent. The body, in other words, produces an amount of carbon dioxide roughly equal to the amount of oxygen it absorbs. By maintaining this continuous exchange of gases, the blood and cells of the body maintain a certain minimum level of oxygen. This prevents an excessive buildup of carbon dioxide.

Because the body constantly uses oxygen and produces carbon dioxide, the levels of these two gases in the blood always change. When the carbon dioxide level reaches a certain level in the alveoli, it stimulates the *respiratory center*. The respiratory center then stimulates the diaphragm and chest muscles to contract, which causes you to inhale. This, of course, lowers the carbon dioxide level in the alveoli. The respiratory center stops stimulating the diaphragm and chest muscles, the muscles relax, the alveoli naturally contract, and you exhale. As the carbon dioxide level builds up, the whole process involuntarily repeats itself.

CHANGING THE BREATHING RHYTHM

You can consciously override the involuntary control of breathing when, for example, you are talking or holding your breath. There are many ways to either slow down or accelerate the breathing rate, all of which have important effects on the exchange of oxygen and carbon dioxide. Changing the breathing rhythm is harmless as long as the balance of gas exchange stays within certain limits. But too much or too little of either gas can cause problems.

TOO MUCH CARBON DIOXIDE AND TOO LITTLE OXYGEN

Almost anything that interferes or hinders the normal breathing process can lead to a buildup of carbon dioxide in the blood. When you stop exhaling, the air in the dead-air space has a high level of carbon dioxide. When you start inhaling, you inhale this air first. The natural dead-air space in your windpipe, however, is small enough so carbon dioxide never builds up. An extremely long or large snorkel, however, can double or triple the size of this dead-air space. If you don't breathe deeper to maintain the right exchange of gases, carbon dioxide levels will climb.

A snorkel or regulator with a lot of breathing resistance will change your breathing and change the effort required to do the work of breathing. When this happens, the body might be producing more carbon dioxide than it can give off, so carbon dioxide gradually builds up.

Most of us have experienced carbon dioxide excess from swimming or running too fast. The "out-of-breath" feeling comes from the respiratory center working overtime in response to a large buildup of carbon dioxide. This can lead to shortness of breath and fatigue. On land, this isn't much of a problem, but, under water, it can be serious. If you feel unusually "hungry" for air and tired or weak from working too hard—stop, rest, and breathe deeply.

"Skip breathing" is a term that refers to a technique that divers once thought would conserve air. Instead of breathing regularly, the diver "skips" every other breath or exhales twice on each breath. Unfortunately, the technique does *not* work and it can be dangerous. Skip breathing apparently uses only one-half the amount of air, but it really leads to a buildup of carbon dioxide. This, of course, eventually leads to a greater than normal breathing rate. Always avoid skip breathing or other so-called techniques of "conserving" air while using scuba.

Certain advanced and commercial breathing devices use gas mixtures and rebreathing systems instead of ordinary compressed air. Any breakdown or misuse of these systems can also lead to carbon dioxide buildup.

Many things that hinder or slow down the exchange of gases not only cause a buildup of carbon dioxide, but also cause a decrease in the amount of oxygen in the blood and cells of the body. This oxygen deficiency in the body's tissue is called *hypoxia*. Whether it comes from an equipment breakdown or improper breathing, the signs and symptoms of hypoxia are the same.

Both carbon dioxide excess and hypoxia can cause heavy breathing, headache, and unconsciousness. Hypoxia can also cause nausea. Carbon dioxide excess can cause muscular cramps and fatigue. The treatment for both is increased ventilation of the lungs and giving 100 percent oxygen if necessary.

CONTROLLED HYPERVENTILATION

Breath-hold divers have used *hyperventilation* for years to help them stay underwater longer. By inhaling completely and exhaling completely three or four times before surface diving, you can "blow off" carbon dioxide. This lets you begin a breath-hold dive with very low carbon dioxide levels in the alveoli. Since the respiratory center in the brain is stimulated by a high carbon dioxide level, you will not feel the need to breathe as quickly after hyperventilation.

Hyperventilation must be very carefully controlled. Never hyperventilate more than three or four times before each surface dive. More than this can reduce the carbon dioxide level too much. Your body, during the surface dive, uses up oxygen. It is possible to use oxygen to the point of hypoxia before the carbon dioxide level gets to a level that tells you to breathe. This is called "shallow water blackout." When you feel the urge to breathe, head for the surface. Never ignore the need for air.

UNCONTROLLED HYPERVENTILATION

Simple anxiety and physical stress can cause hyperventilation whether the diver wants it or not. Unfamiliar equipment or a strange and unusual diving environment is sometimes enough to cause hyperventilation. Treating uncontrolled hyperventilation is easy—become aware of your breathing rate and slow it down if you find yourself breathing too fast and shallow. Consciously maintaining a slow, deep breathing pattern for a short time will help get the carbon dioxide level back to normal.

PANIC AND EXHAUSTION

Panic is defined as a sudden overpowering fear. You lose control, you cannot think, and you therefore take incorrect actions. You focus on one particular task or action that may or may not have anything to do with escaping the problem. No matter how well you are trained or experienced, you are not immune to panic. The best way to prevent panic is to understand it.

Fear is an ordinary, healthy response to danger. A fear of falling off a cliff is normal; stepping back from the edge of the cliff is a normal response. If the fear of falling becomes panic and causes you to freeze at the edge of the cliff, you have lost control. This is not a healthy response.

Avoiding panic, then, is largely a matter of controlling ordinary fear. If "something goes wrong" during a dive, you should accept the normal fear for what it is and do what has to be done to right the situation. Running out of air, difficulty with strong currents, unusually negative buoyancy from a full collecting bag, extreme cold, getting tangled in kelp, and equipment problems: these are all problems with sensible and logical solutions. To solve the problem, however, you must have your wits about you. Panic is never a solution.

Sure signs of panic in either yourself or your buddy are a wide eyed look and very rapid breathing. The breathing may look like hyperventilation but, when the diver is panicking, it is rapid and *shallow*, not deep. This may eventually lead to a buildup of carbon dioxide and a decrease in oxygen in the blood and tissues. This soon causes exhaustion which makes everything worse. Panic increases and a vicious cycle ensues which can easily lead to disaster. Panic, in fact, is probably the leading cause of drowning and near drowning in sport diving and drowning is undoubtedly the greatest cause of fatal diving accidents.

If, at any time during a dive, you feel at all anxious or are having difficulty in any way, stop and think. Relax and breathe slowly and deeply until you have solved the problem and regained complete control. Know your physical limitations and don't exceed them when diving. For a complete discussion on controlling diver stress and panic, see the Advanced Manual.

FIRST AID FOR NEAR DROWNING

When the exchange of oxygen and carbon dioxide completely breaks down, it is called *asphyxia*. When asphyxia occurs in water it is called drowning. A fatal drowning accident begins when the victim stops breathing and loses consciousness, often after panic and exhaustion have set in.

Whatever the cause, a drowning or near-drowning victim will have two definite symptoms: loss of consciousness and lack of breathing. His heart may or may not be beating. The heart can continue to beat for several minutes even though the victim has stopped breathing. The most important element in first aid is time. Of all the cells in the body, brain cells are the most sensitive to a lack of oxygen. If heartbeat and breathing have stopped for more than four to six minutes, permanent brain damage is likely. It is extremely important to begin mouth-to-mouth artificial respiration *immediately*. Do not hesitate for any reason.

MOUTH-TO-MOUTH ARTIFICIAL RESPIRATION

Artificial respiration supplies oxygen to the victim's body until normal breathing resumes. Specific procedures for the mouth-to-mouth method are basically the same, whether the victim is on land or in the water. Follow these steps, as shown in figure 2-19.

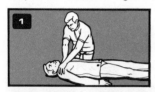

1. Determine if the victim is responsive. Make sure the victim is not breathing before you continue. If other people are within hearing distance, call for help.

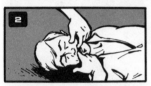

2. Place the victim on his back and clear his mouth of any foreign matter with your finger.

   THINK A, B, C

3. AIRWAY. Open the airway by tilting the victim's head back. Place one hand on the forehead and the fingertips of the other hand under the bony part of the jaw near the chin. Tilt the head without closing the mouth. Maintain an open airway. CAUTION: All neck movement should be avoided if a neck or spine injury is suspected.

4. BREATHING. To check the breathing, place your ear over the victim's mouth, and look, listen, and feel for breathing. If the victim is not breathing, pinch the nose, seal the mouth, and give two full slow breaths. Watch the chest to see if it is rising. After exhaling, turn your head to the side, and listen for the victim to exhale. Watch his chest to see that it falls.

5. CIRCULATION. Check the pulse first by locating the Adam's apple. Then, slide your fingers to the groove on the victim's neck on the same side that you are kneeling. Feel the carotid pulse for 5-10 seconds.

6. If the victim has a pulse but is not breathing, begin rescue breathing. Maintain an open airway and seal the mouth and nose as before. Blow air into the victim's mouth until the chest rises, then watch the chest deflate after each breath. Continue rescue breathing at a rate of 1 breath every 5 seconds (12 breaths per minute).

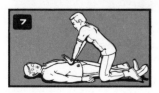

7. If the chest is not rising and falling, the airway may be obstructed. Retilt the victim's head and attempt once again to ventilate the airway. If you are still unsuccessful, perform the Heimlick Maneuver. If the airway is still blocked, open the victim's mouth and sweep deeply with your index finger from one cheek to the other. Repeat the entire sequence until you are successful.

Fig. 2-19   Mouth-to-Mouth Artificial Respiration

Mouth-to-mouth respiration should begin as soon as you realize your buddy is not breathing and you are both stabilized at the surface. The wet suit and buoyancy compensator supply almost immediate buoyancy when the weight belt is released. Once you establish buoyancy, place your hand through your buddy's armpit and hold onto the tank valve, pack, BC, or the back of your buddy's neck, as shown in figure 2-20.

Fig. 2-20 Mouth-to-Mouth Artificial Respiration in Water

CARDIOPULMONARY RESUSCITATION

If the victim's heart has stopped beating, then blood circulation will also have to be restored. Cardiopulmonary resuscitation (CPR) is a combination of mouth-to-mouth artificial respiration and external cardiac compression.

Cardiac compression is a mechanical method of compressing or pushing on the heart from outside the body, as shown in figure 2-21. When you press down on the lower breastbone, you squeeze the heart between the breast-

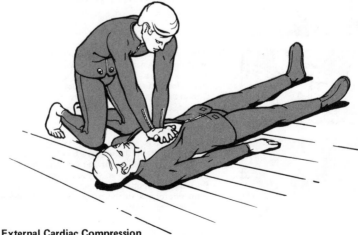

Fig. 2-21 External Cardiac Compression

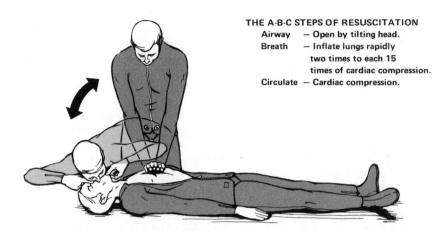

THE A-B-C STEPS OF RESUSCITATION

Airway — Open by tilting head.
Breath — Inflate lungs rapidly
two times to each 15
times of cardiac compression.
Circulate — Cardiac compression.

Fig. 2-22 Cardiopulmonary Resuscitation

bone and the backbone. This forces blood out of the heart and into the arteries. When you stop pressing, blood automatically refills the heart through incoming veins. Constant repetition (approximately 60 times per minute) of this squeeze-release process keeps the heart beating artifically.

One properly trained rescuer can perform both heart (cardio) and lung (pulmonary) resuscitation, as shown in figure 2-22. CPR can also be performed by two rescuers with even greater effectiveness.

Detailed directions for performing CPR are not provided here because the procedure requires special supplemental training in recognizing cardiac arrest. Performing compressions on a functioning heart can cause irregular heartbeats or stop the heart completely. Instruction involves practice on manikins and performance of the skill both individually and as a team. Unless rescuers have repeated experiences performing CPR, they will need periodic training. Agencies such as the American Heart Association, the American Red Cross, and the YMCA offer courses in cardiopulmonary resuscitation. Such instruction is highly recommended. For a complete discussion on diver rescue techniques, see the Advanced Manual.

CLEAN AIR

Sport divers should never breathe anything but clean, dry, filtered air. It must be free from carbon monoxide, carbon dioxide, oil, vapor, and other impurities. (See Appendix for Air Purity Standards Table.) Scuba tanks should never be filled with anything except ordinary air. Avoid other gases or gas mixtures.

From the time air is compressed by an air compressor until you inhale it from the regulator mouthpiece, there are a number of ways it can become contaminated. Here is a list of ways to prevent contamination:

1. Make sure the compressor is located in a pollution-free area. Carbon monoxide from gasoline engine exhaust (automobile, electric generator,

boat, compressor engine, etc.) must not enter the compressor. Carbon monoxide gas combines with red blood cells 200 times more rapidly than oxygen. This prevents oxygen from getting to the body's tissues and also poisons living cells. Carbon monoxide poisoning can lead to unconsciousness and death.

2.   Lubricate compressors and regulators only with special lubricants specified by the manufacturer. The wrong oil or grease used in the wrong place can find its way into the lungs and cause lipoid pneumonia, a lung infection caused by oil in air. Ordinary oils should never be used on a scuba regulator.

3.   Before the air leaves the compressor, it must be filtered to remove any excess dangerous gases, water, oil, particles, and odor. Air compressors used in automobile filling stations do not have these filters and strict cleanliness requirements. This is why it is important to fill tanks only at reputable diving air stations.

4.   High-pressure air from the compressors is often stored in special cylinders or storage tanks, as shown in figure 2-23. To prevent moisture or contaminants from entering the scuba cylinder, make sure the valve openings on both the storage system and the tank itself are clean and dry. Otherwise, moisture can be injected into the cylinder.

Fig. 2-23 High-Pressure Storage Cylinders

The act of breathing and the process of respiration do the work of supplying the cells of the body with life-giving fuel. Without fuel or with the wrong kind or amount of fuel, the body's machinery breaks down. It stops working. This is why divers have such a sensitive awareness of the breathing process. Make a point of developing this awareness, of understanding and appreciating all aspects of why and how people exchange oxygen and carbon dioxide on land and under water.

section C

descending and ascending

● EFFECTS OF PRESSURE CHANGE
● BOYLE'S LAW
● SQUEEZES
● AIR EMBOLISM

EFFECTS OF PRESSURE CHANGE

Even though people today live in a "pressurized" environment, pressure is rarely noticed until it changes. A customary change in pressure usually occurs while driving a car up or down steep hills. Most of us feel the change in our ears. Divers become aware of changes in both air and water pressure almost as soon as they enter the water. These changes are important, and to handle them effectively, you must understand how water pressure and air pressure affect each other, and how both affect the body.

AIR PRESSURE AND WATER PRESSURE

To say that air and water exert pressure is to say that they have weight. A cubic foot of air, for example, weighs a little over an ounce, and a cubic foot of salt water weighs 64 pounds. In the United States, pressure is usually measured in pounds per square inch, which is abbreviated "psi."

At sea level, ordinary air pressure exerts a force of 14.7 psi. A column of air, in other words, one inch by one inch wide extending as high up as the atmosphere (about 60 miles) "presses" toward the earth with a force, or weight, of 14.7 pounds, as shown in figure 2-24. This air pressure measurement of 14.7 psi is also called one *atmosphere* of pressure.

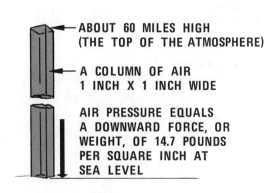

ABOUT 60 MILES HIGH
(THE TOP OF THE ATMOSPHERE)

A COLUMN OF AIR
1 INCH X 1 INCH WIDE

AIR PRESSURE EQUALS
A DOWNWARD FORCE, OR
WEIGHT, OF 14.7 POUNDS
PER SQUARE INCH AT
SEA LEVEL

Fig. 2-24 Air Pressure

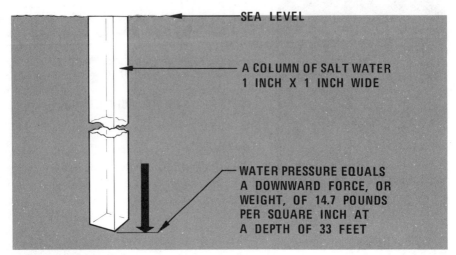

Fig. 2-25 Water Pressure

Salt water, because it is so much heavier than air, exerts one atmosphere of pressure in a mere 33 feet, as shown in figure 2-25. Fresh water exerts one atmosphere of pressure every 34 feet. As you can see, a column of salt water one inch by one inch wide and 33 feet tall has a weight and exerts a pressure of 14.7 psi.

The amount of pressure depends on how much air and water is pressing down at any given time, as shown in figure 2-26. At an altitude of 18,000 feet, for example, there is only one-half the amount of air pressure that there is at sea level. Air pressure at this altitude is 7.35 psi, or one-half atmosphere. At an underwater depth of 66 feet, there are two atmospheres of water pressure (29.4 psi) and one atmosphere of air pressure (14.7 psi). Together, the water and air pressure exert a total of three atmospheres (44.1 psi).

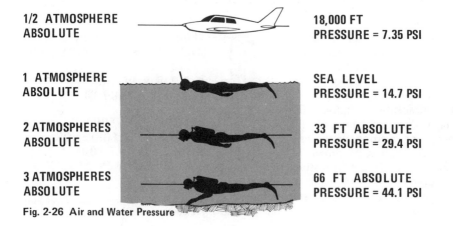

Fig. 2-26 Air and Water Pressure

Absolute pressure refers to a measurement of the *total* pressure exerted under water, including both water and air pressure. At 33 feet, for example, the absolute pressure would be two atmospheres absolute (one atmosphere of water and one atmosphere of air), or 29.4 psi absolute (14.7 psi of water and 14.7 psi of air). Unless indicated otherwise, pressure measurements given in pounds per square inch will usually refer to *absolute* pressure.

Ambient pressure is another term used to express the total or absolute pressure surrounding a diver. It is the pressure a diver feels at any given depth. At sea level, for example, the ambient pressure is 14.7 psi. At 33 feet under water, the ambient pressure surrounding a diver is 29.4 psi.

Gauge pressure refers to the measurement given by pressure gauges. They measure the difference between surrounding air pressure and the pressure inside a scuba cylinder or air compressor. The zero mark on a pressure gauge, therefore, really represents air pressure at normal atmospheric pressure. At sea level, this is 14.7 psi. On the pressure gauge, then, 500 psi refers to 500 psi over atmospheric air pressure.

INCREASING PRESSURE

When you descend below the surface, pressure increases by one atmosphere every 33 feet. The effects of this increasing pressure are easy to see. Take, for example, two standard, one-gallon containers, as shown in figure 2-27. If you fill one with water and one with air and carry them to 132 feet (five atmospheres absolute, 73.5 psi), the effects of increasing pressure are obvious. Nothing happens to the water-filled can, but the increasing pressure crushes the air-filled container.

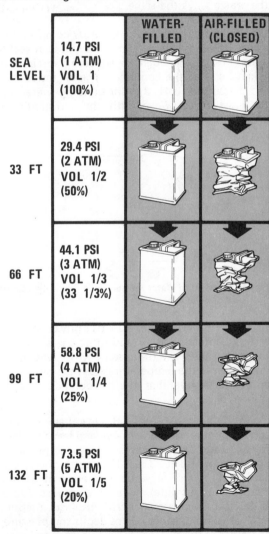

		WATER-FILLED	AIR-FILLED (CLOSED)
SEA LEVEL	14.7 PSI (1 ATM) VOL 1 (100%)		
33 FT	29.4 PSI (2 ATM) VOL 1/2 (50%)		
66 FT	44.1 PSI (3 ATM) VOL 1/3 (33 1/3%)		
99 FT	58.8 PSI (4 ATM) VOL 1/4 (25%)		
132 FT	73.5 PSI (5 ATM) VOL 1/5 (20%)		

Fig. 2-27 Effects of Increasing Pressure

The reason for this is that water is virtually incompressible. You can't "squeeze" it smaller or force it into a smaller space. Figure 2-28 illustrates how the increasing pressure is transmitted through the walls of the container directly into and through the water inside the container. No matter how great the pressure, the water stays the same size.

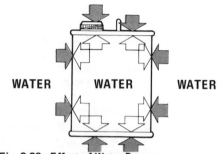

Fig. 2-28 Effect of Water Pressure on a Water-Filled Container

Air, or any gas for that matter, *is* compressible. Applied pressure squeezes it into a much smaller volume. As you can see in figure 2-29, the force of five atmospheres is enough to squeeze the air into a space that is one-fifth the original size of the container. The air inside the container is squeezed until the air pressure equals the surrounding water pressure. When the air in the container is *equalized* with the surrounding water pressure, the squeezing action stops.

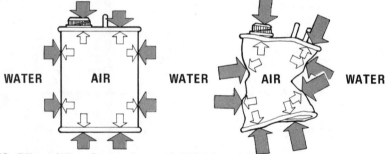

Fig. 2-29 Effect of Water Pressure on an Air-Filled Container

BOYLE'S LAW

In 1610, Robert Boyle, a British physicist and chemist, noticed how pressure affects containers of air and other gases. He found the same thing happens in the same way every time, so he wrote what is now known as "Boyle's Law." It states that if the temperature stays the same, the volume of the gas gets smaller at the same rate that the surrounding pressure increases. (See Gas Laws in Appendix.)

Figure 2-30 shows how Boyle's Law works. If you take the one-gallon container, turn it upside down, and leave the cap off so water can enter the can freely, water will compress the air as pressure increases. When the absolute pressure doubles at 33 feet (two atmospheres absolute, 29.4 psi), the volume of air is cut in half as water fills one-half of the container. At 66 feet (three atmospheres absolute) the air is compressed to one-third of its original volume, at 99 feet (four atmospheres absolute) the air is squeezed to one-fourth its original volume, and so on as depth and pressure increase. When you return the container to the surface, the air expands to its original volume.

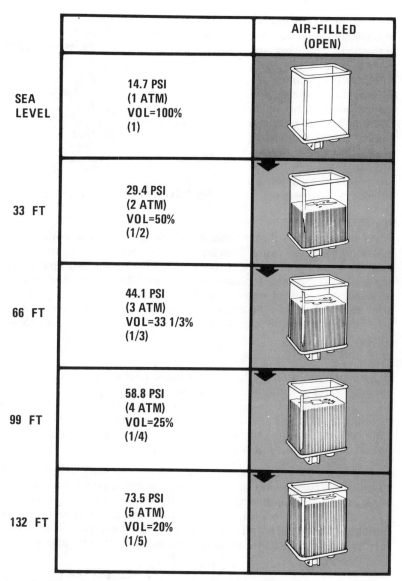

		AIR-FILLED (OPEN)
SEA LEVEL	14.7 PSI (1 ATM) VOL=100% (1)	
33 FT	29.4 PSI (2 ATM) VOL=50% (1/2)	
66 FT	44.1 PSI (3 ATM) VOL=33 1/3% (1/3)	
99 FT	58.8 PSI (4 ATM) VOL=25% (1/4)	
132 FT	73.5 PSI (5 ATM) VOL=20% (1/5)	

Fig. 2-30 How Boyle's Law Works

Boyle's Law is significant for the diver in several ways. Most of your body can be thought of as a large liquid-filled "body balloon." Like the water-filled container, nothing happens during descent. Increasing pressure is simply transmitted into and through blood, bone, and solid tissue without damaging anything. No one knows exactly how much pressure the human body can withstand, but it is deeper than 1,500 feet. This is far beyond any reasonable sport diving depth.

Boyle's Law really comes into play in the air spaces of the body. There are air-filled spaces in the ears, sinuses, lungs and airways, and stomach and intestines, as shown in figure 2-31. All of these spaces tend to respond to pressure in the same way the air-filled gallon container does—they are all subject to "squeezes."

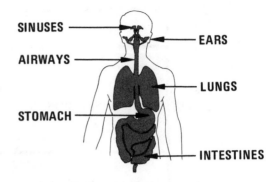

Fig. 2-31 Air-Filled Spaces in the Body

SQUEEZES

Boyle's Law implies that air spaces will tend to equalize with the surrounding, or *ambient*, pressure. This equalization can take place in two ways. The space itself can get smaller or more air can be put into the space as pressure increases. At 33 feet, for example, the air-filled gallon container is either squeezed to a size of one-half gallon or it would hold two gallons of air in order to equalize with the ambient water pressure of two atmospheres. Your body uses both methods to equalize pressure and to prevent problems with squeezes.

Ear Squeeze

The middle ear is an air space connected to the back of your throat by the *eustachian tube*. (Note figure 2-32.) An ear squeeze occurs when increasing water pressure pushes against the eardrum without being equalized. In extreme cases, the pressure can break the eardrum. Sometimes a rupture can occur in the inner ear. An inner ear rupture can cause permanent deafness if a physician is not seen immediately.

Putting more air into the middle ear space is the way to equalize pressure. Yawning or swallowing sometimes opens the eustachian tube enough to allow air to enter the middle ear. Usually, it is necessary to equalize the ears by holding your nose, closing your mouth, and gently blowing air from your throat, up the eustachian tubes, and into the middle ear. (See Part I, Section A.) If you cannot equalize, ascend a few feet and then try again.

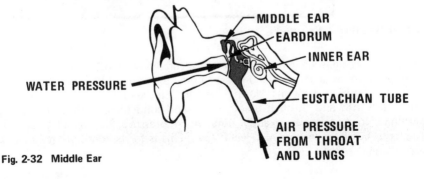

Fig. 2-32 Middle Ear

Anticipate ear squeeze. Start equalizing as soon as you feel any pressure change. Don't wait for discomfort to start; begin equalizing before and immediately after entering the water. For the best results, descend on a line and equalize every two feet. Colds, allergic reactions, infections, eating mucous-producing foods such as dairy products, and a number of other things can close the eustachian tube. This sometimes makes it impossible to equalize, so if you ever have trouble equalizing, don't continue the dive.

Sinus Squeeze

Another set of air spaces is located in the nasal areas around the eyes, as shown in figure 2-33. These spaces, or sinuses, are surrounded by bone and lined with a membrane connected to the nasal cavity. Like the middle ear, they must be filled with extra air during descent to prevent a painful sinus squeeze.

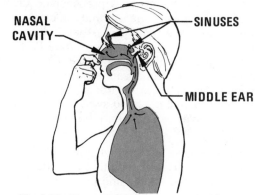

Fig. 2-33 Sinus Air Spaces

Usually, when you equalize your ears, air will also pass from your nasal cavity into the sinuses. Colds, allergies, and infections, however, sometimes swell the nose and sinus membranes which prevents air from passing into the sinuses.

Some divers use decongestants, nose drops, sprays, or pills to open the sinus passages. Problems can result, however, if the decongestant effect wears off too soon. Also, some decongestants contain antihistamines which make some people drowsy. In any case, if you have trouble with your sinuses, it is better to postpone diving activities than to use drugs.

Lung Squeeze

Compared to the middle ear and sinus cavities, the lungs are flexible. When you descend, the increasing water pressure ordinarily reduces the size of the lungs and compresses the air inside until it is automatically equalized with ambient pressure.

Breath-hold divers have gone below 300 feet with no damage to their lungs. However, if a diver sinks lower in the water after extensively exhaling involuntarily from coughing, for example, lung squeeze may occur. This is because the water pressure would be great enough to compress the empty lungs. Constant breathing with scuba equipment continuously replenishes the lungs with adequate air which, in turn, eliminates the possibility of lung squeeze.

Stomach and Intestine Squeeze

Digesting food often produces gas in the stomach and intestines. Air spaces or air pockets in the stomach and intestines are "squeezed" harmlessly during descent because they are surrounded by flexible tissue. If gas continues to form at depth, however, it will expand when you return to the surface. This can be painful and may call for a slow ascent. To prevent this kind of a squeeze, stay away from gas-producing foods before diving.

Equipment Squeezes

Artificial air spaces next to the body can cause squeezes the same way internal air spaces can. The mask squeeze, for example, can damage tissues around and in the eyes. A preoccupied diver might not notice the pain caused by the mask squeeze until the damage has been done. It's important, therefore, to make a point of exhaling through your nose into the mask to equalize pressure during descent. (See Part I, Section A.) Never wear goggles or earplugs while scuba or skin diving. The air spaces created by these devices cannot be equalized, so the eye tissues or eardrums can be easily damaged. Air can also be trapped in the outer ear by a hood. To prevent hood squeeze, pull the hood away from the head permitting water to flow in. Also, small holes can be cut in the hood next to the ears.

Tooth Squeeze

The tooth squeeze is extremely rare. In theory, it is caused by a small pocket of trapped gas in a decayed tooth or underneath a cracked filling. If this air bubble is isolated, increasing pressure squeezes the soft pulp of the tooth into the space. This theory, however, has never been proved. It is possible that pain in the mouth during descent or ascent is associated with sinuses in the upper jaw near the teeth.

VERTIGO

Vertigo or "twirly bends" happens when cold water enters the middle ear after an eardrum ruptures. It may also be caused by pressure imbalance in the ears. Dizziness, disorientation, and nausea are some of the symptoms of vertigo. These should stop when the water warms in the ear. In the meantime, you should breathe normally and hang on to something until the feeling passes or stop diving if the pain persists.

DECREASING PRESSURE

During ascent, when pressure decreases, air naturally expands. Figure 2-34 shows what happens to two one-gallon containers filled with air from a scuba tank at a depth of 132 feet (five atmospheres absolute, 73.4 psi). Since air at this depth is compressed to only one-fifth of its sea level volume, the gallon containers hold five gallons of sea level air. As the cans ascend, the air expands to five gallons.

The first container in figure 2-34 is left open, so that expanding air escapes into the surrounding environment during ascent. The second container is sealed at 132 feet after being filled with scuba air. As it ascends, the container begins to bulge until finally a seam breaks to allow the expanding air to escape. The ears, sinuses, mask, and lungs usually do the same thing that container number one does—the expanding air simply escapes into the surrounding water during ascent. But if the air spaces are closed off like the second container, surrounding tissues can be damaged. Normal breathing during ascents will prevent closing off the lungs and eliminate the possibility of ill effects.

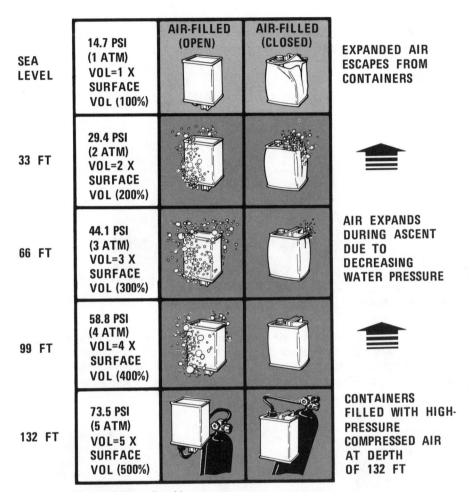

		AIR-FILLED (OPEN)	AIR-FILLED (CLOSED)	
SEA LEVEL	14.7 PSI (1 ATM) VOL=1 X SURFACE VOL (100%)			EXPANDED AIR ESCAPES FROM CONTAINERS
33 FT	29.4 PSI (2 ATM) VOL=2 X SURFACE VOL (200%)			
66 FT	44.1 PSI (3 ATM) VOL=3 X SURFACE VOL (300%)			AIR EXPANDS DURING ASCENT DUE TO DECREASING WATER PRESSURE
99 FT	58.8 PSI (4 ATM) VOL=4 X SURFACE VOL (400%)			
132 FT	73.5 PSI (5 ATM) VOL=5 X SURFACE VOL (500%)			CONTAINERS FILLED WITH HIGH-PRESSURE COMPRESSED AIR AT DEPTH OF 132 FT

Fig. 2-34   Effects of Expanding Air

AIR EMBOLISM

The largest air spaces in the body are also the easiest to close. When you hold your breath, the lungs are shut tight to the outside world. During a scuba diving ascent, unvented lungs can rupture from the expanding air they contain. There are several different ways air can escape. If the air escapes from the alveoli directly into the pulmonary veins, the bubbles may find their way directly into the heart, as shown in figure 2-35. From the heart, they travel up the carotid arteries in the neck and eventually find their way into the small arteries and capillaries of the brain. Embolism comes from the word *embolus*, which means "plug." Sooner or later, the air bubble or bubbles will get stuck in a small artery or capillary and will form a "plug," which cuts off the blood supply to brain tissue. This can be extremely serious, leading to unconsciousness and death.

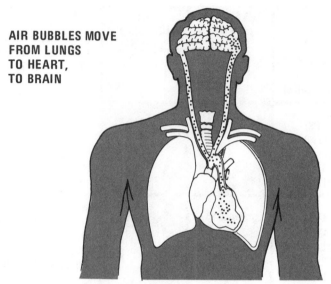

AIR BUBBLES MOVE
FROM LUNGS
TO HEART,
TO BRAIN

Fig. 2-35 Air Embolism

The only treatment for an air embolism is *immediate* recompression in a chamber, as shown in figure 2-36. Here, air pressure is increased quickly to reduce the size of the air bubbles so they won't stop the flow of blood. Then the pressure is decreased very slowly to prevent bubbles and embolisms from forming.

Fig. 2-36 Recompression Chambers

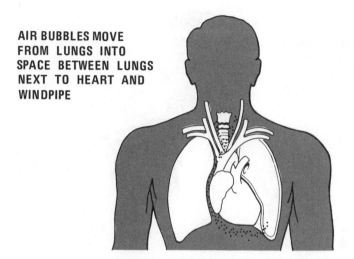

AIR BUBBLES MOVE
FROM LUNGS INTO
SPACE BETWEEN LUNGS
NEXT TO HEART AND
WINDPIPE

Fig. 2-37 Mediastinal Emphysema

Air can also pass out of the alveoli altogether and into the *mediastinum*, or the space between the lungs near the heart and along the windpipe, as shown in figure 2-37. Air in the mediastinum can cause mediastinal emphysema, a problem that brings about chest pain, breathing difficulties, and faintness because of air pressure against the heart.

From the mediastinum area, the air bubbles can travel up along the neck and under the skin in the neck and upper chest region, as shown in figure 2-38. This is called *subcutaneous emphysema*, which may also cause breathing difficulties along with swelling and even changes in voice.

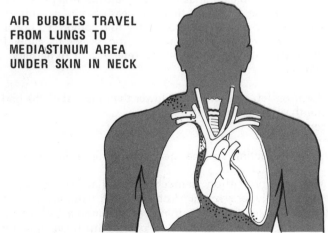

AIR BUBBLES TRAVEL
FROM LUNGS TO
MEDIASTINUM AREA
UNDER SKIN IN NECK

Fig. 2-38 Subcutaneous Emphysema

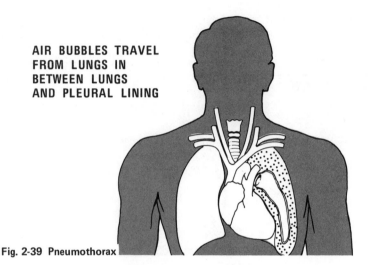

AIR BUBBLES TRAVEL
FROM LUNGS IN
BETWEEN LUNGS
AND PLEURAL LINING

Fig. 2-39 Pneumothorax

Between the lungs and rib cage is a moist membrane called the pleural lining. If air escapes from the alveoli in between the lungs and the *pleural lining*, it could expand and cause the lung or lungs to collapse, as shown in figure 2-39. This is called *pneumothorax*, a rare but serious medical problem. The expanding air in the pleural space not only collapses the lung, but also may press against the heart and affect circulation. Again, chest pain and breathing difficulties occur.

First Aid for Embolism and Emphysema

Symptoms of air embolism occur in a matter of seconds after the diver surfaces and may even occur during ascent. Before losing consciousness, an embolism victim may experience weakness, dizziness, paralysis, changes in vision, chest pain, blood in the mouth, convulsions, and cessation of breathing.

Whenever there is the least suspicion that a diver could have experienced a lung-expansion injury, take the following first aid measures and get him to a recompression chamber as soon as possible. Do not try to recompress a possible embolism victim in the water. The symptoms are too severe to allow for adequate underwater treatment. (See Appendix for reference of Hyperbaric, or recompression, Chambers.)

1. Lay the victim down on left side with head lower than the rest of the body.
2. Give mouth-to-mouth resuscitation if necessary.
3. Administer oxygen.
4. Treat victim for shock.
5. Immediately take the victim to the nearest recompression chamber.

As in all diving accidents, prevention is much more effective than a cure. Anything that could possibly prevent air from escaping naturally from the lungs should be carefully examined. Such things as pneumonia, asthma, lung scars, and even smoking can block the free flow of air out of alveoli and can contribute to the causes of embolism.

It's important to remember that the greatest change in pressure occurs in shallow water. There is a 100 percent increase in pressure in the first 33 feet. In the next 33 feet, from 33 to 66 feet, pressure increases 50 percent, or half the pressure increase of the first 33 feet. From 66 to 99 feet, the pressure increases 33 percent. The deeper you go, the smaller the change in pressure. The danger of embolism, then, is greater in shallow water where the most dramatic changes in pressure exist; cases have occurred in water as shallow as four feet.

The most common cause of air embolism is breath holding. It is entirely natural for an air-breathing creature to hold its breath underwater. In an emergency or panic situation, holding your breath is a powerfully strong instinct. It's important to fight this natural tendency whenever you scuba dive. Never hold your breath when scuba diving. Always breathe naturally and exhale continuously whenever the regulator is out of your mouth.

ASCENT PROCEDURES

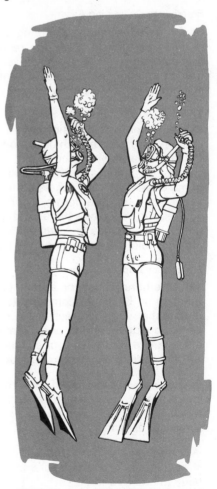

The purpose of learning specific diving procedures is to establish safe habits. You will develop habits whether you want to or not, so it's important to develop good habits from the beginning. Every ascent should follow these steps:

1. Check with your buddy to make sure you both know the dive is over and that it is time to ascend.
2. Check the time.
3. Inflate your BC until you have a slight positive buoyancy.
4. Face your buddy, lift one arm straight up and look toward the surface while ascending, as shown in figure 2-40. Your ascent should be at a rate of 60 feet per minute or less (about the speed of small-size exhaled bubbles). If you ascend without your buddy, turn around slowly to assure no obstructions are in the ascent area.
5. Breathe regularly and continuously all the way to the surface and let expanding air escape from your buoyancy compensator. To help maintain an ascent rate of no more than 60 feet per minute, check your watch and depth gauge during the ascent.

Fig. 2-40 Ascent Procedures

When you reach the surface, inflate your BC completely and switch from regulator to snorkel. As always, be ready to help your buddy in any way. This is especially important at the end of the dive when both divers are tired and when the air supply is at its lowest point.

EMERGENCY ASCENTS

In an emergency, you can ascend by yourself or with the help of your buddy. Listed below are the various options available to make an emergency ascent.

1. Share your buddy's air by the use of an octopus or alternate air source, as discussed in Part I, Section C.
2. Emergency swimming ascent.
3. Emergency buoyant ascent.
4. Buddy breathing ascent. (See Part I, Section C.)

Emergency Swimming Ascent

Begin the emergency swimming ascent with a push off the bottom or with several strong kicks. *Keep the regulator in your mouth, look up, and try to breathe from your regulator as you ascend.* If your buoyancy compensator has an inflating system, use it if necessary, but remember—an emergency swimming ascent depends primarily on kicking, not on excessive buoyancy.

The reduction in ambient pressure as you ascend allows the second stage of the regulator to deliver air from an apparently "empty" tank. As a result, you can probably get a breath or two on your way up. You should, in other words, try to inhale as you ascend, but be careful to exhale at all other times to prevent air embolism. *Never* hold your breath during any normal or emergency ascent. Do not exhale all the air from your lungs. The objective is to keep your lungs at a normal volume. You should try to breathe in and out as you ascend. Keep one hand on the quick-release buckle of your weight belt and be ready to use it. As an extra precaution, you can take your weight belt off and hold it in your hand.

Emergency Buoyant Ascent

An emergency buoyant ascent begins when you ditch your weight belt, inflate your buoyancy compensator, or both. It should begin if you have any doubts that you can reach the surface by buddy breathing or by swimming. Unlike buddy breathing or swimming ascents, the buoyant ascent does not allow you to control your rate of ascent as easily. This increases the possibility of embolism and decompression sickness.

Because of your increased speed during ascent, it is even more important to look up at the surface (to maintain an open airway) and to exhale more rapidly. You should also dump air from your buoyancy compensator to help slow your ascent.

When you are about 10 to 20 feet from the surface, throw your arms out, shoulders back, and feet forward while arching your back. This flares your body to create a large surface area and drag to slow your ascent speed, as shown in figure 2-41.

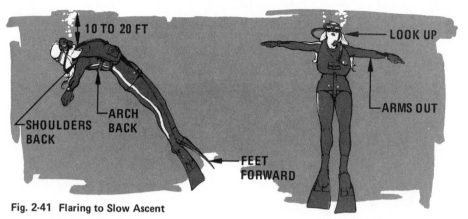

Fig. 2-41 Flaring to Slow Ascent

Selecting an Emergency Ascent

What is the best emergency ascent? There is no simple answer because the best emergency ascent varies with the situation. Each of the basic ascent methods has its own advantages and disadvantages; the diver must practice and master each in order to use any one or all of the methods.

The primary advantage of the emergency swimming ascent is that it is almost identical to a normal ascent. It is fast, simple, and controlled, for you can adjust buoyancy and ascent rates on the way up.

The primary advantage of the emergency buoyant ascent is that it almost guarantees you will arrive at the surface and stay there. The primary disadvantage is that you can ascend too rapidly, which increases the danger of air embolism and decompression sickness.

The emergency buddy breathing ascent has the obvious advantage of supplying you with air throughout the emergency situation. This is especially helpful if the donor buddy has an octopus rig. Buddy breathing with a single hose regulator, however, can be extremely complicated and difficult, especially if the needer is under great stress. Buddy breathing is a skill that requires a great amount of training and practice. Without the appropriate skill level, it can become more hazardous than helpful.

For emergencies in caves or wrecks and under kelp or ice, you will be forced to use buddy breathing with or without an octopus rig. Once you have free access to the surface, you may want to abandon buddy breathing and switch to an emergency swimming ascent. And before you reach the surface, you may want to use an emergency buoyant ascent, thereby using all basic methods of emergency ascent in one emergency situation.

Advances in emergency ascent procedures, buoyancy compensation equipment, and accident research and reporting have done much to increase diving safety. But day-to-day advances continue to depend on good training and repeated practice. Don't be satisfied with just becoming familiar with emergency ascents; *overlearn* these various skills until they become second nature.

section D

depth and time limits

- ● SPORT DIVING LIMITS
- ● NITROGEN NARCOSIS
- ● OXYGEN POISONING
- ● THE BENDS
- ● PREVENTING THE BENDS

EFFECTS OF DIVING TOO DEEP AND TOO LONG

The direct effects of increased pressure on the air spaces inside and outside the diver's body are obvious. Spaces get bigger and smaller almost immediately, and you can either see or feel the changes while they occur. There are, however, less obvious changes. Pressure affects gases and gas mixtures in the body in definite ways, but the effects on the mind and body are sometimes less direct. Even though you may not see or feel these changes as easily, they are equally profound and demand a thorough understanding.

Fortunately, the direct and indirect effects of breathing air under water are measurable and predictable. Because they are predictable, certain depth and time limits can be set for sport divers. Staying within these limits by always monitoring your depth and time devices and tables (See Part II, Section E) is a sure way to prevent problems resulting from effects of pressure. This is especially true when diving in certain areas of extremely clear water, where the bottom, even though 130 feet below, is clearly visible from the surface and "seems" to be in easy reach.

It is suggested that sport divers limit diving to depths of less than 100 feet. Deeper diving requires extensive training and more sophisticated equipment than a certified sport diver may have. The 100-foot limit may sound restrictive, but it really isn't. Many sport divers, in fact, usually dive in waters shallower than 30 feet; they prefer the warmer water and better visibility usually found closer to the surface.

NITROGEN NARCOSIS

What makes 100 feet the suggested limit? Ordinarily, inert gases like nitrogen (or helium) are more or less inactive. They are not consumed or used by the body, and they have no effect on your mind. At depth, the partial pressure of nitrogen increases and it can become "narcotic." Your ability to think and perceive is altered. At depths greater than 100 feet, scuba divers have been known to do strange things as a result of breathing air at a pressure of four or more atmospheres.

SYMPTOMS AND PREVENTION

Beyond 100 feet, nitrogen narcosis can affect your ability to think and make judgments; at 150 feet, you may become somewhat dizzy. Between 200 and 250 feet, you may be unable to communicate or perform simple motor or mental tasks, and below 250 feet, the average diver is more or less useless and becomes a safety menace to himself and others. (Note figure 2-42.)

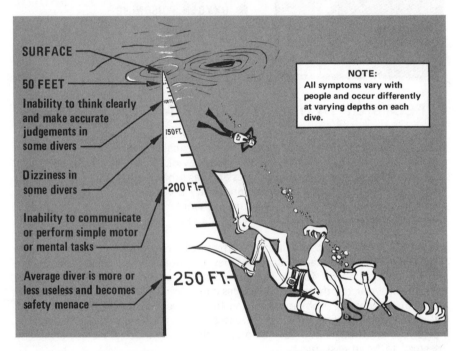

Fig. 2-42 Nitrogen Narcosis Symptoms

Several things lower resistance to nitrogen narcosis. Alcohol, hangover, fatigue, excess carbon dioxide, inexperience, and anxiety tend to reduce a diver's tolerance to high-pressure nitrogen. Also, nitrogen narcosis affects different people in different ways, and any one diver may experience a variety of symptoms inconsistently. But whatever the symptoms, returning to shallower depths is the easiest way to both prevent and treat nitrogen narcosis.

OXYGEN POISONING

Living things need oxygen for survival. An excess of oxygen, however, is just as bad as too little. If you breathe an excess of oxygen for an extended period of time, the outcome can be harmful. Excess oxygen can injure lung tissues and can adversely affect the central nervous system.

PARTIAL PRESSURES

How much oxygen is too much? This depends on three things: the amount, its pressure, and the exposure time. Ordinarily, we breathe a mixture of 78 percent nitrogen and 21 percent oxygen at atmospheric pressure (14.7 psi). Dalton's Law states that the total pressure of a gas mixture equals the sum of the *partial* pressures that make up the mixture. In other words, the sea level partial pressure of nitrogen equals 78 percent of 14.7 psi, or 11.6 psi. The partial pressure of oxygen is 21 percent of 14.7 psi, or 3.09 psi.

Now, oxygen poisoning can occur when the partial pressure of pure oxygen equals two atmospheres absolute, or 29.4 psi (two times 14.7 psi). This could happen if you were breathing pure oxygen (not air) at a depth of 33 feet. It could also happen by breathing ordinary air at a depth of 297 feet, or 10 atmospheres (10 times 3.09 psi). (See figure 2-43.)

100% OXYGEN AT 33 FT. (2 ATMOSPHERES)

OXYGEN/29.4 PSI

PURE OXYGEN BECOMES TOXIC AT 2 ATMOSPHERES, OR 29.4 PSI.

AIR AT 297 FT. (10 ATMOSPHERES)

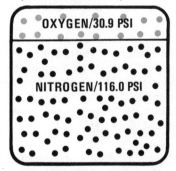

OXYGEN/30.9 PSI

NITROGEN/116.0 PSI

AIR BECOMES TOXIC AT 10 ATMOSPHERES BECAUSE THE PARTIAL PRESSURE OF OXYGEN EQUALS ABOUT 2 ATMOSPHERES, OR 30.9 PSI.

Fig. 2-43 Oxygen Poisoning

Oxygen poisoning will never be a problem to the sport diver as long as he uses clean, dry, filtered air *only* and stays within the 100-foot depth limit for sport diving.

Early symptoms of oxygen poisoning are muscular twitching, nausea, vision and hearing problems, breathing difficulty, anxiety, confusion, unusual fatigue, and clumsiness. These symptoms stop as soon as the partial pressure of oxygen is reduced to below 14.7 psi either by decreasing ambient pressure or by reducing the concentration of oxygen in the breathing mixture.

THE BENDS

"The bends," or decompression sickness, is certainly the most famous of diving illnesses. The story of a diver crippled and bent over with the bends and saved in the nick of time by a recompression chamber, has provided suspense and drama to more than one diving movie. Decompression sickness is a serious diving ailment.

Decompression sickness was "discovered" in the 19th century by laborers who worked in tunnels beneath rivers. The tunnels were pressurized to keep water from flowing into the working areas. At the end of the day's work, the workers returned to an ordinary atmospheric pressure. Many of the workers developed pain in their joints and some became paralyzed. The malady became known as "caisson disease."

The disease of the tunnel workers remained a mystery and a problem until 1907 when Dr. J. S. Haldane determined a method of "stage decompression" to prevent decompression sickness. By bringing anyone who has been in a high-pressure environment back to a normal atmospheric pressure in gradual stages, decompression sickness does not occur.

A slow decompression eliminates the bends by preventing the formation of small pockets of nitrogen in the blood and tissues. According to Henry's Law, gases will enter into a liquid in proportion to the partial pressure of the gas. If you double the partial pressure of nitrogen, for example, the amount of nitrogen that can be dissolved in the blood and tissues of the body also doubles. If you triple the pressure, blood and tissues will hold three times the amount of nitrogen.

Nitrogen dissolved in the body is harmless as long as it stays dissolved. Nitrogen, oxygen, carbon dioxide, and other gases transfer into and out of the bloodstream in the lungs constantly whether you are diving or not. But if you reduce the ambient pressure too quickly, the dissolved nitrogen can come out of solution and form tiny bubbles in the blood and tissues of the body.

The classic example of dissolved gas coming out of solution is a soda pop bottle, shown in figure 2-44. With the cap on, no bubbles are visible because the liquid is under pressure and the "carbonation" bubbles (carbon dioxide gas) are too minute to be seen. When you take the cap off, the pressure is suddenly reduced. The soda pop bubbles. The bubbles seem to come from nowhere. They will

Fig. 2-44 Gas Coming Out of Solution

continue to expand until the soda pop "goes flat." A "flat" bottle of soda does not bubble because the partial pressure of the carbon dioxide gas dissolved in the liquid equals the partial pressure of the gas at ambient pressure in the air surrounding the liquid.

A bubbling, carbonated beverage decompresses in much the same way liquids and tissues of the body decompress during the bends. The symptoms of decompression sickness vary, depending on where the victim gets "hit" (where bubbles form in the body,) as shown in figure 2-45. Symptoms begin within an hour in most cases, but may not begin for six or more hours.

A hit in the brain causes *blindness, dizziness, paralysis, unconsciousness, and convulsions.* *Pain* is experienced if bubbles form in the joints, muscles, or bones; the bloodstream is affected with blocked circulation. *Paralysis and loss of feeling* means that the diver may have been hit in the spinal cord. *Labored breathing, coughing,* and a *burning chest pain* are signs of lung decompression sickness, while the *skin will itch or break out* in a rash if bubble formation takes place there.

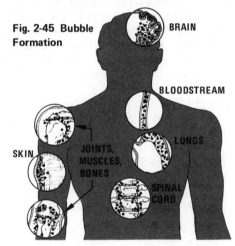

Fig. 2-45 Bubble Formation

BRAIN

BLOODSTREAM

SKIN

JOINTS, MUSCLES, BONES

LUNGS

SPINAL CORD

PREVENTION

The U.S. Navy has set up a No-Decompression Limits Table (see figure 2-46) listing the number of minutes you can theoretically stay at certain maximum depths and still avoid decompression sickness. The first two vertical columns of this table show the number of minutes and the corresponding depths. For example, at 35 feet, you must return to the surface before 310 minutes have passed to avoid stage decompression. At 60 feet, your no-decompression limit is 60 minutes.

Even if you stay strictly within these limits, however, safety cannot be guaranteed. One reason is that all the U.S. Navy diving tables are based on evaluations of a uniform group of trained, healthy, military men, whereas sport divers range widely in physical condition and ability. Recent Doppler ultrasound bubble detection research also has confirmed that sport divers should be more conservative when using the Navy tables. The results of this research are indicated by the shaded areas in figure 2-46.

Several other factors also help contribute to the formation of bubbles and reduce the limits set forth in the No-Decompression Limits Table. Anything that reduces or hinders blood circulation can prevent nitrogen from quickly entering and leaving the blood, such as age, extreme fatigue, alcoholic intoxication, old injuries, extremely hot or cold water showers, and dehydration.

Obesity presents a special problem with decompression sickness. Fat absorbs about five times more nitrogen than blood or other tissues of the body. It takes longer for fatty tissues to become saturated with nitrogen, and it also takes longer for the nitrogen to leave these tissues during decompression.

Other things you need to consider and allow for when calculating your no-decompression limits are the intake of certain drugs, metabolic stresses such as loss of sleep, hypercoagulability or blood that readily coagulates, high altitude diving, and work rate at depth. Skip breathing can also bend you because carbon dioxide builds up and widens the blood vessels, enabling nitrogen to be picked up faster and released to the blood faster. How often you dive also affects how susceptible you will be to getting the bends. If you dive a lot, you are less susceptible. In certain studies, a 50 percent drop in the susceptibility to the bends occurs after 5 to 7 days of diving and a 75 percent drop happens after 10 to 14 days.

It is important to note that even though the No-Decompression Limits Table indicates that you can dive as long as you wish at depths of 30 feet or less, it is best to avoid extreme exposures even at shallow depths and, as a general rule, to be more conservative than the table, especially if you fall into any of the categories listed.

NO-DECOMPRESSION LIMITS AND REPETITIVE GROUP DESIGNATION TABLE FOR NO-DECOMPRESSION AIR DIVES

Depth (feet)	No-decom-pression limits (min)	A	B	C	D	E	F	G	H	I	J	K	L	M	N	O
10		60	120	210	300											
15		35	70	110	160	225	350									
20		25	50	75	100	135	180	240	325							
25	(245)	20	35	55	75	100	125	160	195	245	315					
30	(205)	15	30	45	60	75	95	120	145	170	205	250	310			
35	(160) 310	5	15	25	40	50	60	80	100	120	140	160	190	220	270	310
40	(130) 200	5	15	25	30	40	50	70	80	100	110	130	150	170	200	
50	(70) 100			10	15	25	30	40	50	60	70	80	90	100		
60	(50) 60			10	15	20	25	30	40	50	55	60				
70	(40) 50			5	10	15	20	30	35	40	45	50				
80	(30) 40			5	10	15	20	25	30	35	40					
90	(25) 30			5	10	12	15	20	25	30						
100	(20) 25			5	7	10	15	20	22	25						
110	(15) 20			5	10	13	15	20								
120	(10) 15			5	10	12	15									
130	(5) 10			5	8	10										
140	10			5	7	10										

Sport Diver Limit

Note: Shaded area shows recommended no-decompression limits from ultrasound study. No-decompression limits in parentheses correspond with shaded area.

Fig. 2-46 No-Decompression Limits

Ascent Rate

The U.S. Navy Standard Air Decompression Tables are based on an ascent rate of 60 feet per minute. The smaller exhaled bubbles ascend at about this rate, so always stay below your smallest exhalation bubbles to avoid too fast an ascent, as shown in figure 2-47.

Bottom Time

The no-decompression limits are given in minutes of bottom time. You are technically "on the bottom" from the time you begin your descent until the time you begin your ascent directly to the surface, as illustrated in figure 2-48. For example, you descend to 25 feet for 10 minutes. Then you descend deeper to 50 feet for 15 minutes. After this, you ascend back to 25 feet for five minutes, and then ascend directly to the surface.

After a dive like this, your "bottom time" is 30 minutes at 50 feet, even though you actually spend only 15 minutes at 50 feet. Bottom time, in other words, refers to the *total* time of the dive from the beginning of the descent to the beginning of the direct ascent. The depth of the dive always refers to the deepest point of the dive, no matter how briefly you stay at that depth. Bottom time and depth are also defined in Part II, Section E.

ASCEND AT 60 FEET PER MINUTE

Fig. 2-47 Ascent Rates

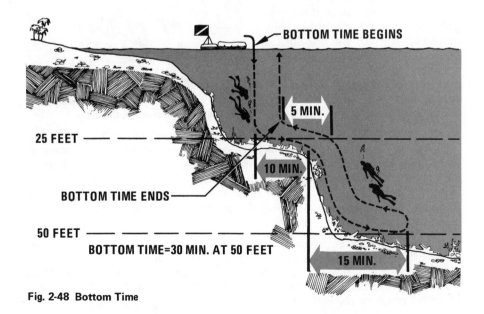

BOTTOM TIME BEGINS

5 MIN.

25 FEET

10 MIN.

BOTTOM TIME ENDS

50 FEET

BOTTOM TIME=30 MIN. AT 50 FEET

15 MIN.

Fig. 2-48 Bottom Time

HIGH ALTITUDE DIVING

Diving in mountain lakes or other high altitude waters increases the possibility of decompression sickness. When you ascend from a dive at a high altitude location, the atmospheric pressure is lower than it is at sea level. This results in a greater difference between water pressures at depth and air pressures at the surface. Because of this, some decompression computers and depth gauges are inaccurate above sea level. Also, the U.S. Navy Decompression Tables are inaccurate either above sea level or in fresh water. If you plan to dive at high altitudes, you should use a set of high altitude dive tables that have been approved by your certification agency.

FLYING AND DIVING

The decompression tables are designed for use at sea level. Airplanes, however, are rarely pressurized to sea level pressures (usually 8,000 feet), and this can cause serious decompression problems for a diver partially saturated with nitrogen. According to the U.S. National Oceanic and Atmospheric Administration, a scuba diver should wait for a surface interval long enough to be classified as a Group D diver (see Part II, Section E). A much safer procedure, if you have made no-decompression dives, is to wait 12 hours before flying in a pressurized aircraft. If you plan to fly above 8,000 feet in a nonpressurized aircraft, or if you have made decompression dives, wait 24 hours. Since pressurized aircraft can lose cabin pressure, you may want to wait 24 hours before flying.

The only effective treatment of decompression sickness is immediate recompression in a recompression chamber. Figure 2-49 is an illustration of one. Recompression reduces the size of the nitrogen bubbles and forces them back into solution. Then, the pressure is slowly reduced inside the chamber according to the U.S. Navy Standard Air or Oxygen Treatment Tables to allow the diver to decompress gradually.

Fig. 2-49 Recompression Chamber

At the first sign of possible symptoms of decompression sickness, do not hesitate to seek treatment. Time is critical. Before diving, make sure you and your buddy know the location and phone number of the nearest recompression chamber. A reference to help locate recompression chambers is provided in the Appendix. Underwater recompression should be considered only in an extreme emergency and only if it is impossible to get to a recompression chamber.

The indirect effects of pressure can be easily avoided. The depth and time limits of sport diving need not inhibit even the most adventurous buddy team. Sport divers have little reason to go beyond reasonable limits. Most underwater life lives well within the warm and lighted depths above 100 feet. This is where diving is most enjoyable, interesting, and safe.

section E

repetitive dives

- RESIDUAL NITROGEN
- DIVE PROFILE
- DIVE TABLES
- DECOMPRESSION DIVING

RESIDUAL NITROGEN, MORE THAN ONE DIVE, AND DECOMPRESSION DIVING

Your body normally contains a certain amount of nitrogen dissolved in the blood and tissues. Whenever you dive, your body absorbs more nitrogen because of increased pressure underwater. The blood and tissues can continue to absorb nitrogen for about 24 hours under pressure. After 24 hours, the body is said to be "saturated" with nitrogen—it cannot hold any more, so absorption stops. When you return to a lower pressure at the surface, the nitrogen slowly leaves the blood and tissues through alveoli in the lungs. The body continues to give off nitrogen until the gas dissolved in blood and tissues returns to normal.

RESIDUAL NITROGEN

The extra nitrogen that stays in your body after the dive is called "residual nitrogen." The U.S. Navy Decompression Tables are more or less based on the simple fact that nitrogen will stay in solution and will not form bubbles as long as the partial pressure of nitrogen is not immediately reduced more than one-half. However, the latest ultrasound studies indicate that very small bubbles are formed and remain in the blood even though a diver stays within the no-decompression limits of the dive table. These bubbles are usually harmless and are eventually filtered out by the lungs.

To guard against the possibility of developing decompression sickness, it is recommended that you do not dive to the maximum limits of the no-decompression table. As an added measure of safety, you should stop at 10 feet for at least one to three minutes after every no-decompression dive. Ultrasound studies have shown this technique helps deplete most or all of the small bubbles.

MORE THAN ONE DIVE

The No-Decompression Limits and Repetitive Group Designation Table for No-Decompression Air Dives (see Appendix) tells you how long you can stay at certain depths in *salt water* and return to the surface without decompression stops. But what if you want to make another dive soon after the first one? Your body contains a certain amount of residual nitrogen from the first dive, so you will have to take this into consideration on your second dive. The U.S. Navy uses two tables (see Appendix), to let you account for residual nitrogen in two or more dives in salt water.

The No-Decompression Limits and Repetitive Group Designation Table and the Residual Nitrogen Timetable for Repetitive Air Dives have instructions and examples to help you use them. Although many examples in this course are worked using the U.S. Navy limits, you should plan to use the more conservative ultrasound limits for actual dive calculations.

A TYPICAL REPETITIVE DIVE

Figure 2-50 is a diagram of two dives. A buddy team plans to make one dive in the morning and one after lunch. They descend at 11 a.m. to a maximum depth of 73 feet and swim along the bottom toward shore. The bottom gets slightly shallower as they swim until they run into a vertical, underwater cliff. They ascend along the face of the cliff until they discover an underwater ledge at 55 feet.

After finding the ledge, they agree to ascend as planned. They both note the time and begin a direct ascent to the surface at 11:22 a.m. After eating lunch and refilling their tanks, the buddy team begins their descent at 1:07 p.m. They explore the underwater ledge at a depth of 55 feet for 25 minutes. The ascent from 55 feet to the surface begins at 1:32 p.m.

Before, during, and after these two dives, the buddy team used the U.S. Navy Tables to plan and recheck both the time and depth of each dive. To use and understand the tables, you must become familiar with several important terms:

> *Bottom time* refers to the total elapsed time starting from when the buddy team begins their descent until they begin a direct ascent to the surface. (See also Part II, Section D.)
>
> *Depth* is the deepest point reached during a dive.
>
> *Surface interval time* is how long you stay on the surface between dives.
>
> *Repetitive Dive* refers to any dive that begins within 12 hours of surfacing from an earlier dive. This applies to most sport dives. If you accumulate a lot of bottom time, take longer surface intervals than the tables require. If the surface interval between dives is 10 minutes or less, consider both dives as one long dive with a bottom time equal to the total bottom times of both dives.

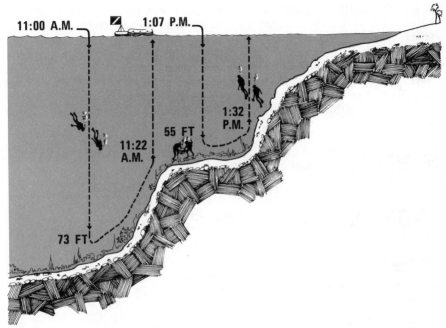

Fig. 2-50 A Typical Repetitive Dive

THE DIVE PROFILE

To plan and analyze repetitive dives, the buddy team sketches a dive profile, as shown in figure 2-51. It is a simple diagram of one or more dives and a convenient way to record time, depth, and information from the decompression tables. The profile shown here is the one the buddy team uses for the dive illustrated in figure 2-50.

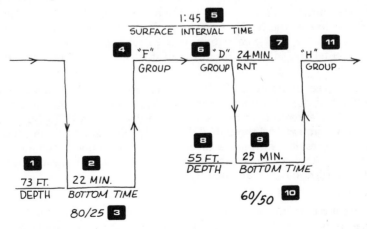

Fig. 2-51 The Dive Profile

The buddy team knows, before arriving at the dive site, that the maximum depth of this particular location is about 75 feet. In order to stay within the no-decompression limits, they consult the No-Decompression Limits and Repetitive Group Designation Table, as shown in figure 2-52. Looking at the first two columns, they find that any dive between 70 and 80 feet is considered a dive to 80 feet (item 1) with a maximum bottom time of 40 minutes (item 2). If they went to the maximum depth, in other words, they would have to ascend within 40 minutes. They agree to end the first dive well before this time limit is up.

NO-DECOMPRESSION LIMITS AND REPETITIVE GROUP DESIGNATION TABLE FOR NO-DECOMPRESSION AIR DIVES

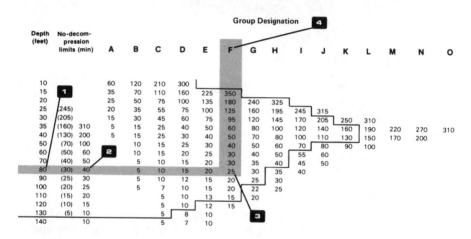

Depth (feet)	No-decom- pression limits (min)	A	B	C	D	E	F	G	H	I	J	K	L	M	N	O
10		60	120	210	300											
15	1	35	70	110	160	225	350									
20		25	50	75	100	135	180	240	325							
25	(245)	20	35	55	75	125	160	195	245	315						
30	(205)	15	30	45	60	75	95	120	145	170	205	250	310			
35	(160) 310	5	15	25	40	50	60	80	100	120	140	160	190	220	270	310
40	(130) 200	5	15	25	30	40	50	70	80	100	110	130	150	170	200	
50	(70) 100		10	15	25	30	40	50	60	70	80	90	100			
60	(50) 60	2	10	15	20	25	30	40	50	55	60					
70	(40) 50		5	10	15	20	30	35	40	45	50					
80	(30) 40		5	10	15	20	25	30	35	40						
90	(25) 30		5	10	12	15	20	25	30							
100	(20) 25		5	7	10	15	20	22	25							
110	(15) 20			5	10	13	15	20								
120	(10) 15			5	10	12	15									
130	(5) 10			5	8	10										
140	10			5	7	10										

Group Designation 4

3

Fig. 2-52 No-Decompression Limits Table

Since the actual depth and bottom time of the first dive is 73 feet for 22 minutes, they enter this information on the dive profile (items 1 and 2 in figure 2-51). Returning to the No-Decompression Table for the 80-foot depth, they find that the *exact or next greater* time, over 22 minutes, is 25 minutes (item 3). They next enter this information in the profile: "80/25" (Fig. 2-51, item 3).

The shaded area in figure 2-52 (No-Decompression Table) illustrates that a dive to 80 feet for 25 minutes puts the dive team in repetitive group "F" (item 4). They enter this information in the dive profile (Fig. 2-51, item 4). The repetitive groups "A" through "O" actually represent a system for cataloging how much residual nitrogen a diver contains in his body after a no-decompression dive. An "A" diver, for example, has very little residual nitrogen, while an "O" diver has a great amount.

The surface interval time between dives is one hour and 45 minutes. They enter this time on the dive profile (Fig. 2-51, item 5). While the buddy team is on the surface, they are constantly giving off nitrogen. When they begin the repetitive dive, therefore, their bodies contain less residual nitrogen than they did at the end of dive one. To get credit for this decrease in residual nitrogen, they turn to the second table, the Residual Nitrogen Timetable for Repetitive Air Dives, as shown in figure 2-53.

Since the dive team ended dive one as "F" divers, they enter the Residual Nitrogen Timetable at "F" on the slanted left-hand side of the table. The paired numbers, to the right, refer to minimum and maximum surface interval times.

RESIDUAL NITROGEN TIMETABLE FOR REPETITIVE AIR DIVES

*Dives following surface intervals of more than 12 hours are not repetitive dives. Use actual bottom times in the Standard Air Decompression Tables to compute decompression for such dives.

Repetitive group at the beginning of the surface interval

Group	Z	O	N	M	L	K	J	I	H	G	F	E	D	C	B	A
A																0:10 / 12:00*
B															0:10 / 2:10	2:11 / 12:00*
C														0:10 / 1:39	1:40 / 2:49	2:50 / 12:00*
D													0:10 / 1:09	1:10 / 2:38	2:39 / 5:48	5:49 / 12:00*
E												0:10 / 0:54	0:55 / 1:57	1:58 / 3:22	3:23 / 6:32	6:33 / 12:00*
F											0:10 / 0:45	0:46 / 1:29	1:30 / 2:28	2:29 / 3:57	3:58 / 7:05	7:06 / 12:00*
G										0:10 / 0:40	0:41 / 1:15	1:16 / 1:59	2:00 / 2:58	2:59 / 4:25	4:26 / 7:35	7:36 / 12:00*
H									0:10 / 0:36	0:37 / 1:06	1:07 / 1:41	1:42 / 2:23	2:24 / 3:20	3:21 / 4:49	4:50 / 7:59	8:00 / 12:00*
I								0:10 / 0:33	0:34 / 0:59	1:00 / 1:29	1:30 / 2:02	2:03 / 2:44	2:45 / 3:43	3:44 / 5:12	5:13 / 8:21	8:22 / 12:00*
J							0:10 / 0:31	0:32 / 0:54	0:55 / 1:19	1:20 / 1:47	1:48 / 2:20	2:21 / 3:04	3:05 / 4:02	4:03 / 5:40	5:41 / 8:40	8:41 / 12:00*
K						0:10 / 0:28	0:29 / 0:49	0:50 / 1:11	1:12 / 1:35	1:36 / 2:03	2:04 / 2:38	2:39 / 3:21	3:22 / 4:19	4:20 / 5:48	5:49 / 8:58	8:59 / 12:00*
L					0:10 / 0:26	0:27 / 0:45	0:46 / 1:04	1:05 / 1:25	1:26 / 1:49	1:50 / 2:19	2:20 / 2:53	2:54 / 3:36	3:37 / 4:35	4:36 / 6:02	6:03 / 9:12	9:13 / 12:00*
M				0:10 / 0:25	0:26 / 0:42	0:43 / 0:59	1:00 / 1:18	1:19 / 1:39	1:40 / 2:05	2:06 / 2:34	2:35 / 3:08	3:09 / 3:52	3:53 / 4:49	4:50 / 6:18	6:19 / 9:28	9:29 / 12:00*
N			0:10 / 0:24	0:25 / 0:39	0:40 / 0:54	0:55 / 1:11	1:12 / 1:30	1:31 / 1:53	1:54 / 2:18	2:19 / 2:47	2:48 / 3:22	3:23 / 4:04	4:05 / 5:03	5:04 / 6:32	6:33 / 9:43	9:44 / 12:00*
O		0:10 / 0:23	0:24 / 0:36	0:37 / 0:51	0:52 / 1:07	1:08 / 1:24	1:25 / 1:43	1:44 / 2:04	2:05 / 2:29	2:30 / 2:59	3:00 / 3:33	3:34 / 4:17	4:18 / 5:16	5:17 / 6:44	6:45 / 9:54	9:55 / 12:00*
Z	0:10 / 0:22	0:23 / 0:34	0:35 / 0:48	0:49 / 1:02	1:03 / 1:18	1:19 / 1:36	1:37 / 1:55	1:56 / 2:17	2:18 / 2:42	2:43 / 3:10	3:11 / 3:45	3:46 / 4:29	4:30 / 5:27	5:28 / 6:56	6:57 / 10:05	10:06 / 12:00*
NEW GROUP DESIGNATION →	Z	O	N	M	L	K	J	I	H	G	F	E	D	C	B	A

REPETITIVE DIVE DEPTH	Z	O	N	M	L	K	J	I	H	G	F	E	D	C	B	A
40	257	241	213	187	161	138	116	101	87	73	61	49	37	25	17	7
50	169	160	142	124	111	99	87	76	66	56	47	38	29	21	13	6
60	122	117	107	97	88	79	70	61	52	44	36	30	24	17	11	5
70	100	96	87	80	72	64	57	50	43	37	31	26	20	15	9	4
80	84	80	73	68	61	54	48	43	38	32	28	23	18	13	8	4
90	73	70	64	58	53	47	43	38	33	29	24	20	16	11	7	3
100	64	62	57	52	48	43	38	34	30	26	22	18	14	10	7	3
110	57	55	51	47	42	38	34	31	27	24	20	16	13	10	6	3
120	52	50	46	43	39	35	32	28	25	21	18	15	12	9	6	3
130	46	44	40	38	35	31	28	25	22	19	16	13	11	8	6	3
140	42	40	38	35	32	29	26	23	20	18	15	12	10	7	5	2
150	40	38	35	32	30	27	24	22	19	17	14	12	9	7	5	2
160	37	36	33	31	28	26	23	20	18	16	13	11	9	6	4	2
170	35	34	31	29	26	24	22	20	17	15	13	10	8	6	4	2
180	32	31	29	27	25	22	20	18	16	14	12	10	8	6	4	2
190	31	30	28	26	24	21	19	17	15	13	11	10	8	6	4	2

RESIDUAL NITROGEN TIMES (MINUTES)

Fig. 2-53 Residual Nitrogen Timetable

Reading from left to right (Fig. 2-54), they find that their time, one hour and 45 minutes, puts them in the fourth column from the right side of the table, or the box containing 1:30 (minimum time in that designation) and 2:28 (maximum time). Following the column downward, the buddies find they have given off residual nitrogen to move from the "F" group designation to the "D" group designation.

The buddy team has less residual nitrogen in their bodies, but they still have some nitrogen that must be taken into account for the second dive. The new

RESIDUAL NITROGEN TIMETABLE FOR REPETITIVE AIR DIVES

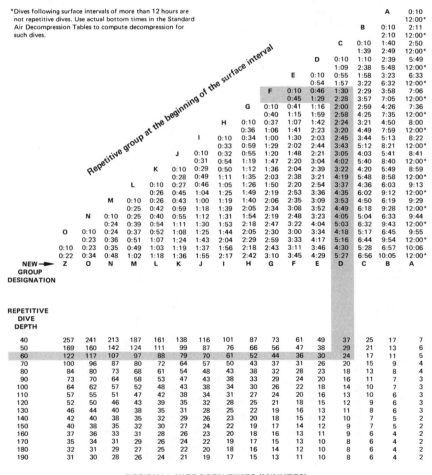

Fig. 2-54 Residual Nitrogen Timetable

group designation letter "D" is added to the dive profile (item 6, Fig. 2-51). Then, they turn to the lower half of the Residual Nitrogen Timetable shown in figure 2-54. The purpose of this part of the table is to convert the group letter and the depth of the next repetitive dive into minutes of residual nitrogen time that the buddy team must consider that they have already spent on the bottom *before* they begin the next repetitive dive. Depths for the next dive are listed on the far left-hand column.

The shaded area in figure 2-54 shows that a "D" diver going to a repetitive dive depth of 60 feet will have a residual nitrogen time of 24 minutes. The residual nitrogen time (RNT) is added to the dive profile (item 7, Fig. 2-51). This means that our buddy team must *start* their second dive to 55 feet as though they had already been at this depth for 24 minutes.

Now, to make sure that they don't go beyond the no-decompression limits, they go back to the No-Decompression Limits Table (See figure 2-55) and find that a dive to 60 feet (55 actual feet) will have a maximum bottom time of 60 minutes.

NO-DECOMPRESSION LIMITS AND REPETITIVE GROUP DESIGNATION TABLE FOR NO-DECOMPRESSION AIR DIVES

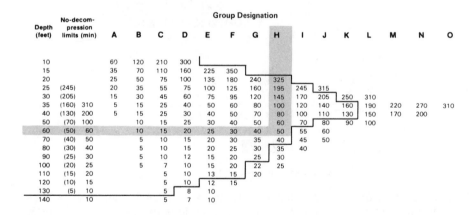

Depth (feet)	No-decompression limits (min)	A	B	C	D	E	F	G	H	I	J	K	L	M	N	O
10		60	120	210	300											
15		35	70	110	160	225	350									
20		25	50	75	100	135	180	240	325							
25	(245)	20	35	55	75	100	125	160	195	245	315					
30	(205)	15	30	45	60	75	95	120	145	170	205	250	310			
35	(160) 310	5	15	25	40	50	60	80	100	120	140	160	190	220	270	310
40	(130) 200	5	15	25	30	40	50	70	80	100	110	130	150	170	200	
50	(70) 100			10	15	25	30	40	50	60	70	80	90	100		
60	(50) 60			10	15	20	25	30	40	50	55	60				
70	(40) 50			5	10	15	20	30	35	40	45	50				
80	(30) 40			5	10	15	20	25	30	35	40					
90	(25) 30			5	10	12	15	20	25	30						
100	(20) 25			5	7	10	15	20	22	25						
110	(15) 20				5	10	13	15	20							
120	(10) 15				5	10	12	15								
130	(5) 10				5	8	10									
140	10				5	7	10									

Fig. 2-55 No-Decompression Limits Table

In order to stay well within the no-decompression limits, the buddy team decides to limit their actual bottom time to 25 minutes (item 9, Fig. 2-51). Since they are beginning the repetitive dive with a residual nitrogen time of 24 minutes, their total bottom time will be 25 plus 24 minutes, or 49 minutes. This is 11 minutes short of the U.S. Navy no-decompression limit and within the ultrasound limit.

At the end of the repetitive dive, the two divers use the No-Decompression Limits Table to find their repetitive group designation, as shown in figure 2-55.

The shaded area in the table shows that their second dive of the day was to 60 feet for 50 minutes (55 actual feet and 49 actual minutes) which makes them "H" divers. The "H" repetitive group designation is entered on the profile at the appropriate place where it can be used for another repetitive dive if they decide to make one (item 11, Fig. 2-51).

DECOMPRESSION DIVING

The sample repetitive dive situation just described illustrates two dives made *within* the no-decompression depth and time limits. Decompression diving should not be performed by sport divers. If you want additional information on decompression diving and deep diving, consult the Advanced Manual. The following example will give you a brief outline of how the dive tables are used for decompression diving. The buddy team wants to dive to 73 feet for a total bottom time of 48 minutes. They must make a stage decompression stop during their ascent to prevent nitrogen bubbles from forming in their bodies.

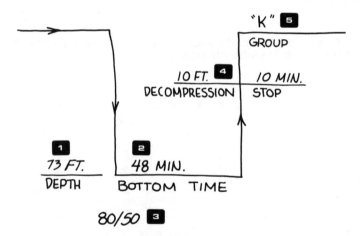

Fig. 2-56 A Typical Decompression Dive Profile

The U.S. Navy Standard Air Decompression Table gives the depths and times of decompression stops during ascent. This table is used whenever a buddy team goes beyond the depth and time limits of the No-Decompression Limits Table. A decompression stop may be anywhere from 50 to 10 feet deep for a period of one minute to over an hour. Figure 2-56 shows a dive profile for a typical stage decompression dive.

The actual depth and bottom time of the dive is 73 feet for 48 minutes. This is entered on the dive profile (items 1 and 2, Fig. 2-56). Turning to the Decompression Table in figure 2-57, the buddy team finds that the exact or next greater depth and time for this dive is 80 feet for 50 minutes. Entering the table from the left side at this depth and time (80/50), they find it will take one minute and 10 seconds to ascend to the first decompression stop at 10 feet.

U.S. NAVY STANDARD AIR DECOMPRESSION TABLE

Depth (feet)	Bottom time (min)	Time first stop (min:sec)	Decompression stops (feet) 50	40	30	20	10	Total ascent (min:sec)	Repetitive group
40	200						0	0:40	*
	210	0:30					2	2:40	N
	230	0:30					7	7:40	N
	250	0:30					11	11:40	O
	270	0:30					15	15:40	O
	300	0:30					19	19:40	Z
	360	0:30					23	23:40	Z
	480	0:30					41	41:40	Z
	720	0:30					69	69:40	Z
		0:40							*
		0:40							
80	40						0	1:20	*
	50	1:10					10	11:20	K
	60	1:10					17	18:20	L
	70	1:10					23	24:20	M
	80	1:00				2	31	34:20	N
	90	1:00				7	39	47:20	N
	100	1:00				11	46	58:20	O
	110	1:00				13	53	67:20	O
	120	1:00				17	56	74:20	Z
	130	1:00				19	63	83:20	Z
	140	1:00				26	69	96:20	Z
	150	1:00				32	77	110:20	Z
	180	1:00				35	85	121:20	Z
	240	0:50			6	52	120	179:20	Z
	360	0:50			29	90	160	280:20	Z
	480	0:50			59	107	187	354:20	Z
	720	0:40		17	108	142	187	455:20	Z

Fig. 2-57 Standard Air Decompression Table

When they reach a depth of 10 feet, they have to stay there with the chest area at that exact depth for 10 minutes before making a direct ascent to the surface. At the far right-hand side of the table is the repetitive group designation. In this case, the buddies will be "K" divers when they surface. The ascent time (at a rate of 60 feet per minute) is not considered as part of the decompression stop time. This information is then entered in the dive profile (Fig. 2-56, items 3 through 5).

AIDS TO DIVE PLANNING

Dive tables come in a wide variety of shapes, sizes, and construction. Some are designed for use out of the water, while others can be taken with you during the dive. The common bond between all of these aids is to help you control the amount of nitrogen in your blood and to become a safe, intelligent diver.

The dive table shown in figure 2-58, incorporates all of the standard U.S. Navy dive tables you need for no-decompression and decompression diving. The table also has a simple-to-use dive profile that eliminates the need to memorize how to figure your repetitive dives. The dive profile has spaces to record the initial dive and two repetitive dives (see Fig. 2-59).

The legend below the first dive explains the abbreviations used on the profile. The formulas for computing the adjusted no-decompression limit and the total bottom time are included below the boxes for the second dive. Within the repetitive dive boxes, simple mathematical symbology is used to help remind you of the necessary computations.

Good planning and intelligent use of the decompression tables should almost eliminate the need for decompression in the water. No-decompression diving is safer and more enjoyable; stage decompression, at its best, is not fun.

Sport diving gives human beings a marked admiration for fish. Few creatures are more completely adapted to their environment than fish.

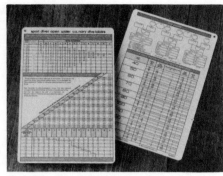

Fig. 2-58 Dive Table

Sport divers, on the other hand, need equipment, skills, knowledge, procedures, and intelligence to adapt to both their natural and underwater environment. You must know how your body works in both air and water to really understand physical sensations, breathing, and the direct and indirect effects of underwater pressure.

As human beings, we have certain limitations when it comes to entering the underwater environment. Our intelligence not only allows us to overcome and work within these limitations, but also gives us the much greater advantage of appreciating and enjoying our adaptation. No fish, in spite of its almost total adaptation, can possibly appreciate its own home as well as a trained and knowledgeable sport diver can.

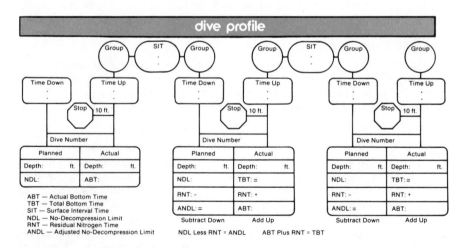

Fig. 2-59 Dive Profile

PART III   the environment

introduction

Once you feel secure in your ability to use diving equipment, and once you understand how water affects your mind and body, you are ready to turn to the environment itself, to its ancient mysteries and its infinite variation.

In some ways, the waters of the world have remained the same for billions of years. Currents flow, waves roll on, and underwater creatures live and die today much as they did centuries ago. From the beginning of human history, man has found the seas a continuing source of myth, poetry, beauty, like that captured in figure 3-1, and awesome terror.

Figure 3-1.

In other ways, however, the waters of the world are always new and different. You will soon find that no two diving locations are exactly the same. Both salt and fresh waters are in constant motion. And life beneath the surface is constantly evolving, shifting, moving, and responding to changes in the environment and the balance of nature.

The underwater environment is a paradox, for it stays the same, yet constantly changes at the same time. Man's intimate and ongoing relationship with the waters of the world, however, might just be at a critical turning point. We have come to learn that the sea is neither bottomless nor eternal; it is, instead, finite and fragile, requiring great care and respect for its complex and delicate ecological web.

Part III introduces the diving environment and its living plants and creatures. It is designed to give you an appreciation for the fluid environment so you can enter it, not as an intruder, but as a friend.

section A

the worlds of diving

- HISTORY OF THE OCEANS
- ECOLOGY
- ENVIRONMENTAL VARIATION
- REGIONAL VARIATION

DIVING ENVIRONMENT: AN OVERVIEW

The oceans cover 70.8 percent of the earth's surface. Thousands of freshwater lakes and rivers contribute even more to the earth's liquid surface. Sport divers, in other words, have a right to feel at home on this particular planet in the solar system. Astronomers, in fact, often call earth the "Water Planet."

Why and how was this planet blessed with the liquid of life? Thinkers and philosophers have long attempted to unravel this mystery, but it remains largely unsolved. We know that earth lies just far enough from the sun to prevent the seas from boiling away into a giant cloud surrounding the planet, but it lies close enough to the sun to keep most of our water in a liquid state.

HISTORY OF THE OCEANS

Attempts at solving some of the mysteries of the oceans began as early as 2 B.C. Posidonius wrote that a depth of 1,000 fathoms had been measured in the Sea of Sardinia, but study of the oceans did not make material progress for some 2,000 years. Study of the oceans only became an independent branch of science in the nineteenth century.

Despite the remarkable advances made in oceanography in the last century and a half, a controversy about how the water got into the oceans still remains. Some geologists think that all of primeval earth's water existed as atmospheric vapor which condensed and fell in great torrents when the earth cooled. Others hold that water gradually accumulated when volcanoes released it as steam or worked to the surface in hot springs.

We may not know the origin of the water on the earth's crust, but we do know that about 85 percent is now in the oceans. The rest is found inland or frozen on the polar icecaps.

Compared to continental land, relatively little is known about the land beneath the ocean. Growing evidence indicates that the rocks underlying the ocean floors are more dense than those underlying the continents. According to the *continental drift* theory, the earth's crust floats on a central liquid core. The continents, being lighter, float with a higher freeboard and are slowly drifting apart. The thinner areas, composed of heavier rock, form natural basins where water has collected.

Along most of the continents' coasts, the bottom gradually slopes down to about 600 feet (183 meters), where it falls away more rapidly to greater depths. This *continental shelf*, as shown in figure 3-2, averages about 30 miles in width, but can vary from nothing to about 800 miles in width. A similar shelf usually extends out from islands or groups of islands.

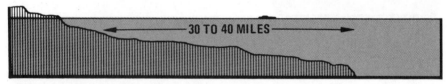

Fig. 3-2 Continental Shelf

In general, the deep sea bottom slopes gradually, averaging about half a degree. But it may slope as much as 45° off a volcanic island. The shape of the ocean bottom looks a lot like the land. Both have steep, rugged mountains, deep canyons, rolling hills, and plains.

ECOLOGY

Ecology is a branch of science that studies the interrelationships of living organisms and their environment. The underwater ecosystem is so interrelated that it is sometimes difficult to distinguish living organisms from their environment: the fish is in the sea, but the sea is also in the fish. It may be more accurate to think of the sea as a living broth, or as a single infinitely complex, living organism. Seawater not only has all the chemical elements needed to sustain life, it also has about 300 times more living space than dry land. As a result, the sea contains vast quantities of organic material.

THE CHAIN OF LIFE

Underwater life is usually divided into three major categories: *plankton* (tiny plants called *phytoplankton* and tiny animals called *zooplankton*), *nekton* (strong-swimming animals, like fish), and *benthos* (plants and animals, such as seaweed, barnacles, and crabs living on the sea bottom).

Either directly or indirectly, nearly all marine life depends upon plankton. By means of photosynthesis, phytoplankton uses sunlight to change chemical nutrients into living cells which become food for zooplankton. Zooplankton becomes food for nekton, which in turn becomes food for benthos. The original chemical nutrients are replaced by animal wastes and plant and animal decomposition, which completes the food cycle and the chain of life.

Underwater plants and animals are so dependent on each other and on their environment, that if we destroy any major link in the food chain, or if we poison the liquid environment and thus kill any part of this living cycle, then we are faced with the real and frightening possibility of all the world's oceans becoming a giant dead sea. Pollution and other threats to the underwater ecosystem are discussed in Part III, Section E.

ENVIRONMENTAL VARIATION

An overview of the diving environment usually gives the impression that the entire underwater world with its basins and life cycles are basically the same. In some respects this is true. A small wave breaking on a pond's shore in Minnesota and an enormous breaker crashing on the shore of Australia both obey the same laws. But a closer look reveals an endless variation in diving environments.

The variables include different bottom types, currents, plant and animal life, color and transparency, and a host of other differences that depend on time and place. All these variables, however, have something in common. In almost all cases, they either depend on, or are closely associated with, differences in temperature.

TEMPERATURE

Geology dictates basic bottom types such as rock, mud, or sand, but water temperature gives a dive site its distinctive quality. Reef-building corals, for example, flourish in tropical and subtropical areas on the eastern shores of continents where the sea's mean annual temperature is at least 74.3°F (23.5°C), as shown in figure 3-3. Corals cannot withstand water temperatures much below 64°F (18°C). Along the colder coasts of North and South America, on the other hand, the great brown algae known as *kelp* thrives, as shown in figure 3-4.

Fig. 3-3 Coral Reef   Fig. 3-4 Kelp

The abundance of marine life also depends on water temperature, although the relationship is an indirect one. The amount of marine life is directly related to the supply of phytoplankton in the water. And the supply of phytoplankton depends on a good supply of sunlight and chemical nutrients. In shallow waters, water movement usually stirs up the bottom and carries nutrients to the sunlit surface, so animal life abounds. Life also thrives in polar regions where the water's surface is supplied with nutrients lifted from the bottom by uprising, warm-water currents. Surprisingly, the warm water tropics produce relatively little phytoplankton, for chemical nutrients tend to sink in the stable waters below the sunlit surface. As a result, warm waters tend to produce an enormous *variety*, while cold waters tend to produce a great *quantity* of marine life.

The effects of temperature on plants and animals are relatively stable and permanent, but water temperature at a given location can change dramatically from month to month. Water temperatures range from 85°F (29°C) in the tropics, to 40°F (4°C) at 100 feet in the Great Lakes, to a low of 28°F (-2°C) beneath polar ice. The average temperature of surface water in the ocean is about 63°F (17°C). Surface temperatures vary an average of about 18 Fahrenheit (11 Celsius) degrees during the year.

THERMOCLINES

Thermoclines are layers of water having different temperatures. They can occur close to the surface or deep in the water. Temperatures can vary 20 Fahrenheit (12 Celsius) degrees between the surface and lower layers. With depth, water temperatures decrease nearly everywhere. Colder water, because it is denser, sinks below warmer water.

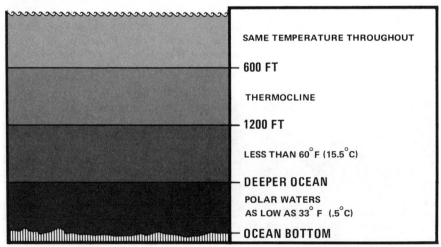

Fig. 3-5 Thermocline

In general, the temperature is the same in the top layer of sea water which can extend as deep as 600 feet. Below this layer is a zone of rapid temperature decrease called the *thermocline*, shown in figure 3-5. Below 1,200 feet, the temperature is less than 60°F (15.5°C). Below this the deeper layers of the ocean are fed by cooled waters that have sunk from the surface in the arctic and antarctic. Temperatures as low as 33°F (.5°C) exist in this area.

OVERTURNS

During the winter and summer months, lakes and oceans usually remain stratified, with definite zones or layers forming above and below the thermocline. Surface water changes in density, however, when temperatures change. Wind or sudden temperature drops in the ambient air can cool surface water to a temperature less than the water immediately below it. When this happens, the surface water sinks to join levels of water having the same temperature and is replaced by the water just below it.

This water, in turn, may be cooled and will also settle, until the rising water is approximately the same temperature as the surrounding air. The cycle then stabilizes. At these times, suspended material often reduces visibility.

UPWELLINGS

Strong surface winds can also cause currents strong enough to mix layers of water. A wind blowing in the right direction can make surface waters flow away from shore and colder bottom waters replace them. This phenomenon is called *upwelling* and is illustrated in figure 3-6. Because of nutrient-rich waters rising from the bottom, upwellings are often associated with huge increases in the plankton population, and corresponding decreases in visibility.

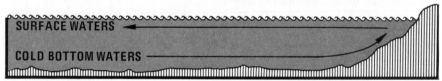

Fig. 3-6 Upwelling

REGIONAL VARIATION

The National Oceanic and Atmospheric Administration designates eight different diving regions in and around the United States, as well as tropical and polar diving regions. These regions are listed in a regional water temperature chart in figure 3-7 and on the map in figure 3-8. All environmental variations, including temperature, visibility, and marine life, give each region its own peculiar characteristics. A discussion of these and other distinctive features of each area follows.

Before diving in any unfamiliar region, you should obtain information about local conditions from divers in the area. It is also a good idea to make at least one checkout dive with a diver who is familiar with the diving region.

REGIONAL WATER TEMPERATURE CHART *
(Degrees in Fahrenheit)   20° 30° 40° 50° 60° 70° 80°

NORTHEAST (Maine through New Jersey)

Spring and summer:	50° to 70°	
Winter:	as low as 28.5°	

(bar spans approx 30° to 70°)

MID-ATLANTIC (Delaware through South Carolina)

Summer:	60° to 75°	
Winter:	as low as 38° to 45° in north; 45° to 55° in south	

(bar spans approx 50° to 75°)

SOUTHEAST (Georgia through Florida coast)

Summer:	as high as 75° to 80°	
Winter:	65° to 70° in south; as low as 50° to 55° in north	

(bar spans approx 60° to 80°)

GULF OF MEXICO (Florida Panhandle through Texas)

Summer:	up to 86°	
Winter:	down to 56°	

(bar spans approx 70° to 86°)

NORTHWEST (Southeast Alaska through Oregon)

Summer:	45° to 50°	
Winter:	34° to 38°	

(bar spans approx 34° to 50°)

MID-PACIFIC (Northern and Central California)

Summer:	48° to 56°	
Fall, early winter:	52° to 60°	
Late winter, spring:	45° to 54°	

(bar spans approx 45° to 60°)

NOTE: Thermocline at 20 to 40 feet during late spring and early summer.

SOUTHWEST (Point Conception to Northern Baja)

Summer:	55° to 70°	
Winter:	50° to 60°	

(bar spans approx 50° to 70°)

NOTE: Distinct summer thermocline at 40 to 60 feet.

POLAR REGIONS

Summer:	40° to 45°	
Winter:	28°	

(bar spans approx 28° to 45°)

TROPICS

Summer:	85°	
Winter:	70°	

(bar spans approx 70° to 85°)

INLAND (Lakes and rivers)

Summer:	55° to 75°	
Winter:	32°	

(bar spans approx 32° to 75°)

NOTE: Thermocline at about 60 feet in late summer; below thermocline, 39.2°, both summer and winter.

*From *THE NOAA DIVING MANUAL*

Fig. 3-7 Regional Water Temperature Chart

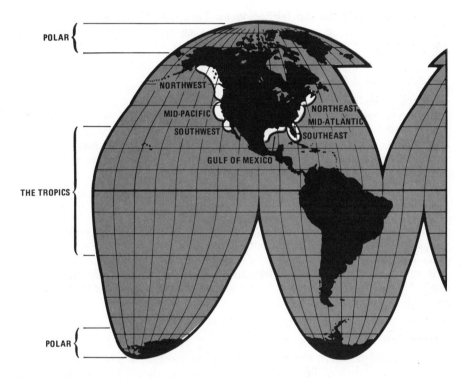

Fig. 3-8 Regional Diving Areas

NORTHEAST

The best diving conditions in the Northeastern region, which extends from Maine to New Jersey, are from June through October. When the sea is calm, visibility of 50 to 80 feet is occasionally seen throughout the year. One to several times each summer, however, visibility is limited to one foot. Surf is usually modest. Sometimes, however, 5- to 10-foot waves on rocky, barnacle-covered rocks must be avoided.

MID-ATLANTIC

Visibility in the Mid-Atlantic region (Delaware through South Carolina) is highly variable, ranging anywhere from 3 to 60 feet, depending on the season, weather, currents, and distance from shore. Moderate surf and sandy beaches make shore entries relatively easy. But you must be alert for strong tidal currents in large rivers and bays.

Stinging jellyfish are sometimes abundant; you must have complete covering when diving around them. Wear gloves when working in these areas.

SOUTHEAST

This region of southern offshore waters which extends from Georgia to Florida's east and west coasts has good to excellent visibility. It drops to 20 or

30 feet closer to shore and farther north. Take special care when diving at the boundary of major oceanic current systems such as the Gulf Stream where high speed currents can be encountered (see page 3-15).

GULF OF MEXICO

This region includes the Florida Panhandle and goes through Texas. Visibility offshore is generally good to excellent, in excess of 100 feet around some reefs. Visibility near shore can be poor, especially near river outfalls, in bays, and in estuaries. Currents can sometimes be of concern to the diver, especially around offshore oil platforms. Weather conditions and resultant running seas are unpredictable and should be watched carefully.

NORTHWEST

Visibility in the waters of southeast Alaska and Oregon varies greatly. It may range from 40 to 80 feet along outside coastlines and around the Aleutians. In bays and straits, visibility is usually about 15 to 20 feet. In southeast Alaska, a late spring overturn and phytoplankton can limit visibility in the top 30 or 40 feet of water to zero. Currents and tides can be strong and unpredictable, with currents running as fast as 10 knots in narrows.

MID-PACIFIC

The waters of northern and central California make up the Mid-Pacific region. In California, north of Point Conception, visibility ranges from about 5 to 50 feet. The main factor controlling visibility in this area is the huge plankton bloom during spring and summer upwellings. Rough seas and river runoffs during winter and spring also contribute to dirty water. Divers can expect to see kelp and at least a two- to three-foot surf when diving in this area. Longshore and tidal currents are common, as are rip currents.

There are five ecological reserves along this area of the California coast, and divers should consult park authorities before diving in these protected waters.

SOUTHWEST

Visibility in the Southwest region extending from Point Conception to northern Baja, ranges from 5 to 10 feet along much of the mainland coast to as much as 100 feet around the offshore islands. Visibility is best during late summer and fall. The mainland coast ranges from sand beaches to high palisade cliffs, with a moderate to heavy surf prevailing along the coast and windward sides of offshore islands. The prevailing longshore current is not dangerous although currents around islands can attain speeds of three to four knots during tidal changes.

Check with the California Department of Fish and Game for the locations of ecological reserves and their current restrictions. And be sure to get proper permits from Mexican customs officials before diving in Mexican waters.

POLAR

Cold waters and cold temperatures are the most important considerations when diving in polar waters. Thick wet suits or variable-volume dry suits are decided advantages.

TROPICS

Visibility in tropical waters is excellent in most cases, generally better than 50 feet. Occasional storms and plankton blooms limit visibility.

FRESH WATER

Visibility in freshwater lakes and rivers can range from about 100 feet in Lake Superior to less than a foot in waters filled with bottom sediment. If possible, stay off the bottom and move slowly in fresh water to maintain maximum visibility. Be prepared to cut monofilament fishlines away from equipment and don't forget that depth gauges are designed for use in salt water and are inaccurate in fresh water. Basic diving techniques, however, are similar in fresh water and salt water.

WEATHER

Weather is a key factor in determining whether a dive is one that is enjoyable or is one that compromises the safety of the dive team. Since most weather is the result of airmass interaction which can be measured, tracked, and predicted, weather should come as no surprise.

AIRMASSES

Airmasses are extensive bodies of air with distinctive temperature and moisture characteristics as the result of where they are formed. Generally, the weather conditions prevailing at a certain location at a certain time are dependent upon either the characteristics of the prevailing airmass, or the interaction between two airmasses.

FRONTS

Airmasses which have different properties of temperature and moisture content do not mix easily. When two distinct airmasses meet, a boundary called a *frontal zone*, or *front*, is formed. Across this zone, temperature, humidity, and wind may change rapidly over a short distance, or the change may be very subtle and take place over a wide area. In any case, the mixing zone between the two airmasses often creates unsettled, stormy weather ranging from low clouds, fog, and rain to thunderstorms, tornadoes, and waterspouts.

HOW TO FORECAST WEATHER

The National Weather Service observes and tracks these airmasses and develops weather forecasts based on their specific characteristics. In coastal areas and around large bodies of water, marine weather reports and broadcasts are excellent sources of information. Television weather reports normally include the type and position of relevant airmasses and frontal activity. Some include radar returns from precipitation and satellite photos of cloud cover. Of course, a forecast of imminent weather is provided.

Radio station reports normally include a synopsis of the present weather and also a forecast. Some radios are able to receive a special continuous NOAA

(National Oceanic and Atmospheric Administration) weather report and forecast which is available throughout the United States and Canada. The weather information received pertains to that specific area. These special weather radios, shown in figure 3-9, may be obtained from home entertainment and electronic stores. The source of weather information is not as important as getting the most up-to-date information.

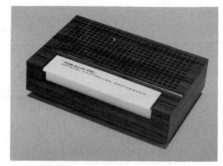

Fig. 3-9 Weather Radio

Weather Trend

Begin to analyze the weather several days before a planned dive. Note the movement of relevant airmasses and any frontal activity which may be developing. Pay particular attention to the forecast to determine whether the dive can be conducted as planned. Continue to monitor the weather as your dive day approaches. Be aware of any significant weather which is developing. This includes thunderstorms, high water, high waves, or other phenomena which may produce undesirable or dangerous diving conditions.

Observe the weather at your dive site. Notice any rapid cloud build-ups or overcasts developing. Be alert to any sudden wind shifts or temperature changes which may signal deteriorating weather conditions. Continue to listen to radio weather broadcasts and note any change in the temperature/ dewpoint spread. The *dewpoint* is the temperature to which air must be cooled to become saturated with water vapor. A comparison of air temperature and dewpoint gives an indication of how close the air is to saturation. Fog should be anticipated when the temperature/dewpoint spread is small, generally five degrees or less. The amount of water vapor actually in the air is measured as relative humidity. An increase in relative humidity indicates that the air is becoming more and more saturated and fog or precipitation may occur. A falling barometer also may indicate a decline in weather conditions. If several of these trend indicators occur simultaneously, a deterioration of the weather condition is imminent. Whenever there is a possibility of fog occurring during your dive, be sure to take a compass and use it for orientation. Then if you surface in a sea of fog, navigation to shore is easy.

Don't get caught short! In some areas of the country the weather can change dramatically in very little time. Good weather at the beginning of a dive can turn to bad weather at the end of a dive. Be aware of any such forecast changes and plan your dive activities accordingly.

DIVING ON THE WATER PLANET

As a sport diver, you should feel fortunate to live on the "Water Planet." Earth, in fact, could be the only planet in the universe with a suitable diving environment and such a great variety of diving regions. The beauty, vitality, color, and exciting motion of the underwater world make it a truly magical environment—a world within a world.

section B

water movement

- TIDES
- TIDAL CURRENTS
- OCEAN CURRENTS
- WAVES
- LOCALIZED CURRENTS

TIDES, CURRENTS, WAVES, AND THEIR EFFECTS ON DIVING

For centuries people have observed the waters of the world with awe. The oceans, in particular, have been a source of inspiration and fear for all who view them. But fear of the oceans stems from misunderstanding the mechanics of water movement. Once you understand the cause and effect of water movement; once you learn to respect the destructive power of the oceans, you can dive confidently with thorough enjoyment.

If you are an inland diver, you will need special instruction before diving in currents and through surf. You need to dive with an instructor or experienced ocean diver. Even divers who regularly dive in areas of the oceans, such as the Florida Keys, need more ocean training prior to diving in such places as the waters of New England, kelp forests, or through the Pacific surf. This section will help you understand water movement and how it can help you.

TIDES

Among the predictable types of worldwide water movement are the tides, which consist of the daily *vertical* rise and fall of water. Tides are actually bulges in the water that are created by the gravitational pull of the moon and sun. When this bulge approaches a given coastline, the water level rises and creates the *high tide*. As the bulge moves away, the water level drops and *low tide* results. When the tide changes direction, there is a period where no vertical motion occurs. This time is referred to as the *stand*. The tidal range, shown in figure 3-10, is the vertical distance between the levels of high and low tide. The tidal flat is the term used to describe the sloping shore that is exposed during low tide.

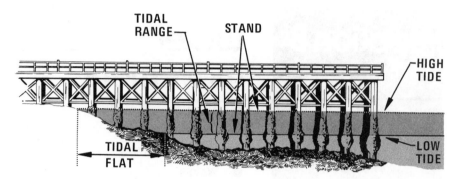

Fig. 3-10 Tidal Definitions

Generally, boaters have a greater interest in predicting the high, low, and stand of the tide than divers. If you would like to know more about predicting the tides, seek out your local U.S. Coast Guard Auxiliary or U.S. Power Squadron and enroll in a basic boating class. Predicting the *tidal current* associated with the tidal movement is of greater value to a diver.

TIDAL CURRENT

The tidal current is the *horizontal* flow of water. As shown in figure 3-11, when the flow is toward land, it is called a *flood current*. When the flow is away from land it is called an *ebb current*. (See figure 3-12.) As the current changes direction, there is a time when no horizontal movement occurs. This point is referred to as the *slack* time.

The somewhat misleading expressions—*flood tide* and *ebb tide*—where the vertical and horizontal flows of water are combined, are not altogether accurate because the time of the high, low, and stand of the tide are rarely the same as the flood, ebb, and slack of the tidal current. The maximum flood

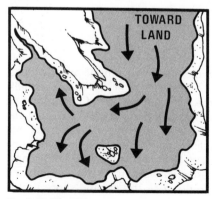

Fig. 3-11 Flood Current

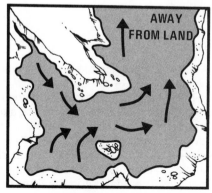

Fig. 3-12 Ebb Current

current does not necessarily occur at the same time as the high tide. The same holds true for the ebb current and low tide as well as the slack and stand.

TIDAL CURRENT TABLES

The flow of the tidal current has been measured over the years at numerous coastal locations. As a result of these studies, a set of four tables have been developed by the National Ocean Service (NOS) that predicts the current speed and direction at various locations, called reference and subordinate stations. Two books are published: one for the Pacific Coast of North America and Asia, and another for the Atlantic Coast. (See figure 3-13.) Sample pages from the NOS Tidal Current Tables are included in the appendix and a brief explanation of their use is included in Part IV, Section B.

Table 1 predicts the time of maximum current and slack water for designated reference stations. Table 2 provides the names of subordinate stations and the corrections that must be applied to the reference stations to find the times, current velocities, and slack for a subordinate station. (Table 3 is not discussed in this manual since it is more applicable to boat navigation and is more difficult to read and interpret than the other tables.) Table 4 covers the duration of the current and the velocity near slack time.

OCEAN CURRENTS

Another part of water movement occurring on a global scale is ocean currents, which are caused primarily by the wind and by the sun's uneven

Fig. 3-13 Tidal Current Tables

heating of the earth's surface. The sun heats equatorial waters faster than polar waters. As polar water freezes, the salt is squeezed out of the ice and falls into the unfrozen water. This cold, salty water is much heavier and denser, and naturally sinks into the deep warmer waters. It pushes the warmer water out of the way, and the result is a movement of water into and away from the warmer deep water, so that water is constantly warmed near the equator and cooled as it returns to the poles. Unceasing ocean currents thus occur all over the planet.

These conditions, together with worldwide wind paterns and the east-to-west rotation of the earth, create six major circular currents in the oceans. One is in each hemisphere of the Pacific, Atlantic, and Indian Oceans.

Currents in the northern hemisphere circulate in a clockwise direction; those in the southern hemisphere travel in a counterclockwise direction.

These "rivers in the sea" may have several names. They may be known as currents, streams, or drifts. All are the same thing, except that drifts are currents which flow in the direction of the prevailing westerlies. Drifts are slower and wider than other rivers in the sea. The Gulf Stream, for example, is the name given to a particular current in the Atlantic Ocean that runs northward along the Florida coast.

Cold polar air acts in the same manner as cold polar water—it tends to descend at the pole and rise after it is warmed near the equator. In fact, this air circulation brings you, as the diver, closer to home in terms of the broad spectrum of water movement, for the wind creates waves, surf, and wind currents.

WAVES

Waves form in essentially two ways: they are either generated by wind or by some geologic disturbance beneath the surface of the water (submarine earthquakes and volcanic eruptions).

WIND WAVES

Wind waves are always born in the same way—whether it happens in the middle of the ocean or on the surface of a small pond. First the wind disturbs the surface of the water, as shown in figure 3-14. When the surface is disturbed, ripples appear (item 1). These ripples are actually caused by changes in air pressure on the surface and the frictional drag of the moving air. The ripples, though small, resist the wind (item 2). The wind pushes against the ripples until they become small waves (item 3). Three things determine how large a wave will become: how hard the wind blows (velocity), how long the wind blows (time), and over what distance the wind continues to blow (fetch). (See figure 3-15.) The harder the wind blows, the more quickly it disturbs the water. The newly-formed wave presents a larger surface for the wind to blow against, and the result is an even larger wave. The longer and harder the wind blows, the larger the wave becomes.

If the wind remains constant, the water reaches a steady state and the waves generated are known as *sea*. Sea persists only as long as the wind keeps blowing and exists only in the fetch area. *Swell waves* develop when the wind velocity decreases or the wave leaves the fetch area. (See figure 3-15.) They have long, rounded crests and are shorter than sea waves.

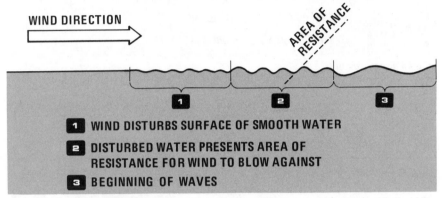

Fig. 3-14 Wave Formation

Because the wind pushes the water for a short distance, the water in a given wave appears to move. But it is actually the *energy* which is moving. The water rises and falls, as shown in figure 3-16. This principle can be illustrated with a length of rope. If you hold one end of a rope extended outward in a straight line along the ground and flip the rope several times, it will send a series of "waves" along the rope. The rope remains in the same place; only the energy moves to the other end.

The energy from waves can travel almost indefinitely if unobstructed. If this happens, waves may grow to enormous proportions, often reaching 40 feet or

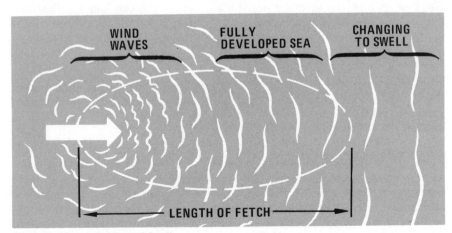

Fig. 3-15 Waves, Fetch, and Swell

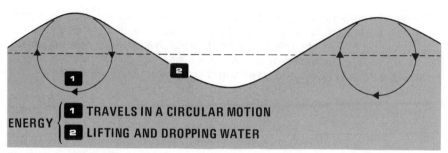

Fig. 3-16 Energy Motion

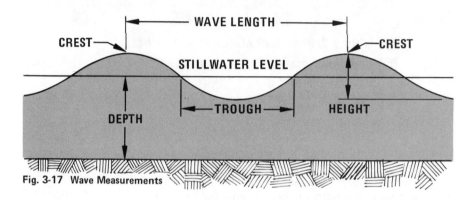

Fig. 3-17 Wave Measurements

more in height. The height of a wave, as shown in figure 3-17, is measured from the *trough* to the crest. The length is measured from crest to crest.

SURF

Wave action is a prime consideration for entering and exiting through surf. Large waves breaking against a beach are powerful and can injure a diver who underestimates this power. However, it is possible to pass in and out of surf safely if you understand how it forms and if you use the proper techniques.

Formation of Surf

The waves created by offshore storms may eventually flatten to the point where they are no longer visible. But the energy is still moving. As the waves approach shallower water near the shore, the motion of the water particles beneath the surface is altered. The wave is said to "feel bottom" when it enters water of depth equal to or less than one-half the wavelength. This makes the wave steeper and shorter.

As the wave height increases, the water particles at the crest orbit with increasing velocity. Finally, the wave breaks at approximately 1.3 times the wave height, when the steepest surface of the wave inclines more than 60° from the horizontal. (See figure 3-18, item 11.) These breaking waves (breakers) make up what is called the *surf*. The *surf zone*, as shown in figure 3-18, item 1, is an area of "white water," or bubbles of entrapped air where the waves have spent their energy.

Waves breaking away from shore generally indicate a submerged reef or sandbar, as illustrated in figure 3-18, items 10 and 12. Waves also break away from shore when the tops of the waves are blown off by strong winds and when they grow in height and steepness until a 1:7 ratio (height to length) is reached. The crests of the waves fall under the force of gravity, causing *broken water* or *white caps*.

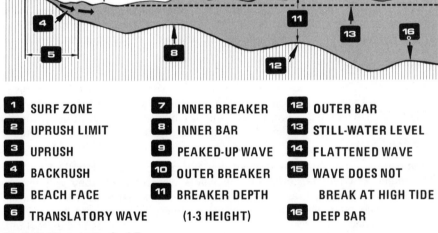

1 SURF ZONE		**7** INNER BREAKER		**12** OUTER BAR	
2 UPRUSH LIMIT		**8** INNER BAR		**13** STILL-WATER LEVEL	
3 UPRUSH		**9** PEAKED-UP WAVE		**14** FLATTENED WAVE	
4 BACKRUSH		**10** OUTER BREAKER		**15** WAVE DOES NOT	
5 BEACH FACE		**11** BREAKER DEPTH		BREAK AT HIGH TIDE	
6 TRANSLATORY WAVE		(1-3 HEIGHT)		**16** DEEP BAR	

Fig. 3-18 Waves in the Surf Zone

The primary problem for divers entering or exiting through surf is the weight of large quantities of water tumbling from the top of the wave to the shore. There can be tons of water in the breaking crest of large waves, as figure 3-19 shows.

Fig. 3-19 Breaking Wave Crest

Fig. 3-20 Spilling Breaker   Fig. 3-21 Plunging Breaker

When the wave rushes up onto the *beach face*, it is called *uprush*. (See figure 3-18, items 3 and 5.) Once the wave has rushed up onto the beach, it must return to sea. This seaward movement of water is called *backrush* (see figure 3-18, item 4). This is not to be confused with the mythical "undertow"—a current said to flow seaward along the bottom and pull swimmers under. Backrush does not last too long or go out too far. However, it can catch an unwary diver and knock him down into the path of another crashing wave.

Sand Beach Entries

It is best to consult local divers concerning surf conditions before diving through surf on an unfamiliar beach. You can also obtain information on the height of the sea from wind data and on bottom configuration from the nautical chart, for wave height and bottom configuration are directly related to surf conditions.

First-hand information comes from actually watching the "beat" of the surf. Depending on how far offshore the waves were created, they will tend to stabilize themselves into even sets. A set of waves is a series of waves of similar size followed by one or more larger waves. Every so many sets, there will be either a particularly large wave or set of waves. Shore entries and exits should be timed to coincide with the smaller waves.

The type of breakers rolling into shore can also be studied before entering through surf. When one breaks slowly over quite a distance, it is a *spilling breaker*. (See figure 3-20.) A *plunging breaker*, as shown in figure 3-21, curls over and breaks in one crash. A *surging breaker* does not spill or plunge, but peaks up. (See figure 3-22.) The steepness of the beach and wave determines the type of breaker. There is a greater tendency for breakers to plunge or surge when the beach slope is steeper.

Fig. 3-22 Surging Breaker

After observing the surf beat and breaker patterns for a short time, you will know when to move into the water. Several procedures must be followed quite carefully. (See figure 3-23.)

SLIDE OR SHUFFLE IN BACKWARD

UNTIL DEEP ENOUGH TO SWIM

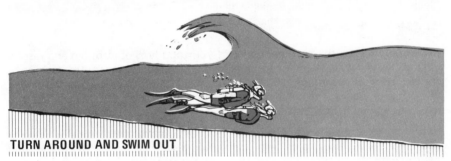

TURN AROUND AND SWIM OUT

Fig. 3-23 Entering Surf

1. You should be fully outfitted with mask and fins on and your regulator in your mouth. In some areas, fins are not put on until you are in the water, but this is the exception. Remember that any gear placed near the water's edge can be carried away easily by a large wave.

2. Hold onto your mask and regulator firmly, especially when breakers hit you.

3. Slide or shuffle *backwards* into the water rather than walking to avoid stepping on stingrays or into holes and for better stability. It is a good idea to bend your knees and stop when a wave hits you in shallow water.

4. Get through the surf as quickly as possible. Make any equipment adjustments either after you pass through the surf zone or return to shore to make them.

5. When you are deep enough to swim, turn around and swim out through the surf with your regulator *in your mouth*. The surf disturbs a great deal of sand; your regulator will be filled with sand if it hangs loose.

6. The power of a wave is concentrated in the surface area, as illustrated in figure 3-24. To avoid fighting that power, simply swim through or under the wave, not over it. Swim as low as possible, next to the bottom, to pick up the back current to help you.

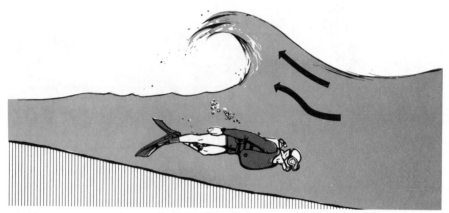

Fig. 3-24 Swim Under Waves

Once you are past the surfline, you and your buddy should rejoin and rest by inflating your buoyancy compensators before proceeding. Any extra items to be carried, such as spearguns, and so forth, should be tied to a float and *pulled* through the surf rather than pushed. You should *push* the float when you return to exit so it won't hit you.

Returning to shore is easier than entering. Just outside the surfline or the area where the waves begin breaking, you should stop, rest, watch the waves, and swim in with the smaller ones. Once you can touch bottom, don't stand up. Let the water carry you as far up on shore as possible. Keep your regulator in your mouth as you did on entry to keep it clear of sand. Lie on the beach and relax until you are certain you are up as far as the water will carry you. When the water rushes back and leaves you on dry ground, *crawl* out of reach of the water, then stand up.

Freshwater Entries

Freshwater entries are essentially the same as for the ocean, but there is a noticeable lack of heavy surf, although it is possible to have large unstable waves which require the similar techniques.

Rocky Shore Entries

You should not attempt to stand or walk when entering surf from a rocky shore, for it is dangerous to be knocked down in such an area. Enter the water when you see the backwash of the last large wave of a series. Once this backwash carries you past the rocks, swim in a prone position while facing the next wave. So you will not be pulled back into shore, hold onto a rock or kick. Then kick on out to sea.

Exit on the backside of the last large wave in a series. Again, grasp a rock to avoid being carried back out to sea with the backwash, then catch the next wave to take you into shore. Be extremely cautious when crawling over slippery rocks.

Coral Reef Entries

Entries around coral reefs should be made at high tide. Wear coral shoes or hard-sole neoprene boots when walking on coral. Reefs are delicate and pocked with holes, making footing treacherous. Shore sides of some reefs have water deep enough for swimming. In this case, you can pass over the inside, calm area because the outer reef will break up the wave action. Follow any channels through the reef into deep water. If no suitable passages are present, wait for a wave and slip over the coral reef.

SURGE

In deep water, wave action has little effect on the horizontal water movement. (See figure 3-25, item 1.) Therefore, a boat will move up and down with wave action, but it generally stays the same distance from shore. The circular motion of water within a wave diminishes proportionately until it vanishes at a depth equal to one-half the wave length or at the bottom, whichever occurs first. As a wave reaches more shallow water, (items 2 and 3), the circular motion flattens to a back and forth movement due to the influence of the bottom. This back and forth movement is called *surge*. The amount of surge depends on the energy contained in the wave passing overhead. Surge is a nuisance to underwater photographers and collectors, and can be dangerous in rocky areas.

CONFUSED SEA

When waves approach the shore from different directions, the result of their interaction is often difficult to predict. This situation usually results in what is called a *confused sea*. If one group of waves arrive at a slightly different speed than another group of waves, the two may offset each other and produce relatively small waves. When the two sets of waves are in phase with each other, they will join forces and create an unusually large wave or group of waves. Since this wave interaction agitates the bottom, visibility may be greatly reduced.

LOCALIZED CURRENTS

Longshore and rip currents are two types of currents occurring in the surf zone. They are generated when waves approach the sea's bottom at an angle, or by an irregular configuration of the bottom. They normally affect only the top few feet of water, and then only for a short period of time.

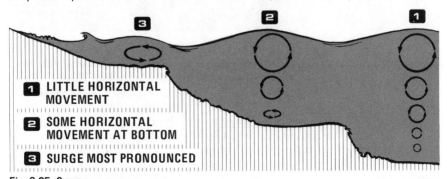

1 LITTLE HORIZONTAL MOVEMENT

2 SOME HORIZONTAL MOVEMENT AT BOTTOM

3 SURGE MOST PRONOUNCED

Fig. 3-25 Surge

LONGSHORE CURRENTS

Longshore currents flow parallel to a beach and are generated from waves approaching the shore at an angle. You find them most frequently along straight beaches. Their speed seldom exceeds one knot, but it does vary, according to the height of the breakers, decreasing wave period, increasing breaker line angle with the beach, and increasing slope of the beach.

RIP CURRENTS

Water can't continue after it moves toward shore, so it must stop and return to open water, as what has previously been mentioned, *backwash*. This returning water always takes the course of least resistance. In the shore configuration shown in figure 3-26, the direction of current is from left to right toward shore. As it reaches the point on the right, it is turned in toward the center. As it approaches the cove's bank, its flow changes to the left. When the two forces meet, they must return to open water in what is called a *rip current*. It's nothing more than a current running back out to sea.

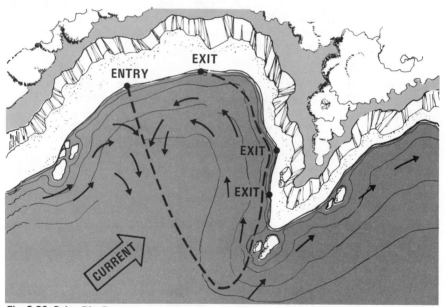

Fig. 3-26 Point Rip Current

Depending on the amount of water flowing in, the rip current may run for a few feet or it may run for some distance, but it dissipates rather rapidly for two reasons. First, it lacks sufficient power to continue on out to sea and, second, oncoming waves or currents help dissipate it. Normally, rip currents spread to the left and right, so a swimmer, rather than swimming against it, should swim at right angles to the current. In the case of figure 3-26, the diver would move to the right side of the current and then catch the incoming current and ride it back into shore. Accidents occur when people try to swim against rip currents. Even very strong swimmers are only able to maintain a maximum pace of less than 1 mph; swimming against a rip current which can range from 3 to 12 mph is a losing battle. It makes sense to swim to the side of the rip current and then catch the current coming back.

When the current moves in along a long straight beach, as shown in figure 3-27, rip currents may appear in several places. Normally this occurs because a trough is formed and the water will be slightly deeper at the point of the rip current. Even along the straight beaches, there must be a point where the water returns to the open sea.

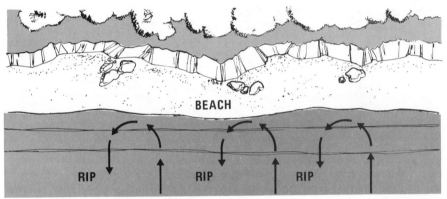

Fig. 3-27 Straight Beach Rip Currents

Figure 3-28 shows the water moving in past two submerged bars. As the water moves in around them and begins to move back out to sea, it will be channeled with some velocity through the opening between the two bars. It could be very dangerous if this channel is narrow and passes through a coral reef. As the flow of water is concentrated in that small channel, it picks up speed and may exceed four or five knots. A diver caught in this could be badly injured. You should swim directly to the inside of the cove to be protected by the bar; the water will turn and carry you back into shore.

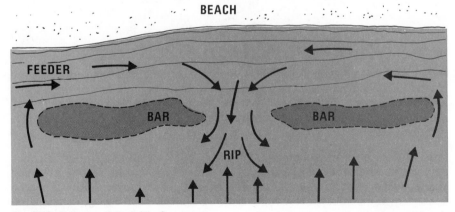

Fig. 3-28 Submerged Reef Rip Current

EFFECT OF CURRENTS ON BOAT DIVERS

Longshore currents are readily apparent when you dive from a boat. When you dive offshore from an island, you normally have one of two conditions: a current running parallel to the shore or no current at all on the lee of the island. When the boat is anchored, it tends to swing into the current, as illustrated in figure 3-29. Before entering the water, the diver should watch the current and estimate its strength. If the current looks strong (greater than one knot) do not dive. If it is not too strong, or if it is a surface current, you can dive safely, if you observe proper procedures.

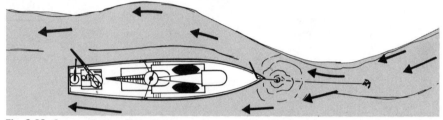

Fig. 3-29 Current Action Near Shore

You should always swim *into* the current at the beginning of a dive, as shown in figure 3-30. You can descend and pull yourself over the rocks *away* from the boat while you have plenty of strength. After the dive, the current carries you back to the boat. It would be a mistake to initially swim downcurrent, only to fight the current on the way back when you are tired.

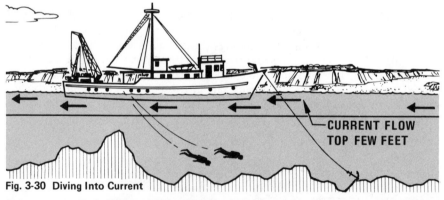

CURRENT FLOW
TOP FEW FEET

Fig. 3-30 Diving Into Current

If you *are* carried downcurrent, you should use certain safety precautions. Wear a good buoyancy compensator so you can rest for long periods of time. Use a whistle to attract the attention of the people on the boat. The sound of whistles carries a great distance above water and you can blow them a long time with little effort.

It is always best to be prepared for the unexpected. You must always remember—the greatest problem comes from fear and its resulting panic. You should possess the proper equipment and training to ensure your safety under any condition. For a complete discussion of boat diving, consult the Advanced Manual.

section C

ocean life

● REEF DEVELOPMENT
● REEF INHABITANTS
● DANGEROUS MARINE LIFE

REEFS AND THEIR INHABITANTS, DANGEROUS MARINE ANIMALS

The ocean depths are a sightseer's dream. Their panorama is so vast, that quite often the inexperienced diver sees very little of it. Life dwells on every rock, however, and unless you familiarize yourself with these life forms, you might miss the most enjoyable part of the dive.

Another thing to consider is—despite their beauty and fascination, some creatures present potential hazards. The diver must study his new surroundings so that he might appreciate and understand them well enough to avoid harm during his underwater explorations.

Underwater animals have one thing in common with their untamed relatives on land—they are wild. Water creatures are neither aggressive nor friendly. They are more or less indifferent to strange invaders in their domain. While some may be a little curious, most are nervous when they see a diver, and you should remember that some are capable of inflicting serious injury when molested. Most injury, however, is the result of accidentally disturbing a sea creature and does not stem from aggression. Because some wounds can be serious, it is important to know exactly which animals you can touch, and which ones to avoid.

This section is designed as a brief introduction to the marine environment: to explain the development of the ocean floors; to make you aware of a few of the creatures there; and to help you avoid the hazardous ones.

REEF DEVELOPMENT

CORALS

Corals are members of the phylum Coelenterata. They are found in both hard and soft forms, as shown in figure 3-31. The hard corals (Scleractinia) are the foundation for the reefs. The soft gorgonian corals (hydroids) are also large contributors to the reef formation.

Corals are bisexual and divide themselves. The way in which they divide determines the formation of the coral. New colonies develop when the coral releases seeds which float along with the current toward shallower water. They settle to the bottom of the shallow water and attach themselves to anything solid. Due to several factors, including water movement, sunlight, and the availability of solid objects, coral is limited to the relatively shallow depths. Some are too delicate to survive in areas of violent water action. Others grow right up to the low tide level and even protrude slightly out of the water.

Corals protect the reef inhabitants. They are also a symbiotic home for the zooxanthellae, an algae which lives in the coral polyps and provides oxygen for the coral animal, which in turn supplies carbon dioxide for the algae. This algae gives coloration in most corals and furnishes the chemistry for the actual formation of the coral structure.

Corals are a source of food for many creatures, and as the animals eat the coral, the pulverized residue becomes sand. Corals are an important part, if not the entire basis for the ecosystem in warm waters, especially where no rocks exist. The reefs provide shelter, food, and protection from its inhabitants' enemies. It is difficult to conceive of oceans without coral reefs.

Numerous coral growths exist; every reef contains a wide variety. There are corals that simply spread themselves over an area of the reef. For sake of simplicity, they can be referred to as blanket corals, an accurate, if not entirely scientific, description. For identification purposes, the corals of interest in this section are those that form recognizable clumps or formations. The following examples illustrate many of the corals that contribute to the general reef makeup. These include hard and soft corals, and sponges. For protection from coral cuts and abrasions, it is a good practice to wear a 1/8" wet suit, gloves, and boots.

Hard Corals

The magnificent elkhorn coral, shown in figure 3-32, grows very fast and forms a large portion of the reefs, particularly in the Caribbean. It is razor sharp and can cause severe cuts. You should immediately attend to cuts or scratches caused by coral, for they often become infected and do not heal easily.

Figure 3-33 shows examples of staghorn coral, some growing and some dead. This coral serves as a home for many small fishes.

The young star coral, as shown in figure 3-34, illustrates the early stages of most coral. Shown in an extreme closeup, the growth is approximately one inch across. Although it appears soft, it is quite hard and abrasive.

You can find many other less spectacular but equally beautiful corals all along the reef, such as, brain coral (figure 3-35), star coral (figure 3-36), and fire coral (figure 3-37). Fire coral demands respect because it has a nematocyst or stinger long enough to penetrate human skin and toxic enough to cause a reaction. The sting feels like a burn—hence the name, fire coral. Its effect varies from a minor rash lasting a few minutes, to large, slow-healing sores.

Fig. 3-31 Hard and Soft Coral

Fig. 3-32 Elkhorn Coral

Fig. 3-33 Staghorn Coral

Fig. 3-34 Star Coral

Fig. 3-35 Brain Coral

Fig. 3-36 Star Coral

Fig. 3-37 Fire Coral

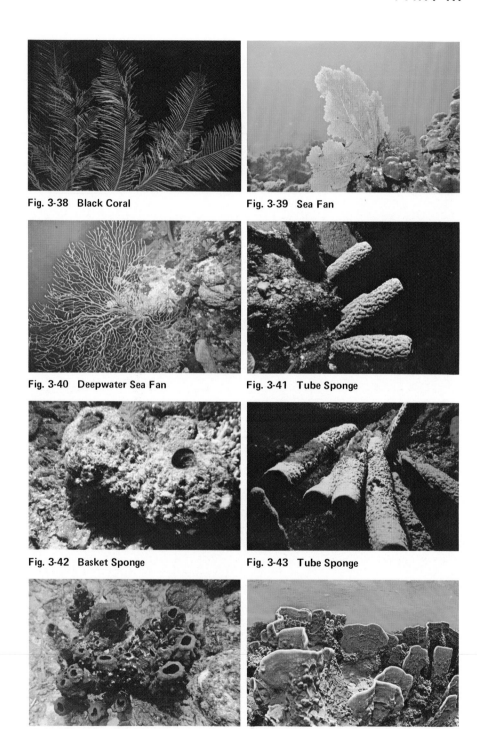

Fig. 3-38   Black Coral

Fig. 3-39   Sea Fan

Fig. 3-40   Deepwater Sea Fan

Fig. 3-41   Tube Sponge

Fig. 3-42   Basket Sponge

Fig. 3-43   Tube Sponge

Fig. 3-44   Basket Sponge

Fig. 3-45   Coral Reef Formation

Soft Corals

The hydroids, or soft gorgonian coral, form another part of the reef-building process. These soft corals are flexible and appear to be a plant form rather than an animal form. There are many soft corals, including the famous black coral, shown in figure 3-38. Hydroids remain flexible while alive, but when they are removed from water, the skeletons become hard and rigid. The sea fan, shown in figure 3-39, is found at all depths and in various forms. Its height ranges from 12 to 24 inches. Collectors have taken and displayed them for many years, however these beautiful creatures grow very slowly and it is unfortunate when they are destroyed for no reason. Coral is much more beautiful in the sea than on a shelf.

The deepwater sea fan, illustrated in figure 3-40, is a huge specimen found in depths over 100 feet. Despite their flexibility, sea fans are delicate. Very large specimens normally are not found in shallow water.

SPONGES

Another large contributor to reef building is the sponge (Porifera). They come in every size, shape, color, and texture. The sponge is animal, not plant, and the forms humans see are sponge skeletons. The actual animal lives inside. Sponges are not edible, but some varieties are used for washing and other household chores. The varieties of sponges are shown in figures 3-41 through 3-44.

REEF FORMATION AND DEPTHS

Three distinct reef formations are illustrated in figure 3-46: the deep reef found at 80 to 100 feet deep; the midreef found in the 20 to 40 foot range; and the shallow reef found from 15 feet up to sea level.

Development of the deep reefs can be seen by first observing the shallow and then the midreef. It appears that the surface of the oceans was once near the level of the deeper reef. The midreef formed as the waters rose. The water then continued to rise to its present level; now we are seeing the development of the shallow reef.

Small individual clumps of one or more coral animal colonies live in shallower waters. In the midreef area, corals have had time to grow together and form larger overlapping clumps. These look like small islands; many are as large as 50 to 75 feet, but they remain as separate and distinct coral clumps. (See figure 3-45 on page 3-30.) In the deep reef, the clumps or small islands have had an

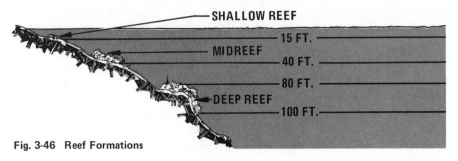

Fig. 3-46 Reef Formations

opportunity to grow together, forming one continuous reef cut intermittently by ravines, and a series of large and small caves created partly by worms. The worms eat into the coral and weaken it, causing breakage. The reefs become honeycombed because the various corals grow and overlap. The resulting effect appears to be solid rock, but, in reality, it is a network of caves and passageways. (Note figure 3-47.)

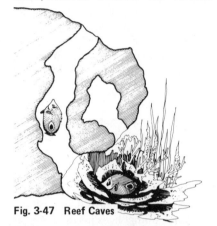

Water temperature also limits the area in which coral can flourish. It requires temperatures above 75°F (24°C). This restricts coral to an area 30° north and 30° south of the equator. Interestingly enough, coral reefs are only found on the eastern shores of the continents. This is thought to be due in part to the upwelling of cold water from the currents on the western side of the continents.

Fig. 3-47   Reef Caves

BOTTOM FORMATION IN COLD WATERS

In the cold water areas which lack the warmth to produce hard corals, bottom formations are comprised primarily of rock, and in some areas, the coastline is protected by kelp beds.

Rocks and kelp provide the same kind of protection for sea animals in cold water regions that coral provides in warmer waters. While cold waters normally don't produce the profusion of different individuals that the warm waters do, the population in terms of numbers of animals in cold water is more intense, especially in the kelp forest.

Kelp has very strong roots and kelp stocks grow from the bottom to the surface in as much as 50 to 75 feet of water. Kelp strands are normally several feet apart, but when they reach the surface, the strands lay in a mat. (See figure 3-48.) They resemble a forest with the leaf-covered branches of the trees intertwining and shutting out the sun in many places. Kelp is a wonderful place to dive. It contains more sea life than one might imagine possible.

There have been stories of divers becoming entangled in kelp. While this is a possibility, it is not probable. The broad flat leaves of the kelp are capable of entangling a diver who struggles, but a diver who remains calm can use a kelp crawl to move through the forest with the greatest of ease. If you do become entangled, kelp can be broken, cut, or removed with the help of your buddy. When you move across kelp, push it down with your forearm and crawl on your hands and knees, as shown in figure 3-49.

Giant kelp beds can be found along the cold water coasts of the North Pacific, the islands of Japan, around the Aleutian Islands extending to Alaska, and along the coast of California.

Fig. 3-48   Kelp Mat

Fig. 3-49   Passage Across Kelp

REEF INHABITANTS

The reef makeup is extremely complex. It ranges from the smallest microorganism in coral to the sponges, shellfish, crustaceans, and the fish and plant life. Large free-swimming pelagic fish that use the reef as a source of food and as a breeding area, also live within the reef's ecosystem. Each animal serves its special function within this underwater environment.

By watching the reef for a period of time, you can clearly see the existing territorial system. In every reef system, a big fish presides over an entire section of the reef. This fish is the reef master. Under its control, the reef is divided into territories. The size of the territory depends upon the size of the fish, extending down to the smallest fish that inhabits no more than a few square inches.

To the new diver, the most apparent reef inhabitants are fish. Reef fish can be divided into two categories: edible and inedible. What is edible in one part of the world may not be edible in another part. To be certain, check with the local residents.

EDIBLE REEF FISH

Pictured in figures 3-50 through 3-55 are the common edible fish found on most reefs. It must be realized that the variety of life along the reefs and in the oceans staggers the imagination. It is not the purpose of this text to identify each variety. However, it is possible to point out a few of the most common and easily recognizable fish in each category.

Parrot fish, as seen in figure 3-50, are one of (if not the most) important contributors to the reef. They eat the living coral animals and in so doing, bite off pieces of coral growth and grind it up, making sand. They also eat algae and are the most efficient and unwasteful eaters on the reef. In terms of collective pounds, they are the biggest reef inhabitants. There are over 30 varieties of parrot fish in every conceivable color. They are considered edible, but, depending on their diet, they may be poisonous in some areas.

Members of the porgy tribe have a similar appearance, differing mostly in color. They weigh between two and four pounds and are found throughout the Caribbean. The most outstanding example of the porgy tribe is the blue, yellow, and black porkfish, shown in figure 3-51.

The grouper, as shown in figure 3-52, is very common, but it is highly prized for its food value. It grows to great size, but is harmless to divers. Large groupers are found in deeper water and are quite shy. The grouper has two cousins, the black sea bass and the jewfish which are even larger, weighing 800 or more pounds.

The squirrel fish is aptly named. Its big brown eyes give it an almost comic look, as seen in figure 3-53. Although they are edible, they are not a very good source of food, because they are quite small (8 to 10 inches long) and very bony.

Fig. 3-50 Parrot Fish

Fig. 3-51 Porkfish

Fig. 3-52 Grouper

Fig. 3-53 Squirrel Fish

Fig. 3-54 Red Snapper

Fig. 3-55 Amber Jack

Snapper can be found in many varieties including the red snapper, dog snapper, mangrove snapper, and yellowtail snapper, to name a few. The fish shown in figure 3-54 is a red snapper. They range in size from quite small up to over 100 pounds and are usually edible.

The jack family forms a large part of the pelagic free-swimming fish that skirt the reefs. They are characterized by the amber jack, shown in figure 3-55. They are large and powerful, reaching weights up to 100 pounds. They may be several feet in length. Jacks normally travel in schools and while they are edible and quite delicious, it is unlikely that a diver would ever have the opportunity to spear one.

Fig. 3-56   Puerto Rican Butterfly   Fig. 3-57   Spot Fin Butterfly

Fig. 3-58   French Angel   Fig. 3-59   Gray Angel

Fig. 3-60   Queen Angel   Fig. 3-61   Pisaster Star

Fig. 3-62   Yellow Feather Star   Fig. 3-63   Sea Urchin

INEDIBLE REEF FISH

The variety of inedible reef fish seems endless. The warm seas of the Caribbean and South Pacific provide a breeding ground for fish of every conceivable shape, size, and color.

The butterfly and angel fish are two of the friendly reef fish that are often confused. The Puerto Rican butterfly, shown in figure 3-56, is also known as the banded butterfly. It is from five to seven inches long. Reef fish of this type are quite tame and appear to have very few, if any, natural enemies. The same is true of the spot fin butterfly, shown in figure 3-57.

The angel fish are among the most beautiful on the reef and are certainly the most graceful. The French angel, shown in figure 3-58, is black with bright yellow scales. This fish almost glows in its brilliance, and like the butterfly fish, it is quite tame. A cousin, the gray angel, shown in figure 3-59, has almost no fear of man and can be touched occasionally. If left undisturbed, this angel fish will swim around oblivious to divers. The queen angel, shown in figure 3-60, is the most beautiful of the angel fish. It is extremely graceful and brilliant. Its dazzling colors change with each shift of light.

INVERTEBRATES

Fish are the reef inhabitants the diver sees first, but they comprise only a small part of the total population. Another common reef inhabitant is the starfish. The pisaster star, shown in figure 3-61, is one of the most common. They are bottom dwellers, found clinging to rocks or crawling across the bottom. Their main food is shellfish and barnacles. While the pisaster star is what you normally think of, a starfish may have up to 20 arms, like the yellow feather star, shown in figure 3-62. Its skeleton is a loose meshwork of calcareous plates or rods. When it dies, the skeleton becomes rigid and can be preserved—making it a natural for collectors.

Another large reef contributor, the sea urchin, is shown in figure 3-63. The sea urchin is nature's pin cushion, because it has needlelike spines that protrude from its body in all directions. Beneath the spines is a small globular shell containing ova, which is considered a delicacy. However, this food must come from the correct species. Some urchins will cause illness, although it isn't known if it is caused by poison, bacteria, or an allergenic reaction.

There are two layers of spines; the largest of the poison spines serve to protect and feed the urchin. Near the body, down between the long spines are the pedicellariae, small pincer-like organs that keep away larvae and minute creatures. There are many varieties of urchins which vary in color, size, and appearance. Sea urchins are normally found tucked away in the cracks and crevices of reefs and along the rocks in shallow water.

The sea anemone is a colorful marine animal that looks like a plant. It is in the same phylum as coral, jellyfish, and hydroids. They range in size from a fraction of an inch to over one foot in diameter. Many are brightly colored and look like flowers, as shown in figure 3-64, but they contain a nematocyst and poison capable of killing small fish.

Featherduster worms, shown in figure 3-65, are further evidence in the overlap of appearance between plant and animal. The dusters' flowerlike plumage is used to breathe and attract food. They are less than eight inches high and many are barely visible. They are found on the bottom in sand or growing in coral and appear to be more plentiful in shallow water. As you might imagine, they are quite fragile and retract at the slightest touch. Another example is the spiral Christmas tree worm, shown in figure 3-66.

Crustaceans

Careful observation in the little nooks and crannies of the reef will expose many creatures like the coral shrimp pictured in figure 3-67. This tiny coral shrimp is only about one inch long and is nearly transparent. This animal contributes little to the reef—except as food for others. They are primarily nocturnal and their transparency helps protect them from enemies.

The hermit crab, shown in figure 3-68, is considered a long-tail crustacean, but the tail lacks the skeletal protection of its relatives, the lobster and shrimp. For protection, it adopts the discarded shell of other marine animals. The hermit may begin life in the smallest of shells and as it grows, will try many shells until one is found that fits properly. The largest hermits can be found in huge conch shells.

Figure 3-69 shows a California spiny lobster. It differs from the Maine lobster, shown in figure 3-70, in that it has no large front claws and a larger tail. The spiny lobster grows to over 20 pounds, although 12 pounds is considered large.

It is known that lobsters shed their shells periodically but nothing is known about their growth rate, and commercial incubation attempts have been futile. The fine taste of lobster has created such a demand that the supply is dwindling. They are increasingly more difficult to find, and most coastal fish and game departments are controlling the number taken. Commercial fisherman make the greatest catches with their highly efficient traps.

Shellfish

The contribution of shellfish to the marine ecosystem is significant. Among the most common are the scallops and oysters. (See figure 3-71.) They are a good food source and are commercially cultivated.

The conch, as shown in figure 3-72, is also an excellent food source and can be found crawling along the bottom in warm water areas of the world. Abalone, as shown in figure 3-73, is another commercially desired food source. It thrives in the colder water regions and is found clinging to rocks in the cracks and crevices along the shore.

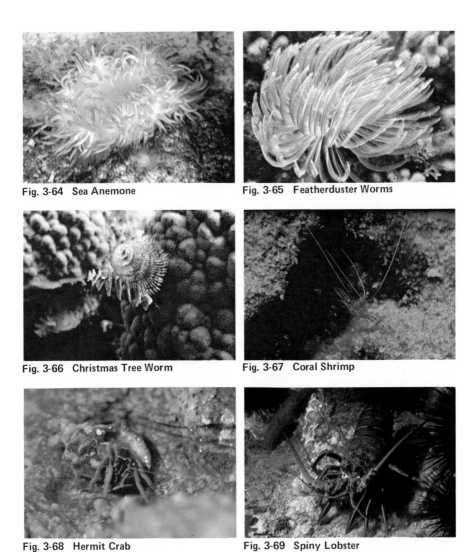

Fig. 3-64   Sea Anemone

Fig. 3-65   Featherduster Worms

Fig. 3-66   Christmas Tree Worm

Fig. 3-67   Coral Shrimp

Fig. 3-68   Hermit Crab

Fig. 3-69   Spiny Lobster

Fig. 3-70   Maine Lobster

Fig. 3-71   Scallops

Fig. 3-72   Conch

Fig. 3-73   Abalone

Fig. 3-74   Sculpin

Fig. 3-75   Stonefish

Fig. 3-76   Lionfish

DANGEROUS MARINE ANIMALS

It has been noted that while some fish are capable of inflicting serious wounds, there are very few that are aggressive. Although some of the more exotic and dangerous animals don't frequent the American coastline, there are common ones you should learn to recognize and avoid.

The California sculpin (Scorpaena guttata), pictured in figure 3-74, is an extremely timid poisonous fish found along the west coast of the United States and in many other parts of the world. The sculpin is also known by a variety of names, including: scorpionfish, rockfish, sea pig, bullroute, waspfish, bullhead, and blob. It hides under rocks most of the time—the only way you can see one is to watch carefully. The sting is not fatal, but if you are stung, the best first aid is to apply hot water directly to the wound.

The stonefish (Synanceja), shown in figure 3-75, resembles the sculpin, but it is much more dangerous. Like sculpins, they are shy and use their poison only for defense. They are not a problem to divers along United States coasts, however, because they live mostly in the South Pacific.

When handled and released, the stonefish will simply sink to the bottom, but if you molest it, the fish will tend to move its dorsal fin toward you. Again, the best first aid is to quickly apply extremely hot water and an injection of Emetine Hydrochloride directly into the wound within 30 minutes.

The lionfish (Dendrochirus zebra) is beautiful and carries a powerful sting. (Note figure 3-76.) Fortunately, lionfish are shy and brightly colored, which makes them easy to avoid. First aid procedures are the same as for the sculpin.

Stingray (Dasyatis americana) is the name generally given to the butterfly ray, bat ray, round ray, and to the true stingray. Some variety of each of these rays may be found in American waters. Rays live in the bottom and remain camouflaged.

Only the bat ray, shown in figure 3-77, is considered a free swimmer. Rays differ mostly in shape. They all have a flat body with winglike fins and a long tail. The stinger rests along the top of the tail, as shown in figure 3-78. If

Fig. 3-77 Bat Ray

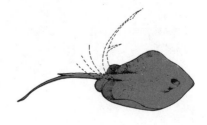

Fig. 3-78 Tail Stinger

molested, the tail is looped over the top of the body causing the stinger to point forward. In this position, it may be driven into the intruder. The greatest danger from stingrays lies in the fact that they camouflage themselves on the bottom. When you move on the bottom, it is wise to look carefully and make sure nothing is there. First aid includes soaking the wound in hot water.

The puffer (Diodon holocanthus), shown in figure 3-79, isn't poisonous unless you eat it. Every part of the world has fish which are dangerous if eaten, but only the puffer is universally considered poisonous.

The appearance of the barracuda (Sphyraenidae) causes its terrible reputation. It may reach a size of six feet and exceed 100 pounds, as shown in figure 3-80. It moves with lightning speed and has razor-sharp teeth, but there have been very few authenticated reports of attacks on humans. The real danger of barracuda exists while spearfishing. They are attracted by water motion and blood. Barracuda meat is considered excellent, but it can be poisonous.

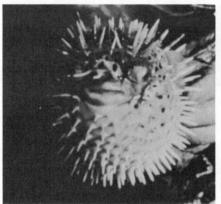

Fig. 3-79 Puffer   **Fig. 3-80 Barracuda**

Fig. 3-81 Moray

There are over 10 species of morays, three are common in United States waters. The moray is nocturnal—only a small percentage is ever seen. Their length varies greatly among the different species, but they may reach six feet and weigh 25 to 35 pounds. The moray's appearance is ferocious because of its needlelike teeth and the way it opens and closes its jaws. (See figure 3-81.) The jaw movement is a breathing process and while morays could bite if molested, they are quite shy and want nothing to do with divers.

The phylum Coelenterata includes three classes: Hydrozoa, Scyphozoa, and Anthozoa. These classes contain familiar names like jellyfish, sea wasps, Portuguese-man-of-war, sea anemones, and coral. They are known as cnidarians because of their ability to sting. All members of the phylum contain a poisonous stinging mechanism and are capable of inflicting various degrees of discomfort.

The stinger is known as a nematocyst. When you touch animals containing a nematocyst, the sharp, whiplike stinger releases and forces poison into the victim. Only a very few have a nematocyst long or strong enough to penetrate human skin. Of those that do, only two or three are capable of any discomfort. The Portuguese-man-of-war (Hydrozoa Physalia physalis), shown in figure 3-82, has a bad reputation and is considered dangerous due primarily to its great numbers.

The creature is completely at the mercy of the wind and its float serves to support thousands of individual cells joined in the appendages trailing below. Each cell contains a nematocyst and contact produces hundreds of little stings, resulting in a burning sensation. Take care of stings immediately by leaving the water and removing the tentacles and as much venom as possible with a cloth, seaweed, or sand. Then apply baking soda, diluted ammonia, or alcohol.

There are 9,000 varieties of jelly-fish (Schyphozoa). All contain the same nematocyst system found throughout this phylum. Unlike the Portuguese-man-of-war, the jellyfish, as shown in figure 3-83, are swimmers. They propel themselves by alternately sucking in and expelling water, much like the opening and closing of an umbrella, creating a jet effect. The true jelly-fish also contains a central digestive system and forms tissue and organs. The first aid is the same as for the man-of-war.

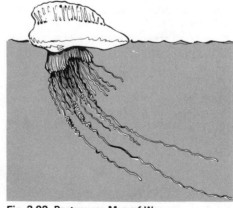

Fig. 3-82 Portuguese Man-of-War

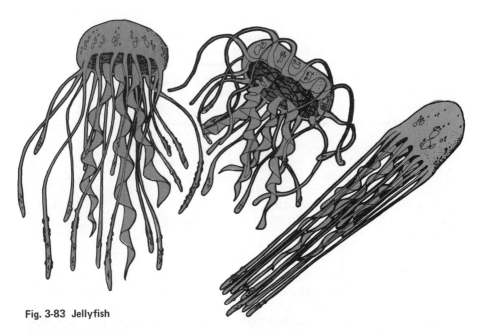

Fig. 3-83 Jellyfish

Cone shells (Gastropoda) are cone-shaped and vary in size from three to five inches. They possess a powerful stinger and are poisonous. Figure 3-84 shows the stinging mechanism which consists of a venom bulb and duct connected to and extending through the stinger. The radula is a small sack containing needlelike teeth which are forced through the stinger into the victim. Cone shells don't attack; stings result from careless handling. Hot water, because it breaks down protein venoms, is a good treatment for spine and venom wounds. If you cannot positively identify a shell, pick it up by the large end and always wear heavy leather gloves to avoid injury.

Barnacles are another form of marine life to avoid. They, like the cone shell, are incapable of attacking. They are free-swimming in the larval state and attach themselves permanently to foreign objects such as wharf piles, rocks, and the bottom of ships, in the adult state.

A calcified shell of several pieces protects the creature, as shown in figure 3-85. This shell is very sharp and jagged and can cut a diver who brushes against it.

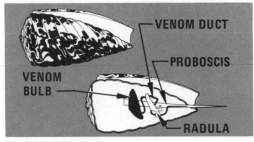

Fig. 3-84   Cone Shell Stingers

Fig. 3-85   Barnacle

Sharks (Selachii) are the most feared fish in the sea. Common species include the blacktipped bull, hammerhead, lemon, mako, nurse, reef, requiem, sand, sharp nose, tiger, and white tip, some of which are shown in figure 3-86. The rare white shark is the most dangerous species.

Fig. 3-86 Sharks

Sharks are fast, strong, and they are nature's garbage disposal. They eat constantly—anything in the water is a potential dinner. There are so many small easy things to eat, that larger aggressive animals (like humans) are not normally on their menu. The shark is really quite cowardly, despite its strength and continuous feeding habits. In fact, sudden movement in their direction will generally send them away. Sharks seem to be attracted to low frequency vibrations, the kind emitted by weak or sick fish. A human swimming on the surface emits the same frequency and for that reason, surface swimmers are in the greatest danger.

HANDLING MARINE LIFE

The best way to handle unfamiliar aquatic life is *very carefully*. The defenses of marine life include size, speed, camouflage, barbs, stingers, and teeth. Most species that would seem to permit handling also have effective defense mechanisms. Therefore, as a general rule, look at, photograph, follow, but don't touch. Generally, you pose more of a threat to their existence than they do to yours. Adhering to this philosophy will keep you both out of trouble and protect and preserve the marine environment for all of us. As such, the greatest threat of injury will be caused by inadvertently and accidently bumping into or stepping on something with spines, barbs, or sharp edges. The majority of serious diving accidents are the fault of the diver and not the marine environment.

Ocean life continues to be fascinating and sometimes mysterious to those who seek to unlock its endless array of secrets. By constantly learning more about the oceans, we will be able to enjoy and use them without exploiting them or their inhabitants.

section D

fresh waters

- **LAKES**
- **RIVERS**
- **QUARRIES**
- **CAVES**
- **FRESHWATER LIFE**

DIVING AREAS AND FRESHWATER ANIMALS

When you mention freshwater diving, you are likely to find any number of reactions. For some reason, most people only associate diving with oceans. The nondiver finds it hard to imagine where you would dive inland and the saltwater diver tends to look upon the freshwater diver with disdain.

Since many divers in the United States live inland, most of their diving naturally takes place in fresh water. Simply because you live inland doesn't mean that freshwater diving is less challenging or exciting than its salt-water counterpart.

DIVING AREAS

Fresh water offers a great variety of locations for diving. There are lakes, rivers, sandpits, quarries, caves, sinkholes, springs, and even swamps. In fact, any place where there is water means possible diving to the real diver.

Fresh water provides an array of places to dive, and the activities can be just as varied and in some cases, more varied than in the oceans. Exploring can be very rewarding; some rivers and streams offer the diver an opportunity for prospecting. Spearfishing can be excellent in fresh waters where it is permitted and the collecting potential is outstanding. Photography, too, can be rewarding in most fresh waters, and of course, many of the marine sciences can be applied to fresh water.

Freshwater divers should never feel inferior to ocean divers. Their skills must be just as, if not more finely developed than saltwater diving skills. Activities like cave and ice diving require a degree of capability and training that many ocean divers never find necessary. (See Part IV, Section D.)

While it is true that fresh water lacks the sea's variety of colorful life, a wide assortment of fish, crustaceans, and shellfish do live there. A nearly endless variety of diving sites is also found in fresh water. Every small stream and pond is a new and different environment; each demands and deserves your attention as a diver.

LAKES

Lakes are the largest source of inland diving, ranging in size from a few acres to the huge freshwater seas in the northern part of the United States, the Great Lakes.

Fig. 3-87 Lakes

Artificial lakes of every size are being developed all over the United States. These lakes or reservoirs are generally built by damming rivers. As the lakes form, a whole new ecosystem evolves. The diver exploring reservoirs can witness a chain of life that differs from natural lakes.

Because of the relative newness of manmade lakes, most of the diving activities there involve exploring, spearfishing, and photography. You find very few artifacts in manmade lakes, although there is normally a great deal of aquatic life. You may discover "treasures" in the form of lost boats, motors, and fishing tackle. This type of diving is not only fun, but also can be financially rewarding.

Natural lakes offer the greatest diving potential. They are normally clear and, depending on their location, offer the greatest potential for finding old relics. With the constant desire for memorabilia and antiques, there is hardly a better place to look than in natural lakes. The early settlers used the lakes as a handy disposal and because fresh water doesn't rust metals like salt water does, most metal items can be salvaged in nearly their original condition.

Wherever railroads were built over natural waters, there is increased potential for finding artifacts. The railroaders had a habit of throwing waste such as old bottles into the water. You may be able to chance upon items lost during the construction of railroad bridges across lakes and rivers. Fresh water gives the diver an opportunity to find long forgotten items in good condition. It is rumored more than one Colorado mountain lake contains gold from old wrecked trains.

The Great Lakes are large enough to handle oceangoing vessels and there are countless numbers of wrecks containing valuable artifacts and treasure.

RIVERS

Rivers can be a lot of fun. No matter where you live in the United States, there is probably a river near you. While not all rivers are deep or clear enough to justify diving, many offer good diving potential.

Fig. 3-88   Rivers

In the areas where gold is possible, like the Rocky Mountains and the California mountain ranges, gold dredging is an exciting and sometimes rewarding hobby. You can also come across artifacts, because the rivers have long been dumping places for man's waste.

Photography is another fascinating sport in the rivers. Rivers offer an opportunity for unusual photographs of life that is not normally seen in the lakes. Freshwater sciences (limnology) can be applied in the rivers in many forms and there is also the pure recreational potential of rivers.

Quiet river pools are deep and offer the best diving. The less turbulent areas beneath waterfalls should not be neglected, however, because they are the most likely spot for gold and artifacts to settle. In many cases, they have the clearest water.

SANDPITS AND QUARRIES

A sandpit or quarry is a small pond artificially formed by removing its natural deposits. Actual rock quarries contain large pieces of mined rock, and the bottom is usually rock, covered with a fine silt. Rock quarries are generally clear, and they may be quite deep. Spearfishing and general exploring can be quite exciting in quarries with fish life.

Fig. 3-89 Quarries

Sandpits are formed when sand is removed from a small existing spring area; the bottoms are normally sand, covered with a light layer of silt. Sandpits offer possibilities for photography, spearfishing, and occasional fossil hunting.

One thing that should be remembered about freshwater lakes and rivers is that the land animals in the area depend on that water for sustenance and because of the broad range of land animals, amphibians, and fish life that depend on the waters, nature can be observed at every level, much more readily than at the ocean. In fact, a complete land/water ecosystem can be seen, particularly in the dry land areas where water is more of a rarity.

NATURAL CAVES

Natural caves are normally above water and speleologists are the people who explore caves. They occasionally run into water which, depending on the cave's formation, may block an entrance to another part of the cave. The surfacing of an underground river may also block an entrance, but in any event, it is quite often worth exploring. So, for the speleologist who wishes to explore the additional cave area, diving is essential.

Fig. 3-90 Caves

SINKHOLES

Sinkholes can be extremely deep and long. They quite often contain fossils and artifacts and offer excellent opportunities for photography. A number of the sinkholes in Florida contain actual bones and remnants, such as sharks' teeth; however, they are rather dangerous to dive in and require a great amount of special training.

SPRINGS

Springs are like sinkholes and they, too, may contain fossils, artifacts, and some unusual life. In both springs and sinkholes, the water is normally quite clear and warm, having a constant temperature of 72°F (23°C). In some areas, like the mountains of Wyoming and Colorado, there are springs which have a high mineral content and extremely warm water, sometimes over 100°F (38°C).

MINES

Abandoned mines can provide exciting diving and are quite often very clear. Many contain relics which makes exploring and photography a natural activity. Because of high mineral content, there may be no animal life. Mines are normally deep and at the base of the open pit, there is often a mine shaft. Depending on the condition and size of the shaft, it may offer interesting, exciting diving.

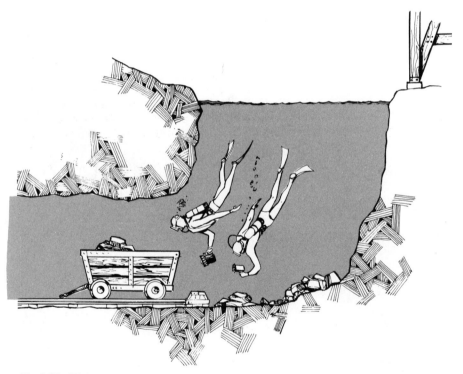

Fig. 3-91 Mines

COMMON FRESHWATER ANIMALS

The fresh waters of the United States lack the immense variety of fish found in the oceans. Depending on the location and water temperature, however, you can find a considerable variety in fresh water.

Fresh water, like salt water, contains edible and inedible fish. In most cases, the fish are edible, but due to their eating habits or water conditions, are not desirable. Undesirable fish are referred to as nongame or scrap fish. Whether or not a fish is a scrap or game fish depends partly on the area of the country. What is considered a scrap fish in one place may be considered a game fish in another.

The purpose of this section is to allow the new diver to identify the inhabitants of his new environment. For that reason, the text will be limited to the fish that might normally be seen by a diver. There are, of course, many fish, like trout, that may exist in great numbers in the lakes where you dive, but which are never seen.

GAME FISH

Largemouth Bass

The largemouth, as illustrated in figure 3-92, is found in almost every state in the United States, in Canada, and Mexico. It can change color according to its surroundings; this color may range from a light brown to almost black. The largemouth is frequently confused with the smallmouth, but it differs, in that the jaw point of the largemouth extends back beyond the eye, while the smallmouth's jaw ends directly beneath the eye. The average size of largemouth bass caught in cold waters is from one to two pounds. In warmer waters the fish may run as large as one to six pounds with a 9 or 10-pounder being possible.

Smallmouth Bass

You can also find smallmouth bass in almost every state, as well as Canada and into Mexico. Like the largemouth, the color of the smallmouth varies according to the terrain. The dorsal fin of the smallmouth appears to be one long fin instead of the two fins of the largemouth. The smallmouth, as shown in figure 3-93, is smaller than its cousin and averages about 1 to 1-1/2 pounds. Five pounds is common, but it is rare to find a smallmouth bass weighing over 10 pounds.

Smallmouth cling close to rocks in lakes and are found around partially submerged boulders and pools in streams.

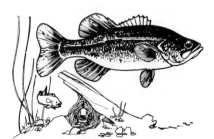

Fig. 3-92 Largemouth Bass

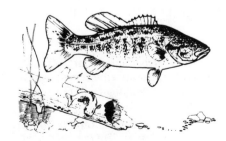

Fig. 3-93 Smallmouth Bass

White and Black Crappie

White and black crappie, as illustrated in figure 3-94, are found in nearly every state in the United States. The white crappie is more numerous in the south and the black crappie is more prevalent in the north.

Both fish are spotted and have vertical stripes. The black crappie is heavier than a white crappie of the same length. The black has seven or more dorsal spines while the white has seven or less. They average 1 to 1-1/2 pounds, although some may be two pounds, with the largest reaching five pounds.

Crappies are primarily lake fish. They run in schools, close to shore along the points. They can be seen occasionally around weeds and in the open water.

Walleye

Walleye are excellent sport fish and are commonly known as walleyed pike, even though they are members of the perch family.

Walleye are found in almost every state, with the exception of the far west and extreme south. Their color varies, but it usually runs from gray-green to almost white. The walleye is different from the true pike in that it has two separate dorsal fins and exceptionally large eyes. (See figure 3-95.) It has strong canine teeth and an upper jaw which extends to a point beneath the rear margin of the eye.

Walleye range in size from an average of two to five pounds, up to 22 pounds. They tend to be a school fish and are normally found around the thermocline. They may swim in water a few inches deep. They are primarily nocturnal and prefer the sandy bottoms near dropoffs in clear waters.

Yellow Perch

Yellow perch are found from southern Canada to the Carolinas. In recent years they have been introduced on the Pacific coast and elsewhere.

Perch are distinguished by six to eight prominent vertical bands. They have a humpback appearance and the two dorsal fins are distinctly divided as shown in figure 3-96. Perch normally weigh less than one pound but may range as high as four pounds. They are normally found in great numbers in schools, and while they are considered lake fish, they may be found in streams and rivers.

Northern Pike

The long, streamlined northern pike is sometimes referred to as freshwater barracuda, primarily because of its appearance. It is a voracious eater, and has canine teeth. (See figure 3-97.)

Pike are found throughout the world, but they prevail in the northern part of the United States. Their color runs from olive gray to almost white; it also varies according to the terrain.

Fig. 3-94 White and Black Crappie

Fig. 3-95 Walleye

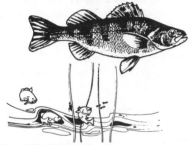

Fig. 3-96 Yellow Perch

Fig. 3-97 Northern Pike

Northerns average from two to four pounds, but may run as high as 46 pounds. There are unauthenticated reports of northern pike weighing over 100 pounds. The pike is a solitary fish which hides along weed beds around logs and other places.

Muskellunge

The muskellunge, or muskie, the largest member of the pike family, is found mostly in the northern part of the United States, Canada, and as far north as Alaska. (Note figure 3-98.) Its color ranges from dark slate gray to a greenish brown. The general appearance is similar to the northern pike, but it can be distinguished by scales on the upper half of the cheeks and gill covers.

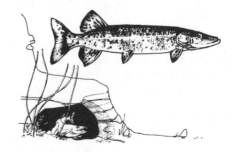

Fig. 3-98 Muskellunge

The average muskellunge weighs 15 to 25 pounds. Fish of 75 pounds have been reported and it is believed some could weigh 100 pounds. Like a northern pike, the muskie is a solitary fish which lays in concealed spots along weeded areas next to logs. Both the northern and muskellunge have been known to eat water fowl and small animals that live around the water.

Pickerel

Pickerel, though similar to muskellunge and northern pike, are much smaller. (Note figure 3-99.) They may be found in the south, even in Florida, and they flourish in streams and rivers as well as lakes. Their feeding habits are much like the northern's.

Channel Cat

The catfish family contains over 1,000 species, but channel cat is considered the sportiest member.

The channel cat, shown in figure 3-100, is found from Canada to Florida, to the gulf states, and into northern Mexico. Their color is slate gray with a slight silvery gray along the sides. None of the catfish have scales. The single spine of the dorsal and pectoral fins is extremely tough and sharp and has the ability to lock in place, which makes catfish dangerous to handle. The whiskers on a channel cat are quite long and the tail fin is very forked. They range from one to two pounds in weight. However, 10-pounders are fairly common and the largest known is 55 pounds.

Channel cat may be found in slow-moving muddy bottom waters, but they normally prefer clean, swift-moving streams and rivers. They are primarily nocturnal feeders and hide under rocks during the day.

Blue Catfish

The blue cat, illustrated in figure 3-101, is the largest catfish in the United States and is found from southern Canada, down to the Appalachians, and into the gulf states. It is also very populous in the Mississippi and its tributaries. The coloring is a solid dark blue-grey fading into silver-white on the belly. The average size is from two to five pounds, although 10 to 20-pounders are common in certain waters. Blue catfish as large as 160 pounds have been reported.

The blue cat prefers larger lakes and rivers and slow-moving quiet waters. Mostly bottom feeders, they feed at night like the other members of the family. During the day they can be found tucked away under rocks in lakes or under the ledges of deeper river pools.

Flathead Catfish

The flathead, as shown in figure 3-102, is found from South Dakota to Pennsylvania and down through Texas and Alabama. Like the blue catfish, it grows to a very large size with 30 to 50-pounders being fairly common. Specimens of 100 pounds have been reported. It differs from the blue catfish because the tail is rounded rather than forked.

Trout

Trout are by far the most beautiful and colorful of the freshwater fish. They range in size from the small brook trout of a few ounces, up to the huge lake

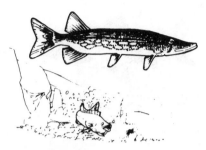

Fig. 3-99 Pickerel

Fig. 3-100 Channel Catfish

Fig. 3-101 Blue Catfish

Fig. 3-102 Flathead Catfish

trout that may weigh as much as 100 pounds. They are found in virtually all waters of the United States and while they prefer and grow larger in colder waters, they swim in the deeper waters of warmer lakes and streams.

There is a great variety of trout, including the rainbow, brown, cutthroat, lake, brook, golden trout, and the steel head. They are illustrated in figures 3-103 through 3-109. Trout are rarely seen by divers. They free swim in open water and are extremely shy and wary.

Fig. 3-103 Rainbow Trout

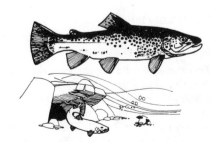

Fig. 3-104 Brown Trout

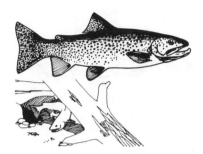

Fig. 3-105 Cutthroat Trout

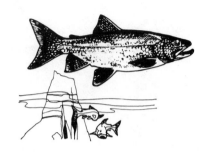

Fig. 3-106 Lake Trout

Fig. 3-107 Brook Trout

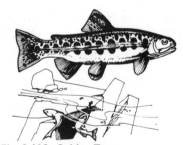

Fig. 3-108 Golden Trout

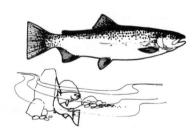

Fig. 3-109 Steel Head Trout

NONGAME FISH

Carp

The extremely hardy carp are originally natives of Asia. They were transplanted here from Europe. They are not generally considered a game fish, but they are edible. Carp can be quite delicious if they are prepared properly, but they are an extremely bony, tough fish. Several varieties exist. One is the mirror carp, shown in figure 3-110. The standard carp in figure 3-111 is a rich golden color and is very streamlined. The mirror carp has the appearance of having lost a number of its scales.

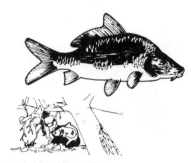

Fig. 3-110 Mirror Carp

Fig. 3-111 Standard Carp

They average from one to six pounds, but may go as high as 55 pounds. They feed on the bottom of streams, rivers, and lakes and must be carefully controlled or they will totally overcome a small body of water and force out the game fish.

Suckers

There are many members of the sucker family, but the white sucker, illustrated in figure 3-112, is the best known. This sucker is found in virtually every state in the United States. Its size ranges from one to two pounds; four pounds is the maximum. It ranges in color from creamy white to silver. Those with a rather pinkish stripe are sometimes referred to as rainbow suckers.

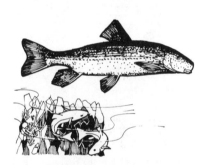

Fig. 3-112 White Sucker

The sucker has a suction-type mouth for bottom feeding. They are found in streams, rivers, ponds, and lakes, and prefer cleaner water. Like carp, they must be controlled.

Gar

Gar are most plentiful in the southern states, but they thrive as far north as southern Canada. Their coloring is an olive green to brown. They are long and thin with alligator-like mouths that contain sharp needlelike teeth.

Garfish grow to a huge size; sometimes they measure as much as seven or eight feet and weigh over 125 pounds. The gar will eat almost anything and are extremely destructive to less vicious fish. They prefer warm sluggish pools and muddy bottoms, but they can be found in rivers and slow-moving streams. There are four common varieties of gar: the alligator, the longnose, the shortnose, and the spotted gar, as shown in figures 3-113 through 3-116.

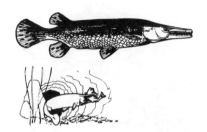

Fig. 3-113 Alligator Gar

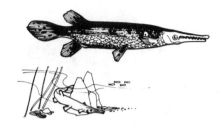

Fig. 3-114 Longnose Gar

Fig. 3-115 Shortnose Gar

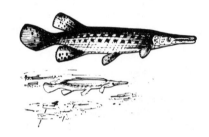

Fig. 3-116 Spotted Gar

While there are many other varieties of freshwater fish, those illustrated are the animals most likely to be seen by divers in the waters of the United States.

CRUSTACEANS

The crayfish is the only noteworthy freshwater crustacean. (See figure 3-117.) The crayfish resembles a lobster, but is much smaller, ranging in size from a few millimeters to eight inches. They are found in almost any type of fresh water, but they prefer clear shallow water. Crayfish are nocturnal. At night they crawl along the water's edge, which makes them fair game for fish and land animals. Crayfish are considered edible and are quite good, but they have limited food value because of their size.

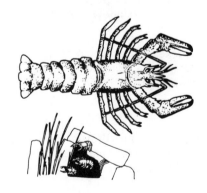

Fig. 3-117 Freshwater Crayfish (Crawdad)

SHELLFISH

Several varieties of freshwater shellfish exist, but only one is of interest—the freshwater clam, as shown in figure 3-118. This three-to-five inch clam lives throughout the United States. Its meat is very good but tough.

Clams found in clear fresh water are the only ones recommended for eating. If you can open them with your bare hands, the clams are probably sick and should not be eaten.

Like their saltwater cousins, freshwater clams bury themselves in the bottom of lakes and ponds. They protrude only enough to breathe and eat. Clams can't hide

Fig. 3-118 Freshwater Clam

from the observant diver because they leave a trail along the bottom when they move from place to place.

As a freshwater diver, you are blessed with a variety of diving locations and activities. You have the rare opportunity to see unexplored places within a few miles of your home and to observe nature on its most fundamental level. The chain of life, from the tiniest water creature to the land animal that depends on the water for its life, is yours to experience.

There is an exceptional and exciting opportunity for the diver to find and recover antique relics and to reward himself intellectually, along with the continuing probability of rewarding himself financially as well.

Fresh water may lack the publicity and glamour of the oceans but it is by no means second best. It rivals and equals the oceans in every sense of the word.

section E

ecology

● THE DELICATE BALANCE OF NATURE
● POLLUTION PROBLEMS
● POLLUTION SOLUTIONS

SOURCES OF PROBLEMS

The balance of nature is really a very simple thing. Every creature, in order to live, must have food. If you remove its source of food, the creature dies. In nature there is a chain of life wherein every living thing, be it plant or animal, provides either food or shelter for every other living thing.

Fig. 3-119 Chain of Life

Fig. 3-120 Clown Fish and Anemone

Occasionally the balance of nature is disrupted by nature herself. Where ideal growing conditions exist, the population of one or more species may increase to huge proportions, far beyond what is normal. When this happens, nature is able to rebalance herself. As the population increases, so does the demand on its food source. As the food source begins to diminish, so does the population, until everything regains its proper balance.

Left undisturbed, nature establishes a system in which the strongest survive. The weak are killed and eaten and the survivors produce successive generations which become more adept at survival. This system constantly improves the species.

All through the oceans you can see large and small creatures helping one another. A good example is the small clown fish which lives inside the poisonous sea anemone. The clown fish attracts other fish which are killed by the anemone. The remains of the victim serve as a food source for the clown fish, so each helps the other. The small cleaner wrasse operates stations throughout the oceans where the larger fish come to have parasites cleaned off their bodies. The large fish even allow the small wrasse to enter their mouths and remove food from between their teeth. They are serving each other, in what is known as symbiosis.

Man, in his effort to provide a better way of life for himself, is constantly upsetting the balance of nature. The dumping of excess waste, the process of construction in and around the water, and the search for natural resources, all disturb the natural chain of life in some way.

Nature has an amazing capacity for adapting to change both on land and in the water. However, if there are enough continuing changes, or changes that are severe enough, nature is often unable to adapt. When a permanent change occurs, it affects more than just a single species; it will interact and all creatures will tend to reduce each other.

COASTAL PROBLEMS

SEWAGE

The dumping of unrefined sewage into rivers or immediately offshore into the oceans is killing much of the marine life. The survivors are becoming mutations and disease is increasing among the fish. The affected creatures aren't fit for human consumption, but, worse, they aren't safe as food for each other. Healthy fish which eat the sick ones are also affected.

Fig. 3-121 Diseased Fish

The sewage pollution is affecting not only the fish living *in* the water, but also the people *around* the water. It causes rivers and beaches to be closed, decreasing recreational areas for swimming and, in some cases, for boating as well.

Fig. 3-122 Pollution

Many popular resort areas in foreign countries dump raw sewage into the rivers which eventually flows to the sea at or near swimming beaches. The result—swimmers in the area contract dysentery or even worse diseases.

CONSTRUCTION

Dumping and landfill along the shoreline to create new real estate disturbs homes of the shallow water animals and also destroys the natural food cycle.

Fig. 3-123   Landfills

Dredging along the coasts also disrupts the food cycle. In coral reef areas, the silt created by dredging drifts, settles along the reefs, and kills the coral. To kill the coral reefs and the shallow water creatures is to upset the chain of life. It affects not only animals in the immediate vicinity, but eventually creatures at greater ocean depths.

INDUSTRY

CHEMICAL DUMPING

Chemical dumping by industry produces much the same results as sewage. It kills marine life and causes deformation and disease. Fortunately, the United States Environmental Protection Agency has strict laws and is enforcing them with heavy fines for offenders. A constant watch, however, must be maintained to avoid chemical dumping not only in the form of direct dumping, but also from accidental runoff of pesticides into our rivers and coastal areas.

CRUDE OIL DAMAGE

Crude oil has caused a great deal of damage to the coastal areas' beauty, recreation, and marine life. Land animals that depend on the sea for their life suffer too.

There have been natural crude oil seepages for millions of years and the oceans have handled them gracefully. However, with the depletion of our natural oil reserves on land, man has reached into the oceans to tap its riches, and regardless of the care taken to safeguard against oil spills, they do happen.

Fig. 3-124   Crude Oil Spills

Until recently, it was believed that most of the oil problems stemmed from exploration and its resulting spills. It is now apparent, however, that another source of crude oil is much more severe and holds a greater potential danger than all the drilling put together.

Oil tankers transport about 2 billion tons of oil each year. They carry crude oil one way across the ocean and then use seawater for ballast on the return voyage. At the end of the voyage, they dump the seawater along with its oily residue back into the oceans. The oil industry estimates that 5 million tons of oil are disposed of in this manner each year and scientists estimate that ballast pumping accounts for five times as much oil pollution as the accidental spills which we hear about. This dumping is not only a matter of course, but is quite legal. Unless something is done, it will have long-range and drastic effects on the natural ecosystem of the oceans.

COMMERCIAL FISHING

Damage caused by pollution, accidental or intentional, is a major problem. Overharvesting of the seas presents an equally great threat to our existence. In recent years, sophisticated electronic equipment has improved the techniques

Fig. 3-125   Commercial Fishing

of long-line fishing boats, trawlers, and purse seiners. New, larger boats are able to process the fish as they are caught. These boats have catching and storage capabilities far beyond what fishermen of just a few years ago ever dreamed possible.

Even with today's improved fishing techniques, in 1972, fishing boats in some areas were able to take only about 10 percent of the amount harvested in 1965. Clearly, the oceans are being depleted of their available resources.

The seas currently provide only a small percentage of the animal protein used by the world. If the demand increases, conservation methods will have to be strictly enforced for fishermen throughout the world. It must be remembered that only about one-tenth of the ocean is really fertile—the rest is virtually barren.

Some forms of sea farming are practical, but not every species can be controlled. Consequently, fishermen must be careful not to deplete the stock of fish beyond chances for natural recovery.

SPORT DIVING

The threat to the oceans by sport divers is minimal. The amount of game the sport diver can take from the oceans by spearfishing or other means is inconsequential in comparison to what a single fishing boat can take. Still, the sport diver has a responsibility to respect sea life and not take just for the sake of taking. Spearfishing is fine for food, but to take fish just for sport is wrong. The same is true of crustaceans and shellfish. To take what you need to eat is a way of life, to take for sport is unique to man and is wrong. Along the coastal waters of the United States, fish and game departments have established limits and seasons. If the seasons are observed, the stocks won't be depleted and can be maintained for all.

Fig. 3-126 Don't Pollute

Sport divers must respect the new environment and avoid unnecessary damage. Don't remove anything natural unless there is a very good reason. Don't break off coral or disturb underwater growths. Remember that it took millions of years to grow the beautiful underwater life and it takes only moments to destroy it. If everyone was careless, before long we would have nothing but an underwater desert.

INLAND PROBLEMS

Problems in fresh water are much the same as in the oceans, including sewage and industrial dumping plus the additional problems created by the widespread use of insecticides.

Chemical fertilizers and runoff from cattle-feeding operations eventually settle in ponds and lakes. The runoffs are creating a problem known as eutrophication. Eutrophication is a process whereby too many nutrients enter a body of water, causing increased plant growth which dies and produces a lethal gas, which in turn kills the animal life.

If the intentional or accidental dumping of nutrients is not curtailed, it is only a matter of time until eutrophication begins to take its toll on larger bodies of water with long-range and disastrous effects on freshwater animal life as we know it today.

SOLUTIONS

It would be a wonderful thing if it were possible to list the causes of pollution, and then, just as easily, list the solutions to the problems. Unfortunately, such is not the case.

Fig. 3-127 Conserve and Enjoy

The solution to pollution problems are at least as complex as the problems themselves. Ecologists are painfully aware that dramatic action to eliminate the obvious may, in fact, create new problems that are equally bad, if not worse.

One point shines clearly amid the confused quest for answers. Pollution is everyone's problem, and each individual must do his or her part to keep pollution levels down to a point where nature can handle it. Until such time as answers are found, a program of active prevention must be maintained.

PART IV dive activities

introduction

By now you should have a good basic understanding of the equipment required to dive safely. You should also have a clear understanding of how water affects the diver and how the diver can function safely within the new environment.

This part will offer an insight into diving activities. It will discuss how to provide yourself with food from both the sea and from the fresh waters. It will provide further information on collecting techniques for aquariums and preserving specimens, as well as ways to capture your undersea experiences on film. For the more adventuresome diver who seeks the thrill of something more than just the normal open water environment, there is a presentation on cave diving, ice diving, wreck diving, treasure hunting, and other advanced diving techniques.

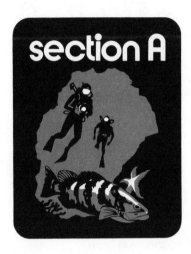

section A

food from sea and lake

- SPEARFISHING
- SHELLFISHING
- CRUSTACEANS
- COMMERCIAL FOOD FARMING

SPEARFISHING, ANIMAL TYPES, AND COMMERCIAL DEVELOPMENT

The seas and lakes provide an ever increasing amount of our daily food requirements. Even more food will be available as commercial fishing and undersea farming techniques improve but care must be taken in everything we do concerning the seas.

Environmentalists have recently made it clear that the seas are showing the adverse effects of too much commercial fishing. There can be little question that the problems they are creating must be solved, but the desire to protect our waters from abuse by large commercial fishing firms should not affect all forms of fishing. This includes a minority of sport divers who fish from the sea.

The sport diver, using selective techniques and careful conservation, does not threaten the ecosystem but can, in fact, help it. He can also help his personal economic situation by supplementing his food supply with what he is able to gather from the water. More important than economics is the thrill and satisfaction of using your own skills to provide your own food.

SPEARFISHING

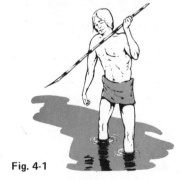

Man has always looked to the sea for food, and one of the oldest methods of securing food was with a spear. Originally, this weapon was used at the surface while standing near or on the shore, as shown in figure 4-1. Man now may go beneath the surface of the water with spearguns. In the beginning, man spearfished *only* for food. Only in the past few decades has he regarded spearfishing as a sport.

Fig. 4-1

Spearfishing offers many challenges, because man must function within an environment that belongs solely to the fish. However, it has recently become painfully apparent that the sea is unable to reproduce at a rate which corresponds with the pressures of commercial fishermen. While spearfishing as a sport has little or no effect in relation to the sophisticated commercial trawlers, each diver must do his share to avoid depleting the precious resources of our oceans. Therefore, it is suggested that spearfishing be used only to take food and not for sport, and that careful conservation methods be employed to protect the fish and allow them to reproduce in their own manner.

SALTWATER TECHNIQUES AND EQUIPMENT

The speargun is the most important piece of equipment and a large selection is available for the spearfisherman. The first spear was a large thin shaft with a point on the end. After a point that would hold the fish was designed, there came the desire for power. The development of rubber reached a stage where it could be used to power the shaft, and the Hawaiian sling was born.

The Hawaiian sling, featured in figure 4-2, resembles a slingshot with the shaft going through the handle and into a notch attached to the rubber. The shaft is pulled back in the manner of a slingshot and then released. It is a free spear (not attached by a line) and is legal only in salt water where the water is sufficiently clear to keep track of any game that may be speared.

While the Hawaiian sling is efficient, its use is difficult to master. In many areas of the world, spearfishing is limited to the use of the Hawaiian sling, and then only while skin diving. No tanks are allowed. (See figure 4-3.)

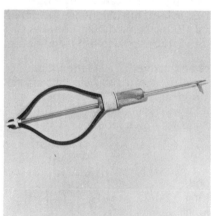

Fig. 4-2 Hawaiian Sling

Fig. 4-3 Using Hawaiian Sling

Rubber Guns

Because the Hawaiian sling must be pulled back and released each time, its power is limited by the strength of its user. To give the user more power, the rubber gun was invented. It is nothing more than a method of holding the shaft secure so that several rubber slings can be attached and released simultaneously at the proper moment. Rubber guns require strength and a good deal of time to load. The number of slings which propel the shaft limit the rubber gun's power. For these reasons, CO_2 guns were invented.

CO_2 Guns

CO_2 guns do have great power, but they also have several drawbacks. They must be recharged each time they are fired, and the gas released into the water creates a disturbance that obstructs the vision of the spearfisherman. Because of these and other problems, including the extreme power and effectiveness of the CO_2 guns, they have been outlawed in most parts of the world.

Spring-Powered Spearguns

The spring-powered gun was designed as a compromise between the CO_2 and rubber gun. A shaft forced against a spring inside the barrel compresses the spring; a trigger mechanism then holds the shaft. When released, the spring throws the shaft. Because the reserve energy of compressed steel is not great, and because salt water had a corrosive effect on the trigger mechanism and spring, the spring gun passed out of favor while the rubber gun remained.

The Pneumatic Speargun

The pneumatic speargun is a compromise between the rubber, CO_2, and spring gun. It offers the advantages of the spring gun because it loads faster than the rubber gun. It is much safer than the CO_2 gun because the gun retains expended air inside. The problem with this seemingly perfect gun is that its power is also limited by the user's strength because it is loaded by forcing the shaft down the barrel against pressure.

No matter what type of speargun you use, treat it with respect. Always load and unload it in the water away from others and never point it at anyone.

FREE-SWIMMING AND ROCK FISH

In areas where the diver is free to choose the type of gun, he should consider the kind of fish to be taken. Fish generally can be placed into two categories: free-swimming fish which move around and hunt for food and bottom or rock fish which frequent reefs and rock outcroppings along coastal areas.

Free-swimming fish usually are found in waters along points and dropoffs. They search for food along protected areas such as coral reefs in warm waters, and rock outcroppings and kelp beds in colder waters. When hunting for fish while skin diving, remember—you can't possibly outswim the fish, they must come to you. Dive to a point slightly below the depth at which the fish normally swim, then just hang motionless in the water. It's important that you move as little as possible. Free swimmers are very spooky and will veer off at the slightest indication of danger. The idea is to shoot up toward the fish rather than down. Remember that free swimmers move quite fast, so you must take a careful lead.

A scuba diver does not always have an opportunity to shoot at free-swimming fish. They don't normally frequent the bottom areas scuba divers like to roam, and the fish may be frightened by exhalation noises.

When shooting large free-swimming fish, special spear points are required, as shown in figure 4-4. These fish possess great power, so the point must be detachable from the shaft. A point secured directly to the shaft would be snapped off almost instantly. There must be a flexible connection, such as a line between the point and the spear shaft. The line should be either strong nylon or cable approximately 18 inches long. Quite often a reel like the one shown in figure 4-5, is attached to the gun and will hold 150 to 250 feet of line. In this way the fish can be played in much the same manner as a fisherman with a rod and reel.

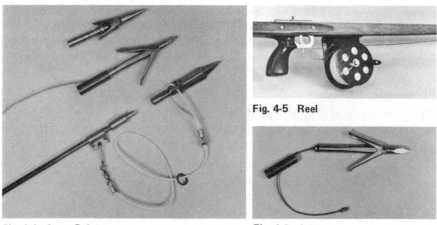

Fig. 4-4 Spear Points

Fig. 4-5 Reel

Fig. 4-6 Cable

Rock fish, or reef fish, present the spearfisherman with a different challenge. Where the diver remains still and allows free swimmers to come to him, he must hunt rock fish. Rock fish are territorial and are seldom found far from a hiding place. When stalking these fish, the diver must move carefully, be very quiet, and peek over every rock and ridge until the fish is located. The diver must move slowly with no sudden motion until he is within the fish's range.

When taking rock fish, you are seldom more than a few feet away, so the ranges are short in comparison to free swimmers. The equipment required is essentially the same except that the shaft should be shorter and heavier. The points used on the spear shaft should still be detachable, but the connecting cord should be made of cable rather than nylon to avoid being cut on rocks or coral, as illustrated in figure 4-6. Reels are not required when shooting rock fish because they don't normally go any great distance, but rather head directly for their hiding places.

FRESHWATER SPEARFISHING TECHNIQUES AND EQUIPMENT

Spearfishing in fresh water is really no different than in salt water. The fish are smaller and not quite as strong.

Many parts of the United States do not allow spearfishing. Of those that do, only a few allow the taking of game fish, even though it has been proven that line fishermen take more fish than spearfishermen. It has also been shown that spearfishermen are much more selective and can actually aid ecology rather than damage it, but until the laws are changed, the diver must adhere to them.

Locating Fish

Fresh water differs from the ocean because the thermoclines change radically according to the time of year and the fish vary in location according to temperature ranges. In the summer you may find fish in rather deep waters, while in the spring and fall they swim in much shallower water.

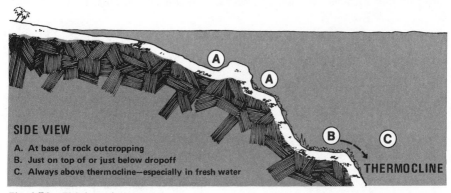

SIDE VIEW
A. At base of rock outcropping
B. Just on top of or just below dropoff
C. Always above thermocline—especially in fresh water

THERMOCLINE

Fig. 4-7A   Fish Locations

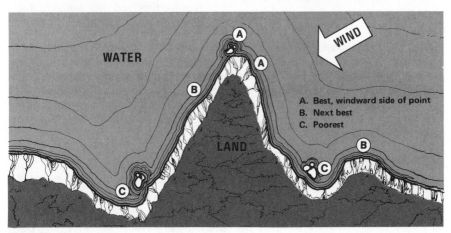

WATER

WIND

A. Best, windward side of point
B. Next best
C. Poorest

LAND

Fig. 4-7B   Fish Locations

Locating the particular fish you desire will vary depending on whether they are territorial fish and remain in a particular area, or if they are hunters which swim around searching for food. The chart in figure 4-7 A and B gives some indication of the areas various fish frequent. By seeking out these areas and using good spearfishing techniques, the diver increases his chance for success.

It is important to remember that fish can outswim the diver and it is fruitless to move along looking for the fish. The diver should remain in the most likely place and wait for the fish to come to him.

Equipment Required

The guns required for freshwater use are considerably smaller than those used in the ocean. The pneumatic spearguns are particularly suited to fresh water because they are fast-loading, extremely accurate, and powerful enough to take any freshwater fish. The points do not have to be detachable. While certain fish (such as catfish) do have enough power to damage your equipment, they are not found in sufficient numbers to warrant the special equipment.

Fig. 4-8   Double-barb Point

The type of spear point used by the freshwater diver is important. It should be a point rugged enough to withstand contact with rocks and employ a double barb to keep the fish on the shaft, as shown in figure 4-8. There must be some method of holding the barbs down so the fish can be removed from the shaft. The freshwater spearfisherman can carry the fish with him, while the saltwater diver must remove fish from the water to avoid attracting any type of predator.

By following these simple rules, the spearfisherman in fresh or salt water has an opportunity to obtain food. Spearfishing should be used for this purpose alone. Remember—the waters are not an endless source of supply for sport and recreation. We must conserve our resources so that future generations will have the opportunity to observe these beautiful creatures in their natural surroundings and to insure that there is a sufficient supply to provide food for their table as well as ours.

SALTWATER SHELLFISH

ABALONE

Many edible shellfish inhabit salt waters. Among the most popular are abalone. They are excellent food and are found from Alaska to Mexico. Because of their excellent taste, they are in great demand and, as a result, supplies have been depleted drastically. Strict controls have been placed on abalone in U.S. waters.

Fig. 4-9 Removing Abalone

California, for example, has strict controls over the depths at which abalone may be taken and the amount and size which may be captured. Methods of taking abalone are also limited in California, for if undersize, or "short" abalone are taken and discarded or improperly replaced, they will either die or be eaten by predators. They are incapable of replacing themselves on their natural habitat of rocks and ledges and are helpless on the open ocean floor.

You should use a legal abalone iron which is less than 36 inches long; it must be straight or curved with a radius not less than 18 inches. The iron should be 3/4 inch or more wide and 1/16 inch or more thick. It should have no sharp edges. To remove the abalone, slide the iron under it at a 15° to 20° angle, while keeping the tip against the rock, as shown in figure 4-9. Once the iron is under the abalone, lift up on the iron.

If you *do* remove an undersize abalone, replace it immediately (with its foot down) in a crevice where it will be protected from strong currents and predators.

CONCH

The conch, pictured in figure 4-10, is another excellent source of food. It is found crawling along the bottom, primarily in warmer waters. It varies in size from very small to several pounds. While there are a number of species of conch, you cannot eat all of them. It is a good idea to check with the local people to determine which are safe to eat.

Fig. 4-10 Conch

OYSTERS, SCALLOPS, AND CLAMS

The common oyster, scallop, and clam are three more ocean delicacies. Oysters and scallops dwell on rocks, while clams are normally found on the bottom, particularly along the shore areas in the mud, or in sand along the beach. Locating oysters, scallops, or clams varies according to the area. Again, checking with local divers is the best idea.

FRESHWATER SHELLFISH

The only shellfish found in fresh water in sufficient quantities or large enough to be of interest to divers are freshwater clams. They live in many lakes throughout the United States and vary in size from two to eight inches in length. Although they are a little tough, they are very tasty. Clams are found on the bottom areas in the bays of lakes and stillwater ponds. To determine if the clam is edible, see if it can be opened easily. Clams which cannot be opened easily are usually healthy, and those which can be opened with your fingers may be sick and should be avoided.

SALTWATER CRUSTACEANS

There are a number of edible crustaceans found in the oceans. Among these are lobster, crab, and shrimp.

LOBSTERS

There are two common types of lobsters. The spiny lobster lives along the west coast of the United States, down through Mexico, into the Caribbean, and up as far north as Virginia. The spiny lobster lacks the claws of the so-called Maine lobster, as illustrated in figure 4-11.

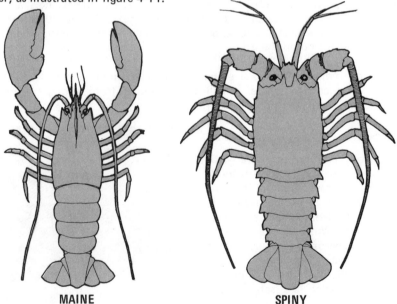

MAINE   SPINY

Fig. 4-11 Lobsters

Lobsters are primarily nocturnal. To locate them during the day you need a good light to search their favorite hiding places—little nooks and crannies along reefs and rock outcroppings. (See figure 4-12.) Lobsters, like abalone, are desirable because of their delicious flavor and have become quite scarce. Divers must pay strict attention to the laws protecting lobsters and take no more than they can eat.

CRABS

Another delicious crustacean is the crab. Crabs can be found virtually all over the world in one form or another. Not all crabs are edible and it is strongly suggested that you check with local people regarding the types available. Crabs and lobsters prefer similar environments. A crab in its natural habitat is shown in figure 4-13. However, they occasionally can be found outside their hideaway during the day. A careful eye must be kept to locate these deceptive creatures.

Fig. 4-12 Spiny Lobster   **Fig. 4-13 Crab**

SHRIMP

Shrimp are almost totally nocturnal and are rarely seen during the day. They range in size from almost microscopic to the size of a small lobster. Shrimp, similar to the one shown in figure 4-14, can be found all over the world. They are highly sought after for food. Their numbers, too, appear to be waning.

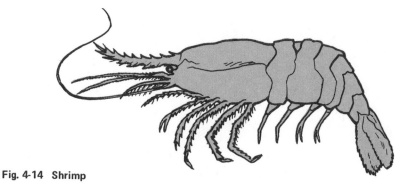

Fig. 4-14 Shrimp

There are a great many edible sea creatures besides those already mentioned. Many are considered delicacies, such as the sea urchin, turtle, squid, octopus, and a number of others which are not readily available to the commercial market. Each type of animal requires special handling and knowledge. Once again, it is suggested that information from local people be obtained prior to taking any creature unfamiliar to you.

COMMERCIAL DEVELOPMENT OF THE SEAS FOR FOOD

There are numerous attempts being made to cultivate the seas for commercial use. Among the most successful sea farming ventures are turtle farming and the cultivation of shrimp and oyster beds. Seaweed is being used as a human food supplement and as a source of minerals and vitamins. New uses are sought daily. Attempts to cultivate lobsters have failed so far. Not enough is known about the lobster's growing and breeding habits to allow man to cultivate it commercially.

The world is just now awakening to the fact that the seas resources must not be indiscriminately wasted. Eventually, through research, man will discover techniques required to cultivate the sea sensibly. It is a new and virtually untapped area that offers a bright future for any young people today who may be interested in doing their part to help solve the world's problems.

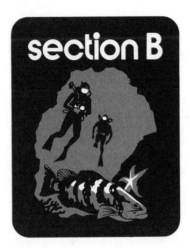

section B

dive planning

- CONDITIONING
- DIVE OBJECTIVE
- DIVE SITE SELECTION
- EQUIPMENT PREPARATION
- ENVIRONMENTAL CONSIDERATIONS
- THE DIVE DAY
- THE DIVE

DIVE PLANNING: AN OVERVIEW

Dive planning is a systematic process of determining where you want to dive and defining the requirements of that dive. Every dive you make requires some degree of planning. A dive in a foreign country obviously requires more planning than a local dive to your favorite site; but they both require planning. Thorough preparation leads to a relaxed, enjoyable, and successful dive. Proper dive planning also takes care of the little things that could easily cause the cancellation of the dive. The old adage that an ounce of prevention is worth a pound of cure certainly holds true for scuba diving. The first time you're a thousand miles from home and lose an "O" ring or break a mask strap, without a replacement, can graphically drive this point home. But, there is more to dive planning than making sure your equipment is in order. In addition to being mentally and physically ready to dive, you need to set a dive objective, select a site, critically evaluate its environment, and develop a plan that will enable you to cope with all the variables of the dive. It may seem like a lot to do but, with a little practice and practical experience, dive planning will soon become routine and even enjoyable.

CONDITIONING

Physical conditioning should be a regular part of your daily activities, whether you are an active diver or not. If you are in shape, only a slight modification of your exercise routine is needed to prepare for the dive. Swimming, snorkeling, a review/refresher course, or any activity that strengthens the

Fig. 4-15 Physical Conditioning

muscles used for respiration or finning are excellent methods of preparing for the dive. (See figure 4-15.) Your honest appraisal of your physical condition and the level of performance required for the dive are vitally important to your health and well being. Age, weight, drugs, alcohol, and smoking all have a substantial affect on your body's ability to function properly underwater. If you are over 40, overweight, or using any drug or medication, a physical examination should be part of your dive planning.

Nutrition is another important factor in preparing for a dive. Certain foods that are high in fats and oils reduce the ability of the blood to transfer oxygen to your muscles and brain. Insufficient oxygen can cause muscle cramps, underwater black-outs, and heart attacks. On the other hand, eating complex carbohydrates, such as whole grains, rice, fruit, and vegetables promotes controlled energy absorption. The night before and the day of your dive, avoid overeating and gas producing foods.

DIVE OBJECTIVE

The objective is simply the purpose or reason for the dive. It can be anything from photography, spearfishing, or lobstering to just looking around and enjoying the underwater scenery. A specific objective ensures that you and your buddy are coordinated and, essentially, doing the same thing underwater. It also enables both of you to plan and equip yourselves for the dive.

DIVE SITE SELECTION

Once you have the dive objective firmly in mind, you can get down to the business of selecting and scouting a dive site, as shown in figure 4-16. Of course, the site must match the dive objective. To find a relevant site, consult your local dive store, a scuba club, or ask experienced divers for recommendations. Make a habit of selecting an alternate site in case changing conditions make your original site unsuitable. The alternate should be within a reasonable travel time from your primary site and, perhaps, be in a sheltered area to preclude rough seas or adverse weather conditions.

SCOUTING THE SITE

With the site selected, you can begin the process of scouting the dive site. This is basically an information search for such things as hazards, local surf, tides, currents, bottom composition, and underwater life. This research helps uncover all the pertinent facts about the dive environment you may encounter. Of course, the easiest way to scout the site is to visit it before the dive for a first-hand observation, as shown in figure 4-17. If this is not possible, you can select one of the various scuba guidebooks available on the market. These books usually are found in dive stores, book stores, or libraries and provide a general description of the dive site. Another excellent source of information is to talk to local divers who have actually dived the spot.

An important element in scouting the site is researching the emergency services available. This includes the telephone number or radio frequency for the U.S. Coast Guard, the number for local emergency medical services, the nearest recompression chamber, and the best mode of transportation to reach the chamber. Another important number to have is DAN (Diver Alert Network). DAN is an emergency information service designed specifically for dive related injuries. When you call DAN, you will be connected with a physician experienced in diving medicine. These physicians assist with diagnosis and initial treatment of the accident, and supervise the referral to an appropriate recompression chamber. It also is a good practice to carry a good quality first aid kit. Make sure it is restocked after every use.

Fig. 4-16 Dive Site Selection

EQUIPMENT PREPARATION

Now that the dive site is selected and researched, you can start to assemble the appropriate equipment for the dive. (See figure 4-18.) It is important to check all your equipment well in advance of the dive day. Taking the time to thoroughly inspect your gear could save you some unscheduled problems and maybe even your life. You'll be much more comfortable detecting a faulty buoyancy compensator while inspecting gear in your living room than you will be discovering it at 95 feet on a dive. Begin early enough so that, if you find any broken or malfunctioning equipment, you will have ample time to have it serviced.

It may be helpful to use an equipment checklist to ensure nothing is overlooked or forgotten. A comprehensive checklist is included in the appendix. You can modify the checklist according to your dive objective and site. If you are planning a spearfishing trip, your equipment requirements will be somewhat different than a photographic dive.

Fig. 4-17 Scouting the Dive Site

Fig. 4-18 Equipment Assembly

Take your time at this stage of the planning; remember, your life will depend on the condition and operation of such things as your regulator, submersible pressure gauge, and depth gauge. If it has been more than six months since your last dive, consider taking your regulator to a reputable dive store for an inspection and adjustment. Also check the inspection dates and hydro-test dates on your tanks. Inflate your buoyancy compensator and check for leaks and proper operation of the inflating system. If you are planning a trip outside the United States, have customs inspect and document the serial numbers on all your equipment to avoid having to pay duty when you return from the trip.

Additional pieces of equipment that often are overlooked include your personal car and the boat that you intend to use. It's pretty disappointing to have to call off the whole dive day due to mechanical problems with the car or boat. Even if you're able to dive, the frustration caused by such problems will detract from your enjoyment of the dive and possibly cause additional problems as your attention is turned from the dive itself.

ENVIRONMENTAL CONSIDERATIONS

Environmental concerns generally focus on two major areas: the weather and tidal currents. The evaluation of these two factors should be accomplished early enough to allow you to make alternate plans, if necessary, and to avoid an unwanted surprise.

WEATHER FORECASTING

About a week before the dive, start monitoring the weather patterns for your dive site. Local radio and television news programs provide general weather information, and are good for visualizing weather trends. National weather programs, such as A.M. Weather and cable weather also are good sources. The National Oceanic and Atmospheric Administration (NOAA), as well as the National Weather Service, provide continuous radio broadcasts that are excellent weather sources.

As the week progresses, continue to update the weather. You should start getting more specific information on the dive site and look for trends in frontal activity and local fog conditions.

PREDICTING TIDAL CURRENTS

Predicting the horizontal movement of water is extremely important if your planned dive is in a coastal area, harbor, or estuary. Carefully timing your dive will allow you to take advantage of the current at both the beginning and end of your dive. It is especially important to have a favorable current at the end of your dive.

The following discussion is an example of how to interpret the Tidal Current Tables using a worksheet and excerpts from the tables in the appendix of this manual. You may find it helpful to review Part III, Section B, to reacquaint yourself with the terminology and the purpose of each table.

Assume you are planning to dive the north end of Agate Passage in Puget Sound on Sunday, January 16. You want to start your dive at the end of the ebb current so that you can take advantage of the weak ebb to take you out and the weak flood to bring you back.

Start with Table 2 and locate Puget Sound and its subordinate stations. (See figure 4-19, item 1.) Substation 1110 is your dive site, the north end of Agate Passage (item 2). The reference station for this location is Admiralty Inlet (item 3) which is located on page 34 in Table 1.

In Table 1 (See figure 4-20), locate Admiralty Inlet and the day of your planned dive — Sunday the 16th. Under the "slack water time" column, notice that there are four times listed (0045, 0746, 1427, and 1702). Two of these times correspond to the slack before the beginning of the ebb current and two are for the slack before the beginning of the flood, as shown by the "E" (ebb) and the "F" (flood) following the knots listings.

You want to start your dive during the slack before the beginning of the flood current, so you select the slack time of 1427. The maximum flood current will occur at Admiralty Inlet at 1544. These values are then entered in the worksheet, as shown in figure 4-21. Note that all times are based on the 24-hour clock, and are local standard times; therefore, you must compensate for daylight savings time, if necessary.

Since the distance from Admiralty Inlet to Agate Passage is considerable, you will need to apply a correction factor to find the actual conditions at your dive site. Return to Table 2 (See figure 4-19), and locate the column labeled Time Differences. In this column are the correction factors for the "Minimum Before Flood" time, which is actually the slack; and the "flood" time, which is the time of the maximum flood current. As shown by item 4, the corrections for Agate Passage are minus 1 hour 28 minutes for the slack, and minus one hour for the flood. The average speed and direction of the maximum flood current are 1.2 knots and 230° (item 5). These values are entered in the worksheet in figure 4-21.

By subtracting the subordinate station corrections from the reference station times, you can determine that, at Agate Passage, the flooding will begin at 1259 in a direction of 230° and reach its maximum velocity of 1.2 knots by 1444. Since the flood current builds gradually to 1.2 knots and you would like to use part of the ebb current to take you out, you turn to Table 4, shown in figure 4-22.

TABLE 2 — CURRENT DIFFERENCES AND OTHER CONSTANTS

Table 2 contains mean time differences by which the reader can compile approximate times for the minimum and maximum current phases at the subordinate stations. Time differences for those phases should be applied to the corresponding phases at the reference station. It should be noted that although the speed of a given current phase at a subordinate station is obtained by reference to the corresponding phase at the reference station, the directions of the current at the two places may differ considerably. Table 2 lists the average directions of the various current phases at the subordinate stations.

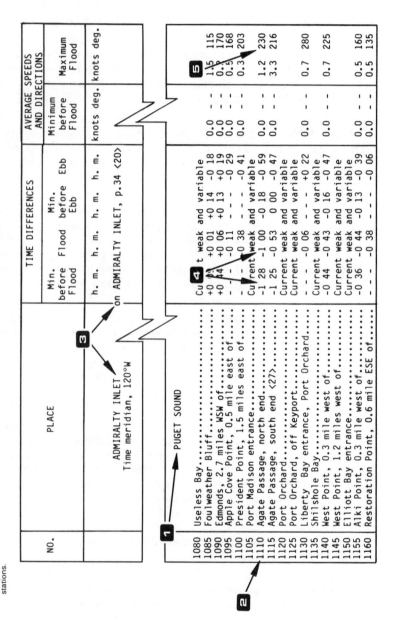

NO.	PLACE	TIME DIFFERENCES				AVERAGE SPEEDS AND DIRECTIONS		
		Min. before Flood	Flood	Min. before Ebb	Ebb	Minimum before Flood	Maximum Flood	
		h. m.	h. m.	h. m.	h. m.	knots deg.	knots	deg.
	ADMIRALTY INLET Time meridian, 120°W	on ADMIRALTY INLET, p.34 <20>						
	PUGET SOUND							
1080	Useless Bay............	Current weak and variable				0.0 --	1.5	115
1085	Foulweather Bluff........	+0 24	+0 01	+0 14	-0 18	0.0 --	0.9	170
1090	Edmonds, 2.7 miles WSW of...	+0 44	+0 06	+0 13	+0 19	0.0 --	0.5	168
1095	Apple Cove Point, 0.5 mile east of...	- -	-0 11	- -	-0 29	0.0 --	0.3	203
1100	President Point, 1.5 miles east of...	- -	-0 38	- -	-0 41			
1105	Port Madison entrance..........	Current weak and variable						
1110	Agate Passage, north end....	-1 28	-1 00	-0 18	-0 59	0.0 --	1.2	230
1115	Agate Passage, south end <27>...	-1 25	-0 53	0 00	-0 47	0.0 --	3.3	216
1120	Port Orchard..........	Current weak and variable						
1125	Port Orchard, off Keyport...	Current weak and variable						
1130	Liberty Bay entrance, Port Orchard....	- -	-0 06	- -	+0 22	0.0 --	0.7	280
1135	Shilshole Bay..........	Current weak and variable						
1140	West Point, 0.3 mile west of...	-0 44	-0 43	-0 16	-0 47	0.0 --	0.7	225
1145	West Point, 1.2 miles west of...	Current weak and variable						
1150	Elliott Bay entrance........	Current weak and variable						
1155	Alki Point, 0.3 mile west of...	-0 36	-0 44	-0 13	-0 39	0.0 --	0.5	160
1160	Restoration Point, 0.6 mile ESE of...	- -	-0 38	- -	-0 06	0.0 --	0.5	135

Fig. 4-19 Table 2 — Current Differences

ADMIRALTY INLET

JANUARY

Day	Slack Water Time h.m.	Maximum Current Time h.m.	Vel. knots	Day	Slack Water Time h.m.	Maximum Current Time h.m.	Vel. knots
1 Sa	0028	0345	3.6F	16 Su	0045	0358	2.6F
	0721	1017	2.5E		0726	1033	2.0E
	1347	1536	0.8F		1427	1544	0.3F
	1718	2139	4.0E		1702	2139	3.0E
2 Su	0116	0433	3.5F	17 M	0118	0430	2.5F
	0804	1108	2.6E		0754	1103	2.1E
	1446	1633	0.8F		1507	1624	0.3F
	1817	2233	3.6E		1744	2216	2.7E
3 M	0206	0521	3.2F	18 Tu	0152	0501	2.3F
	0847	1157	2.7E		0822	1139	2.2E
	1548	1735	0.8F		1548	1713	0.4F
	1922	2329	3.1E		1834	2255	2.4E
4 Tu	0257	0610	2.8F	19 W	0228	0536	2.1F
	0928	1251	2.8E		0848	1213	2.3E
	1652	1845	0.8F		1629	1759	0.4F
	2038				1935	2340	2.1E
5 W		0031	2.5E	20 Th	0309	0613	1.8F
	0352	0700	2.3F		0914	1254	2.4E
	1008	1346	2.9E		1712	1900	0.6F
	1754	1956	0.9F		2052		
	2207						
6 Th		0138	2.0E	21 F		0036	1.7E
	0453	0754	1.9F		0356	0655	1.5F
	1047	1439	3.0E		0942	1336	2.6E
	1852	2110	1.1F		1756	2003	0.8F
	2345						
7 F		0256	1.6E	22 Sa		0143	1.4E
	0601	0848	1.4F		0454	0742	1.2F
	1126	1534	3.1E		1012	1427	2.8E
	1945	2225	1.5F		1842	2113	1.2F
8 Sa	0120	0414	1.4E	23 Su	0004	0300	1.2E
	0717	0950	1.0F		0607	0833	0.9F
	1203	1627	3.2E		1047	1518	3.0E
	2032	2322	1.8F		1930	2222	1.6F
9 Su	0239	0527	1.3E	24 M	0137	0425	1.2E
	0834	1043	0.8F		0729	0936	0.7F
	1241	1712	3.3E		1131	1615	3.3E
	2115				2018	2323	2.1F
10 M		0016	2.1F	25 Tu	0252	0536	1.4E
	0342	0629	1.4E		0849	1042	0.6F
	0945	1135	0.6F		1224	1710	3.6E
	1319	1758	3.4E		2106		
	2155						
11 Tu		0103	2.4F	26 W		0018	2.6F
	0432	0722	1.5E		0353	0640	1.6E
	1046	1224	0.5F		0956	1145	0.7F
	1358	1839	3.4E		1324	1804	3.9E
	2233				2154		
12 W		0144	2.5F	27 Th		0109	3.1F
	0514	0807	1.7E		0444	0733	2.0E
	1138	1308	0.4F		1053	1242	0.8F
	1435	1919	3.4E		1427	1859	4.1E
	2308				2242		
13 Th		0221	2.6F	28 F		0157	3.4F
	0551	0846	1.8E		0530	0822	2.3E
	1224	1348	0.4F		1144	1340	1.0F
	1513	1954	3.3E		1530	1948	4.2E
	2341				2329		
14 F		0254	2.7F	29 Sa		0242	3.5F
	0625	0923	1.9E		0612	0909	2.6E
	1306	1430	0.4F		1233	1433	1.1F
	1549	2029	3.2E		1631	2039	4.1E
15 Sa	0013	0326	2.7F	30 Su	0016	0328	3.5F
	0656	0958	2.0E		0652	0954	2.8E
	1347	1507	0.4F		1323	1528	1.3F
	1625	2104	3.1E		1731	2132	3.9E
				31 M	0103	0413	3.3F
					0730	1039	3.0E
					1413	1622	1.3F
					1831	2221	3.5E

FEBRUARY

Day	Slack Water Time h.m.	Maximum Current Time h.m.	Vel. knots	Day	Slack Water Time h.m.	Maximum Current Time h.m.	Vel. knots
1 Tu	0150	0455	3.0F	16 W	0131	0428	2.1F
	0806	1125	3.1E		0729	1052	2.6E
	1506	1719	1.3F		1440	1650	1.0F
	1935	2314	2.9E		1859	2239	2.4E
2 W	0238	0540	2.5F	17 Th	0207	0458	1.9F ·
	0841	1212	3.1E		0751	1127	2.7E
	1602	1819	1.3F		1517	1731	1.1F
	2043				1955	2326	2.1E
3 Th		0012	2.4E	18 F	0248	0533	1.6F
	0330	0625	2.0F		0815	1202	2.7E
	0915	1301	3.1E		1600	1825	1.2F
	1700	1926	1.3F		2101		
	2200						
4 F		0115	1.8E	19 Sa		0015	1.7E
	0428	0713	1.5F		0336	0614	1.2F
	0949	1352	3.0E		0840	1245	2.8E
	1800	2037	1.3F		1650	1924	1.3F
	2327				2219		
5 Sa		0226	1.4E	20 Su		0120	1.4E
	0537	0809	1.0F		0437	0657	0.9F
	1023	1446	2.9E		0911	1336	2.9E
	1859	2146	1.5F		1746	2033	1.5F
					2348		
6 Su	0056	0349	1.2E	21 M		0240	1.2E
	0702	0905	0.6F		0557	0758	0.6F
	1100	1545	2.9E		0950	1435	3.0E
	1954	2254	1.7F		1846	2150	1.8F
7 M	0215	0507	1.2E	22 Tu	0116	0409	1.2E
	0832	1009	0.4F		0731	0914	0.4F
	1143	1641	2.9E		1044	1543	3.1E
	2045	2351	1.9F		1946	2257	2.2F
8 Tu	0317	0610	1.3E	23 W	0229	0523	1.5E
	0948	1110	0.3F		0853	1027	0.4F
	1234	1732	3.0E		1157	1650	3.3E
	2129				2043	2354	2.6F
9 W		0038	2.1F	24 Th	0327	0627	1.8E
	0405	0703	1.5E		0953	1139	0.6F
	1043	1205	0.3F		1318	1752	3.6E
	1329	1818	3.0E		2137		
	2210						
10 Th		0119	2.3F	25 F		0050	2.9F
	0445	0748	1.7E		0416	0715	2.2E
	1126	1255	0.4F		1041	1240	0.9F
	1422	1859	3.1E		1434	1847	3.8E
	2246				2228		
11 F		0154	2.4F	26 Sa		0139	3.1F
	0519	0821	1.9E		0458	0801	2.6E
	1201	1338	0.5F		1126	1336	1.3F
	1511	1941	3.1E		1542	1943	3.8E
	2320				2316		
12 Sa		0230	2.5F	27 Su		0222	3.2F
	0550	0852	2.1E		0537	0845	2.9E
	1234	1417	0.6F		1210	1430	1.6F
	1556	2014	3.1E		1645	2033	3.8E
	2353						
13 Su		0300	2.5F	28 M	0002	0305	3.1F
	0618	0925	2.2E		0612	0926	3.2E
	1305	1452	0.7F		1253	1519	1.8F
	1639	2048	3.0E		1744	2121	3.5E
14 M	0025	0332	2.5F				
	0643	0954	2.3E				
	1335	1530	0.8F				
	1723	2127	2.9E				
15 Tu	0058	0400	2.3F				
	0707	1024	2.5E				
	1406	1607	0.9F				
	1809	2202	2.7E				

Time meridian 120° W. 0000 is midnight. 1200 is noon.
If three consecutive entries are marked (E) the middle one is not a true maximum but an intermediate value to show the current pattern.
* Current weak and variable.

Fig. 4-20 Table 1 — Daily Current Predictions

TIDAL CURRENT WORKSHEET

DIVE DATE *JAN 16*	MINIMUM SLACK BEFORE FLOOD	MAXIMUM FLOOD
TIME ESTIMATES Reference Station (Table1)	*14:27*	*15:44*
Subordinate Station (Table 2) Correction Factor	*- 1:28*	*- 1:00*
Subordinate Station Time	*12:59*	*14:44*
Duration Correction (Table 4)	*- :23*	
Actual Dive Time (Start)	*12:36*	
CURRENT VELOCITY (Table 2)		
Average Speed		*1.2 kts*
Direction		*230°*

Fig. 4-21 Tidal Current Worksheet

Table 4 allows you to determine the approximate period of time during which weak currents (0.1 to 0.5 knots) will occur for various maximum currents. You determine that diving in a current of .3 knots would be safe. Under the "Maximum Current" column locate 1.2 knots. Since it is not listed, round up to the next value, 1.5 knots. Under the 0.3-knot column you find 46 minutes for a 1.5-knot maximum current. Divide 46 in half to arrive at 23 minutes. You want half of the dive in ebb and the other in flood. By subtracting 23 from 1259 (the beginning of the flood current at Agate Passage), you know that you and your buddy can begin the dive at 1236. This gives you 23 minutes of ebb current to take you out and 23 minutes of flood current to bring you back.

Maximum current	Period with a velocity not more than —				
	0.1 knot	0.2 knot	0.3 knot	0.4 knot	0.5 knot
Knots	Minutes	Minutes	Minutes	Minutes	Minutes
1.0	23	46	70	94	120
1.5	15	31	46	62	78
2.0	11	23	35	46	58
3.0	8	15	23	31	38
4.0	6	11	17	23	29
5.0	5	9	14	18	23
6.0	4	8	11	15	19
7.0	3	7	10	13	16
8.0	3	6	9	11	14
9.0	3	5	8	10	13
10.0	2	5	7	9	11
11.0	2	4	6	8	10
12.0	2	4	6	8	10

Fig. 4-22 Table 4 — Duration of Slack

The National Ocean Service has a word of warning for Tidal Current Table users. The actual times of slack or maximum occasionally differ from the predicted times. This difference may be as much as half an hour and, rarely, even as high as one hour. They go on to state, however, that 90 percent of the slack waters occur within half an hour of the predicted time. The variation can be caused by a number of factors, such as wind, river discharge, or unusual atmospheric pressure. NOS recommends that you reach the dive site at least half an hour before your dive time and observe the conditions, or seek out locals who can better determine them.

THE DIVE DAY

The morning of the dive you need to determine the actual conditions that will, or could, affect your dive. Start with yourself and your buddy. You need to honestly reevaluate your physical condition. Make sure you and your buddy are not suffering from any illness, such as an ear infection or chest cold, that could affect your performance during the dive. Ask yourself, "Is my energy level up to where it needs to be for the type of dive I have planned?" It is important that you are not under the influence of any drugs, alcohol, or a hangover.

PREDICTING THE DIVE CONDITIONS

From your efforts throughout the week, you should have a good idea of the environmental conditions at the dive site. You can reconfirm the actual weather by contacting a weather reporting agency, calling someone close to your intended site, or you can wait and do your own observations at the site itself. Pay close attention to the possibility of storms or fog. These conditions can move in while you are submerged and create a hazardous situation.

After you reach your intended dive area, take a few minutes to assess the existing conditions before you suit up for the dive. (See figure 4-23.) Depending on your observations, you may decide to go to an alternate dive site. The

Fig. 4-23 Evaluating the Conditions

areas you should concentrate on are water visibility, water movement, and wind. Obviously, these are interrelated as they affect diving conditions.

Good visibility is indicated by crystal blue water. Gray or greenish water is associated with reduced visibility. This could be caused by plankton or water movement which stirs up the bottom. Indications of this are high energy waves and/or a confused sea. Tidal currents, wave action, and surge also should be assessed prior to suiting up for a dive. These conditions can cause an exhausting dive and can lead to a dangerous situation.

Wind can cause rough surface conditions and upwelling. A strong off-shore wind can cause surface water to flow away from shore and be replaced by colder water from beneath. When this nutrient-rich bottom water is warmed, an ideal situation exists for the development and growth of plankton. A "plankton bloom" can severely restrict visibility.

In general, conditions which indicate good diving are a light surf with low energy waves and a time interval between waves to allow a reasonable entry. Of course, the absence of longshore currents and rips is desired. The tidal current should be timed to be favorable at the end of the dive. A light breeze and calm surface are signs of little or no surge. Crystal blue water with bright sunshine provides good visibility and underwater illumination.

If your predive observation reveals these conditions, you're in luck. The makings of a good dive are present. Before you make the dive, however, ensure that someone not involved in the dive has a copy of your dive plan. They should know when you expect to return, what to do, and whom to contact if you don't.

THE DIVE

The final check before entering the water includes a physical inspection of each other's equipment, a quick review of the depth and time limits of the dive, setting your watches, observing the sea and current conditions, discussing the type of descent you will use (free or following the anchor line), and any other points that will have a bearing on the success or enjoyment of the dive. (See figure 4-24.)

A dive plan is of little use if it is not followed. In the weeks that preceded the dive, a lot of time was spent gathering equipment, information, and people together to ensure a pleasant, successful dive. Use your dive plan and follow it as closely as possible. The real satisfaction from scuba diving is having a safe, worry-free dive that comes from preparing and following a dive plan.

AFTER THE DIVE

After the dive is the time to sit back, relax, and relive its exciting moments. If consecutive dives are planned, you will need to determine your repetitive dive group and update the dive profile. Then, complete your logbooks, inspect your dive equipment and, if necessary, perform any on-site maintenance.

Fig. 4-24 Final Check

You still need to give some consideration to your body; don't ingest any alcohol or drugs, and don't take a hot shower. All of these things tend to increase circulation, which could cause the nitrogen to come out of solution in your blood.

A dive that is safe, relaxed, and fun doesn't just happen; it is planned. The time you spend planning a dive is well worth the effort. It gives you the opportunity to answer questions while you have the time to research and resolve them logically. So, when the urge to explore the underwater world strikes, take a moment to gather all the available resources, apply the principles of good dive planning, use a checklist like the one shown in the appendix, and follow the safe diving practices in figure 4-25. This will help make each dive an enjoyable, successful, and safe experience.

SPORT DIVER STANDARDS FOR SAFE DIVING

AS A SAFE DIVER I SHOULD:
A. MYSELF

dive within my mental and physical limits

never hold my breath while using scuba

avoid excessive hyperventilation when breath hold diving

descend slowly and equalize my ears every two feet

never dive alone

be familiar with the dive tables and know how to use them

be conservative with the dive tables

be aware of the effects of age, being overweight, and cold in reducing circulation in my body and its ability to deplete nitrogen in a normal way

be aware of the effects of drugs, alcohol, cigarettes, and fatty foods on my body's ability to transfer oxygen

Fig. 4-25 Safe Diving Practices (continued on next page)

let my body deplete nitrogen in a normal manner by ascending no faster than 60 feet per minute

ensure that all possible precautions are taken to clear excess nitrogen from my body by stopping at 10 feet after every dive for one to three minutes

be aware that in an emergency and in current diving a high level of physical fitness is required

B. MY EQUIPMENT

use proper and well-maintained equipment

have my regulator checked and tested periodically

wear a buoyancy control device

use a mechanical inflator on my buoyancy compensator

have a device for monitoring the quantity of air in my scuba tank at low levels

have a device for monitoring time underwater

use only clean, filtered air in scuba tanks

use scuba tanks that have been visually inspected at least once a year

use scuba tanks that have been hydrostatically tested at least once every five years

ensure that my weight belt is never restricted by other equipment by putting it on last

dive with an alternate air source

use a diver's flag and surface support

be aware that depth gauges are not always accurate, can become inaccurate from normal use, and should be tested for accuracy periodically

know my boat and boat regulations

C. ENVIRONMENT

plan my dive according to sea state, actual weather, forecast weather, and my energy level

cancel dives when environmental conditions are questionable

be familiar with the diving location and determine if it is a beginner or advanced dive site

avoid touching unknown creatures underwater

remove killed game from the water as soon as possible

have a dive plan that includes where and how to obtain help in an emergency

D. RESTRICTIONS

be aware of the effects of nitrogen narcosis on my ability to make judgment decisions below 60 feet and that as depth increases, nitrogen narcosis increases

be aware that open water certification is a license to learn and that I should only dive sites recommended for beginners unless under the direct supervision of a divemaster, dive boat captain, or scuba instructor until I have had advanced training in boat diving, dive rescue procedures, and deep diving

never dive below 100 feet

never let an uncertified diver use my equipment

E. DIVE REVIEW

make one or more review dives as needed with a scuba instructor if it has been over 12 months since my last dive and have my logbook signed to show that I am current

strive to improve my diving knowledge by attending diving educational seminars and conventions

F. GOOD CITIZEN

be a good sportsman and obey all fish and game laws

obey all local diving laws

Fig. 4-25 Safe Diving Practices (cont.)

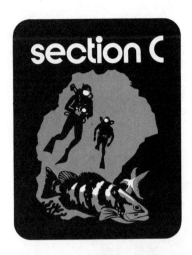

section C

photography

- UNDERWATER HOUSINGS AND CAMERAS
- NATURAL LIGHT PHOTOGRAPHY
- ARTIFICIAL LIGHT PHOTOGRAPHY
- MOVEMENT OF CAMERA AND SUBJECT

EQUIPMENT, NATURAL AND ARTIFICIAL LIGHT PHOTOGRAPHY, AND MOVEMENT

Photography adds a new dimension to diving quite unlike any other diving activity. Divers are blessed with the opportunity to see more wildlife during their short watery visits than they can see on land over a long period of time. There is an endless parade of subjects passing. (See figure 4-26.)

Photography offers the thrill of the hunt because it requires careful stalking and observation to capture your subject on film, as shown in figure 4-27. It also offers a chance to relive each adventure and to share it with others.

LAND CAMERAS IN HOUSINGS
CARTRIDGE TYPES

The popular cartridge type camera, shown in figure 4-28, is an excellent choice for beginning underwater photographers. It is relatively inexpensive and simple to operate. Since many people already own them, they are an

Fig. 4-26 Endless Parade of Underwater Life

Fig. 4-27 Underwater Photographer in Action

excellent first choice for an underwater camera. Cartridge-type cameras are available in pocket or disc models; some of these have more advanced design features, including automatic exposure and automatic advance capabilities in more expensive models.

Housings for cartridge type cameras are shown in figure 4-29 and are the least expensive housings available. They are compact, simple, and dependable. They give the owner an opportunity to experiment in underwater photography at a low cost.

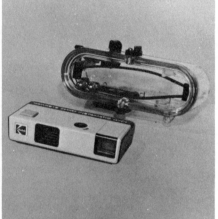

Fig. 4-28   Cartridge Type Camera   Fig. 4-29   Cartridge Type Camera Housing

AUTO 35MM RANGEFINDER TYPE

The auto 35mm rangefinder camera offers a more advanced method of taking pictures. A variety of shutter speeds is available and the exposure can be controlled. It also comes equipped with a flash synchronization and strobe lights can be used. It offers the more versatile 35mm format which provides up to 36 exposures and the cost of film is less because it is in roll rather than cartridge form. Most of the small auto 35mm cameras have automatic exposure control for natural light photography; many have automatic advance capabilities which are excellent for underwater photography.

The auto 35's, like those shown in figure 4-30, are medium price range cameras, which places them between the cartridge-type and the single lens reflex camera in cost. The housings are inexpensive—about the same or slightly more than the cartridge-type housings. They are dependable, small, and easy to handle. For beginning photographers at the experimental stage who demand a little more quality in their pictures, the auto 35mm offers many advantages and excellent results.

SINGLE LENS REFLEX

The single lens reflex camera, or SLR, is the most versatile, available in 35, 120, and 70mm format. The SLR offers interchangeable lenses and through-the-lens

Fig. 4-30 Auto 35mm Cameras

viewing, as illustrated in figure 4-31, so you can see the exact image you will photograph and adjust the focus at the same time. Some models offer large capacity film magazines which let the photographer take up to 250 exposures without changing film. They also provide rapid advance motor drives which give the capability of automatic advancement; a very desirable feature for underwater photography.

A wide assortment of housings is available for SLR cameras. These range from the plexiglass housing, which is reasonably priced and completely reliable, to the very rugged metal housings, indicated in figure 4-32. Metal housings are more durable and longer lasting than plexiglass. Compared to the cartridge and small auto 35's, the SLR camera is by far the most versatile and offers the best quality of photography.

SELF-CONTAINED UNDERWATER CAMERAS

The advent of self-contained underwater cameras, portrayed in figure 4-33, have been a great boon to underwater photography. Many people desire the single lens reflex camera's photographic quality, but are not willing to take their expensive cameras underwater.

Fig. 4-32 Housings for the SLR Camera

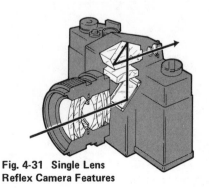

Fig. 4-31 Single Lens Reflex Camera Features

Fig. 4-33 Self-Contained Underwater Cameras

Self-contained cameras are small and easy to handle. They are rugged, dependable, extremely versatile, and have simple controls. These cameras offer interchangeable lenses, close-up attachments, flash synchronization, and complete adjustment of lens openings and shutter speeds.

While the self-contained camera does not offer through-the-lens viewing, it does produce extremely high quality and excellent pictures. The only disadvantage is that you must estimate the distance to the subject.

NATURAL LIGHT PHOTOGRAPHY

PROBLEMS FOR BEGINNERS

Light

Taking pictures underwater is much more difficult than on land. Water bends and absorbs the light rays as you can see in figure 4-34. The ripples on the surface tend to reflect the light and affect the amount of light that enters the water (see Part II, Section A). Because the eyes are able to compensate for the

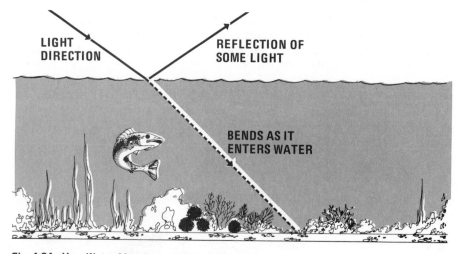

LIGHT DIRECTION

REFLECTION OF SOME LIGHT

BENDS AS IT ENTERS WATER

Fig. 4-34 How Water Absorbs and Bends Light Rays

changes in light, the mind does not notice the changes; whereas the film has a fixed light absorption capability and the coming and going of light can greatly affect the exposure and the quality of the picture.

Most beginners assume the camera is able to capture what the eye sees and are disappointed with their first photographic attempts. Usually, they are too far away or too deep without enough light to expose the film properly. A rough guideline for exposure levels on various cameras indicates that the lower cost cartridge type cameras are effective above the 15 foot level in clear water, and the medium cost cameras, which offer lens opening and shutter speed adjustment, are effective down to 30 feet or more, depending on the clarity of the water.

Color

Another source of disappointment for the beginning photographer is that there is often very little color in their pictures. This is because color is lost very rapidly in water, as depicted in figure 4-35. The colors lost go right through the spectrum. Reds disappear for the photographer within the first 10 feet, then oranges, yellows, greens; near the 60 foot level nothing is left but blues and grays.

Color is affected to a large degree by particles in the water. Depending on what they are, suspended particles determine the color of the water itself. Certain animal life may actually turn the water green or red and that dominance of color affects the ultimate colors in your photograph.

To get maximum color into a photograph, the photographer must get as close to a subject as possible; the amount of color absorbed by the film is a function of not only the depth, but also the distance from the subject. So, to insure that you get maximum color and enjoyment from your pictures, remember to stay in shallow water and get close to your subject.

Fig. 4-35 Underwater Color

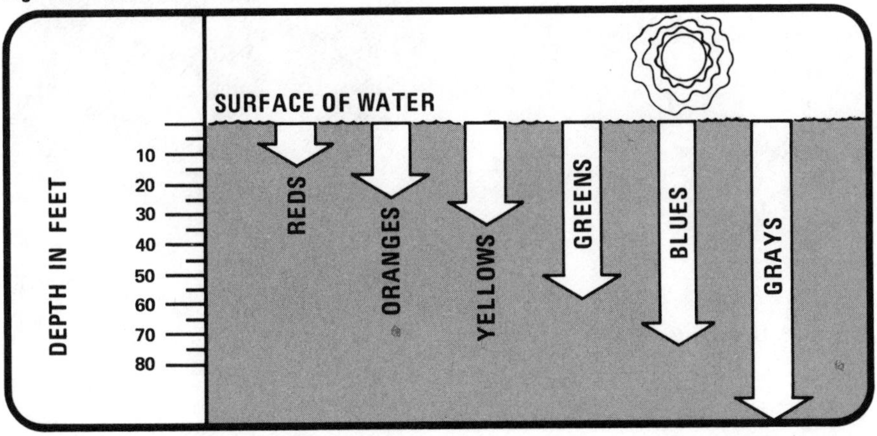

ARTIFICIAL LIGHT PHOTOGRAPHY

The primary reason for artificial light is an obvious one. As light is lost, it must be replaced. At greater depths, both light and color are lost to the naked eye as well as to the camera. A good artificial light source, as shown in figure 4-36, is balanced to the sun's color temperature, and can replace color and produce photographs of startling quality. The colors that exist in the ocean are almost beyond belief in their purity and brilliance.

MOVEMENT

The last and most common of the beginner's problems involves movement of either the camera or subject. It is very disappointing to remember all other aspects of good picture-taking only to wind up with a blurred picture because either you or the subject moved.

Camera movement is very common in natural light photography, and is normally caused by one of several things: slow shutter speed, weak grip on the camera, or the motion of water. Subject motion is normally the result of shutter speed being too slow or the light duration of the flash.

To avoid blurred pictures, weight yourself heavy so you can remain secure on the bottom; weight the camera to neutral buoyancy. If it is too buoyant, it tends to float upwards; if it is too negative, it tends to sink. It is important to maintain a secure hold on both the bottom and camera. Some photographers hold their breath momentarily while they trip the shutter. If you are taking pictures in mid-water you should *never hold your breath*.

Fig. 4-36 Underwater Strobes

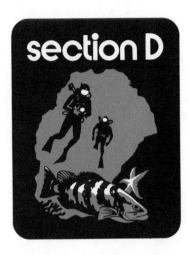

section D
specialty diving

- ● CAVES
- ● ICE
- ● WRECKS
- ● TREASURE HUNTING
- ● SEARCH AND RESCUE

CAVE, ICE, WRECK DIVING, AND SEARCH AND RESCUE

Part of the fascination toward diving stems from the fact that it provides such a wide activity range. We have already explored the various hobbies which may be incorporated into the diving picture. Let us now look at some special diving activities which require a good deal more training and expertise than normal diving in open water.

Cave diving, ice diving, wreck diving, treasure hunting, and, of course, search and rescue, all require their own special brand of excellence. Each represents special diving conditions which introduce additional hazards the open water diver generally does not have to face.

This section offers ideas on how to become involved in something more than just open water diving. It is not intended to provide the technical means to participate in these activities. If you wish to participate in any activities listed, it cannot be emphasized too strongly that you obtain special training from experts.

CAVE DIVING

Caves have always been an irresistible magnet to people. Stemming possibly from the time when people lived in caves, there has always been the desire to explore what's there. With the advent of scuba diving, it became possible to explore underwater caves.

Underwater caves can be found all over the world. In the United States, the greatest concentration seems to be in the southeast. Florida is probably the best known for cave diving and more has been done there to promote cave diving and cave diving training.

TYPES OF CAVES

Caves fall into several categories. There are man-made caves, such as abandoned mines and quarries; there are natural springs and sinkholes. The difference, as shown in figure 4-37, is that mines were originally dry and as they were abandoned, they filled with water. Springs stem from underground rivers bubbling to the surface. A sinkhole is created by an underground river; the ground caves in and creates a hole down to the water's surface.

Cave Characteristics

Springs always have a flow where the water comes out of the ground, and a run where the water flows, creating a stream or river. Sinkholes never have a run, but they may have a flow and a siphon. The flow is the point where the water moves into the sinkhole and the siphon is where it moves out. Because of the siphon possibility, divers must be especially careful in sinkholes.

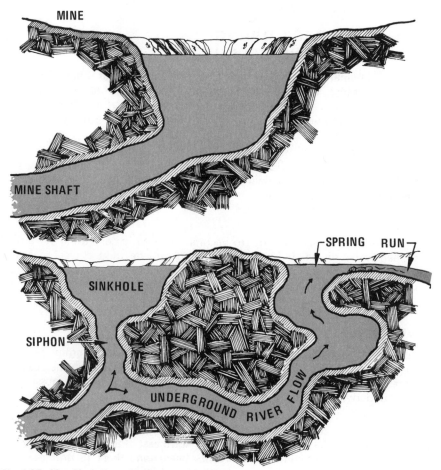

Fig. 4-37 Man-Made Cave, Sinkhole and Spring

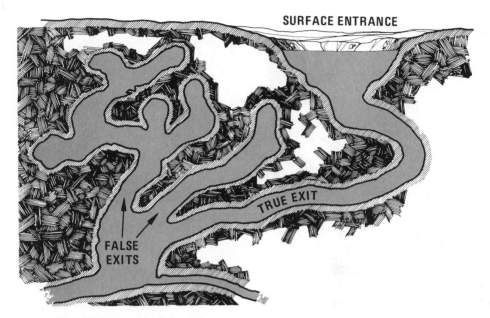

Fig. 4-38 False Exits

In both caves and springs, the entrance is only one of many attempts by the water to reach the surface. (Note figure 4-38.) The diver attempting to exit from the cave is liable to encounter any number of chambers that appear to be exits, but which actually are dead ends.

The floors of most caves are covered with a sediment, a very fine silt which, when stirred, can completely hide the outlet. Safety lines are the only way to insure your safe return to the surface. Another reason for safety lines is that you, as the diver, work in constant darkness even though you use powerful lights to offset the darkness.

ATTITUDE AND TRAINING

A strong mental attitude is required, because the possibility of the lights going out is quite real. If that happens to a cave diver who has a wrong mental attitude, it could spell disaster.

Because of the darkness and sheer uncertainty of what lies ahead in caves, much special training and equipment is required. Whatever prompts you to try cave diving, be certain to properly prepare yourself by seeking professional, specialized training.

Cave diving can be a great joy and thrill, despite its requirements. Caves may contain all sorts of things—from fossils to antiques. The thrill of exploration and the search for contents of caves is endless.

Fig. 4-39 Ice Divers

ICE DIVING

Diving under the ice is very much like cave diving, except it is colder. It requires similar equipment. The diver has only one exit and must use safety lines, as figure 4-39 shows. Because snow often covers the ice, it is very dark and lights are normally required.

Ice diving has a special appeal to the adventuresome diver. It can be done wherever ice forms. In areas where ice diving is done, water is iced over more often that it is open. There is a fascination to see what goes on beneath the ice; however, there is little reason beyond adventure to go ice diving. While the water is sometimes clearer, there is little to see. In cold weather, most fish hibernate.

REQUIREMENTS

In many ways ice diving is even more dangerous than cave diving. The cold does strange things to your mind, to your body, and to your equipment. The cold slows down the bodily functions, so the mind isn't able to react as quickly to any problem that might arise. When the mind does react, there is a physical slowdown that keeps the body from performing needed tasks. In addition, the equipment is subject to freezing and requires special maintenance and care to keep it in top condition.

The watery environment below the ice is totally hostile and the diver must prepare himself to survive in it. He should begin by diving in particularly cold water, training himself to function both mentally and physically under those conditions. He also must have special equipment instruction. Care must be taken to see that the regulator is dry and lubricated and that the tank is filled quite slowly so that no moisture can possibly form. The air must be totally dry to prevent condensation from freezing. The wet suit must be in perfect repair.

Extra layers are required to prevent the cold from creeping through. When adding the extra layers, the diver should have additional practice time in the open water to adapt to the extra equipment.

SAFETY PRECAUTIONS

A great many safety precautions must be taken prior to ice diving. Ice diving is done in teams, as illustrated in figure 4-40. Two divers in the water use the buddy system, and two more divers wait on the surface. You must use safety lines for both divers in the water and safety divers. All divers involved should have a complete knowledge of and be thoroughly drilled in procedure and signals. The reaction time between the line tender and the divers must be immediate. There is no time for trying to determine what was meant by that last tug on the rope. A wrong interpretation or slow reaction could spell disaster.

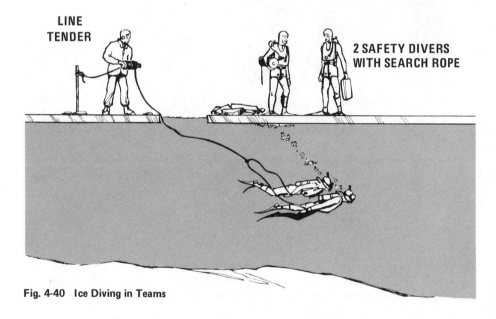

LINE TENDER

2 SAFETY DIVERS WITH SEARCH ROPE

Fig. 4-40 Ice Diving in Teams

If you are interested in ice diving, it is suggested that you seek an established ice diving unit. In most areas of the United States where ice diving has been going on for some time, there are people who have established good solid safety techniques. This reduces existing danger to a minimum. They can provide the special training and information required to ice dive in safety.

WRECK DIVING

Wreck diving has a great deal of fascination for almost all open water divers. The mystery and solitude of a wreck must be experienced to be appreciated. Wreck diving may be conducted in salt water or fresh water, on small boats or large ships, and may include recently sunken vessels or old wrecks with great historical value.

Special training is required because wreck diving is very much like cave diving. Conditions are normally quite poor. The water could be dirty and, in the ocean particularly, it is almost always moving and the water is often quite deep.

When entering a wreck, a diver must be especially careful of internal decay. Even steel ships have a great deal of wood inside them which rots after a period of time. Sometimes the rotting wood requires nothing more than a diver brushing against it to cause its collapse.

Fig. 4-41 Wreck Diving

Wrecks have long been a favorite of divers. They combine adventure with the search for history, and there is always the lure of treasure. Some divers are only interested in the more commercial possibility of salvage.

Whatever your reason for wreck diving, prior to making a dive, learn about the wreck itself. Learn about techniques required, and particularly any special techniques that may be involved for that wreck.

To avoid any possible danger and to insure that the dive will be a success, be sure your equipment is up to par and have sufficient safety equipment. Prior to removing anything from the water, information should be acquired to determine your legal rights to the items you have found. Depending on the area, there are strict laws in effect which govern the diver's right to the items he has located. In fresh water, the prior owner retains ownership at all times. Finding something does not automatically make it yours. Avoid any legal problems that might come up and establish your rights with the proper authorities.

Fig. 4-42 Underwater Treasure Hunting

TREASURE HUNTING

The search for sudden riches has been one of man's failings from the beginning of time, but it has also been one of his great joys. Underwater treasure hunting is no different, and great riches have been taken from the seas.

Treasure does not always come in the form of precious metals, although that is how we normally think of it. It may, in fact, come in the form of artifacts. It may mean prospecting, as shown in figure 4-43. Many divers are involved in dredging for gold in the streams and rivers in parts of the United States where gold is known to exist.

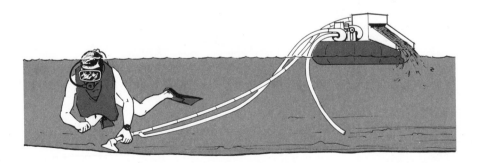

Fig. 4-43 Gold Dredge

While wreck diving for treasure involves a great deal of expense and research time, prospecting can be done on a very small budget. The rewards are more predictable if not as dramatic.

SEARCH AND RESCUE

More and more cities, counties, and states are establishing search and rescue units. These groups have been organized to take care of the least pleasant job in diving, but it is a job that must be done, and it must be done safely.

Water accidents invariably occur during the worst conditions. The water is often dirty, deep, cold, or moving. The bottom may contain plant life. Another problem arises when rescue must be made in icy waters. It could be done at night, but, regardless, rescue always seems to happen under the worst conditions.

When diving problems occur, emotional problems often follow, such as, handling the survivors, organizing the searchers, and maintaining order once the recovery has taken place.

The team efforts may not always involve recovery—they may involve rescue. First aid training is a necessary part of the diver's education as well as a general knowledge of emergency techniques.

Search and rescue diving doesn't appeal to everyone; those who do feel the responsibility and wish to become involved can contact their local law enforcement agencies who can put them in touch with the proper authority in charge of search and recovery teams in your area.

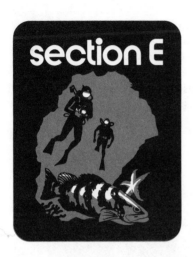

section E

careers

- ● SPORT DIVING
- ● LIGHT COMMERCIAL DIVING
- ● HEAVY COMMERCIAL DIVING
- ● OCEANOGRAPHY
- ● LIMNOLOGY

SPORT DIVING, COMMERCIAL WORK, SCIENCES

Diving is at once the most fascinating and exciting of sports, unique in its flexibility and diversity. It requires careful thought, complete training, and keen intelligence to be performed safely. It provides an ample source of recreation, allowing the diver to combine many of the land sports and hobbies that he might normally engage in with his water activity.

For many, diving represents a way to earn a living at something they really love. The employment opportunities in diving fall into four general categories: sport diving, which includes instruction and such things as writing and photography; light commercial work, which is work that can be accomplished under water with scuba gear; heavy commercial work, which requires mixed gas and/or hard hat gear; and the scientific area, which may include any of the sciences as applied to either oceans or fresh waters.

Whatever underwater employment you choose, you are in continual contact with nature, on the threshold of earth's last frontier. You are a real pioneer and part of the world's future.

SPORT DIVING

INSTRUCTION

There are several ways to earn a living in sport diving. Among these are teaching, writing, and photography. The first step in becoming a diving instructor is, of course, sport diver certification. After gaining further diving experience and perhaps serving as an assistant instructor to a fully certified diving instructor, you would attend an instructor certification course. These courses are offered by a number of local, national, and international schools and organizations listed on page 4-41.

Instructor certification courses last from several days to several weeks. They involve intensive learning experiences in the classroom and in open water and have extremely high standards and rigorous testing procedures.

Some instructor organizations offer student instructors a complete course, not only in diving instruction, but also in retail salesmanship, equipment repair, and

Fig. 4-44   The Instructor at Work

all aspects of effective dive store operation. They also act as dealer associations for the combined diving store and diving school. They aid in communication between dealers, help improve and police business practices, and help maintain high-quality diving education programs. Complete business and education programs like these are offered by the National Association of Scuba Diving Schools (NASDS), National Association of Underwater Instructors (NAUI), Professional Association of Diving Instructors (PADI), and Scuba Schools International (SSI).

Other instructor organizations focus on diver education for the individual, independent instructor who may or may not be affiliated with a dive store. Since these schools place all their emphasis on diver education instead of retail business operations, they are generally shorter, lasting days instead of weeks. As a result, instructor candidates must be mentally and physically prepared before beginning the short and intense training program, for course standards are as rigorous for these as for the more lengthy courses. Diver education courses for the independent instructor are offered by a number of certifying agencies.

For specific details, admission, and course information regarding instructor certification schools, write to the following addresses:

Los Angeles County Underwater Instructor's Association (LACO) 419 East 192nd Street Carson, CA 90746

National Association of Scuba Diving Schools (NASDS) 641 West Willow Street Long Beach, CA 90806

Professional Association of Diving Instructors (PADI) P.O. Box 25011 Santa Ana, CA 92799-5011

Professional Diving Instructors Corporation (PDIC) 1015 River Street Scranton, PA 18505

Scuba Schools International (SSI) 2619 Canton Court Fort Collins, CO 80525

American Canadian Underwater Certification, Inc. (ACUC International) 460 Brant Street, Suite 201 Burlington, Ontario, Canada L7R 4B6

National Association of Underwater Instructors (NAUI) 4650 Arrow Highway Suite F-1 Montclair, CA 91763

International Diving Educators Association (IDEA) 6255 Merrill Rd. Suite B Jacksonville, FL 32211

YMCA National Scuba Program Oakbrook Square 6083-A Oakbrook Parkway Norcross/Atlanta, GA 30093

JOURNALISM

As diving grows, so does the demand for information. Journalism and photography offer a field where the diver can convert his findings, adventures, and knowledge into money and, at the same time, enjoy the sport.

Journalistic areas open to the potential writer are education, adventure, and travel.

Education

Instructors everywhere are hungry for technical information. They are constantly in need of information regarding new teaching techniques and how other instructors are handling problems that arise in training safe divers. In addition, they need equipment information regarding modification and

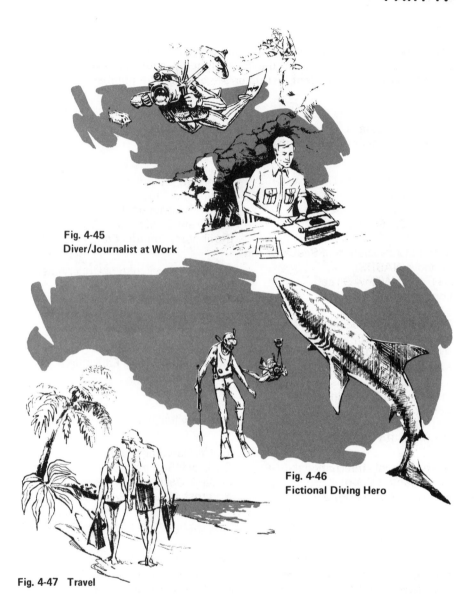

Fig. 4-45
Diver/Journalist at Work

Fig. 4-46
Fictional Diving Hero

Fig. 4-47 Travel

evaluation. Very few instructors are capable of personally purchasing and evaluating each new piece of equipment. Written information regarding personal findings and evaluations is very important.

Adventure

Every sport has its fictional heroes and diving is no exception, see figure 4-46. Many stories, both fact and fiction, are in demand. Every dive is an adventure and special adventures make excellent reading.

Travel

Travel information about different diving areas is important to everyone. Something new appears even in old diving areas. Divers need to know where to go and what to look for, including any special problems that might be involved and how to handle them.

PHOTOGRAPHY

Photography is the only suitable way to present the underwater world visually to the nondiver. Photographs are important because they highlight every article and story. Figure 4-48 is a good example.

Fig. 4-48 Photography

Fig. 4-49 Types of Light Commercial Work

Underwater photographic training begins with basic photography on land. A number of schools in the United States specialize in photography. Once the technique of handling the camera is mastered, most diving equipment stores offer training in underwater camera use. After the diver is familiar with the basic techniques involved, specialized training can be obtained from any of several schools. However, there is no substitute for experience and for the capable photographer, experience is the best teacher.

Almost every publication and television station is a potential buyer for underwater pictures. A career in journalism and photography begins with the basic training received at your local dive school.

LIGHT COMMERCIAL WORK

Light commercial work is normally defined as underwater work accomplished in a short amount of time or in shallow enough water so that decompression is unnecessary. It generally involves inspection of dams, pipelines, cables, and even sewage outfalls, as shown in figure 4-49. It may also consist of such things as salvaging small boats, underwater repair, and even some forms of underwater construction.

To the diver with an imagination, there is an almost endless array of jobs that can be completed with the use of scuba. However, every other certified diver is a potential competitor and, unless there is a big demand in your area, it is not a dependable source of income.

A competent light commercial diver needs advanced training and a keen mechanical ability. A light commercial worker must be a jack-of-all trades, skilled at construction techniques with a good sound knowledge of physics and photography.

Advanced scuba training for light commercial work is available at your local professional school and, of course, on the job. Again, there is no substitute for experience.

HEAVY COMMERCIAL WORK

Heavy commercial work is the highest paid and most hazardous of all commercial diving. Most work is done under adverse conditions where visibility is zero and water temperature may be low. The work involves salvage, repair, maintenance, construction, and may include saturation diving. Salvage work is normally done on ships or anything else worth recovering. Repair, maintenance, and construction work may involve oil rigs, piers, bridges, or any number of underwater objects.

The equipment has become quite sophisticated—beginning with scuba and the Kirby Morgan units and going to hard hat rigs which utilize both compressed air and mixed gas. (See figure 4-50.)

Fig. 4-50
Equipment for Heavy Commercial Work

Fig. 4-51 Scientists Research Earth's Last Frontier

Before applying to one of the many commercial schools, a diver should be thoroughly trained in scuba. You should have a good knowledge of what to expect in heavy commerical work with all its inherent conditions. Instruction includes welding, the use of hard hat and mixed gas units as well as heavy construction techniques.

SCIENCES

It has already been stated that the waters of the world are our last frontier on earth. Diving is one of the tools used by scientists to personally examine the happenings in the underwater world. More sciences now recognize the potential of the oceans and fresh waters. It is quite apparent that additional research must be done to allow us to tap that great potential.

OCEANOGRAPHY

When science is applied to the marine environment, it is known as oceanography; the scientists are oceanographers. The science involved includes such specializations as biology, botany, zoology, geology, geography, and archaeology, to name a few. Many nations have research vessels, similar to that portrayed in figure 4-52, operating on the oceans. They employ sophisticated equipment and highly trained scientists. The oceanographers of the world are attempting to unlock the mysteries of the deep, but they are confined to a very small segment of the ocean floor—primarily the area of the continental shelf.

LIMNOLOGY

Limnology is the application of the sciences to fresh water as opposed to the marine environment, and, just as there is a growing need for oceanographers, there is a great need for limnologists. The fresh waters, like the oceans, hold a key to our future. The challenges are great and exciting.

The most pressing research concerns pollution and feeding the world. Giant steps are being taken toward locating and stopping the causes of pollution in many areas of the world.

If you are interested in a career in the sciences, you must begin with a good solid background in the science of your choice, starting at the junior high level with all of the sciences that are available to you. For specific information, contact your local high school or university. They can supply you with the specific information required to begin a career in oceanography or limnology.

Fig. 4-52   Research Vessel

appendix

CONSIDERATIONS FOR THE DIVING WOMAN

Diving is a perfectly normal activity for *anyone* who is physically fit and mentally able to cope with diving's unique requirements. A woman is as capable as a man of becoming certified and pursuing a diving career. Most of the concerns and considerations of diving are relevant to both sexes. Some, however, are unique to the woman diver.

The shared concerns of diving have been covered in great detail elsewhere in this manual and are mentioned here only briefly. This section is primarily devoted to women, but men can benefit greatly by understanding the concerns and considerations of their female diving buddies. The major ones include equipment, thermal sensitivity, menstruation, the use of oral contraceptives, and pregnancy.

EQUIPMENT

The basic requirements that make diving a safe, enjoyable sport are thorough, competent instruction and obtaining proper, well-fitting equipment. For many years, the only equipment available was designed for men. Finding a perfect fit was a rare exception. Women were forced to alter, or make do, the best they could.

Today, equipment manufacturers are more sensitive to the needs of women than ever before. Custom wet suits, low-volume masks, easy breathing snorkels, back-mounted buoyancy compensators, lightweight regulators, and powerful, flexible fins are only a few examples of the advances in equipment designed specifically for women. The majority of these new designs have benefited both sexes.

A good mental attitude is just as important as training and equipment. While learning to dive, and later while enjoying the sport, maintain a positive and assertive attitude. Ask questions, volunteer when needed, take part in dive site decisions, and assemble and handle your own equipment.

THERMAL SENSITIVITY

Temperature control is another important consideration. Body heat is retained more easily in women than in men due to the presence of more subcutaneous fat and fewer functional sweat glands. A woman's body temperature will be a few degrees higher than a man's before the cooling process of sweating begins. It's not uncommon to experience overheating while suiting up for a dive. Because excessive overheating can be dangerous, cool off in the water for a moment if you feel overly warm.

Women also can become uncomfortably cool more quickly than their male diving buddies because of a larger surface-to-body-mass ratio. This is especially true of lean women with less than 27% body fat. A well-fitting, custom wet suit or dry suit can help alleviate the problem. If uncontrollable shivering begins, get out of the water and obtain warmth.

MENSTRUATION

Another consideration is diving during menstruation. There is no reason why you shouldn't dive if you feel well. The myth of shark attacks is unfounded.

Fluid retention and impaired circulation, however, are concerns. These conditions may increase your susceptibility to decompression sickness. Dive conservatively and shorten your time at depth more than that recommended by the U.S. Navy Dive Tables.

BIRTH CONTROL

Although the method of birth control is a highly personal decision, you should be aware of some of the considerations as they relate to diving. Unfortunately, there is a general lack of adequate and reliable information on the use of contraceptives while diving. Any method that impairs circulation or causes blood clots to form can increase the susceptability to decompression sickness. Again, a wise recommendation to follow is to dive conservatively and avoid decompression dives.

If you are contemplating pregnancy, or suspect that you may be pregnant, don't dive. The Undersea Medical Society has made this recommendation because of the possible harmful effects on the unborn child during its early stages of development.

PREGNANCY

A major concern for women is diving during pregnancy. There is much research yet to be done and not enough documented, reliable information to draw any strong conclusions.

Most of the research has been conducted with animals. The results have varied and are somewhat conflicting. An example is the early experiments on rats and dogs, where it was found that the fetus was more resistant to decompression sickness than the mother. But research on goats and sheep (whose placenta more closely resembles the human), showed a higher incidence of nitrogen bubbles in the blood of the fetus. There has been some controversy as to whether such results were caused by surgical manipulation.

The known and suspected effects of diving during pregnancy are numerous. Increased swelling and sensitivity of mucous membranes in some women cause difficulty when trying to equalize pressure in the ears. Some may experience nausea and vomiting, a potentially dangerous condition for any diver. A pregnant women may be more susceptible to decompression sickness for two reasons: tissue edema (fluid retention) which may effect the ability of the mother's system to rid itself of nitrogen; and increased body fat. Because nitrogen is more soluble in fat, it cannot be eliminated as quickly as it normally would be through conservative use of the decompression tables.

A fetus is susceptible to decompression sickness because of a differing circulation system than is found in the mother. Unlike its mother, a fetus' blood does not pass through the lungs that help to filter some of the harmful nitrogen bubbles. Instead, these bubbles travel more directly to the brain, heart, and other organs, where they can cause serious problems.

A pregnant woman who dives is exposing her unborn baby to an increase in the partial pressure of oxygen, which can cause birth defects. Women who are pregnant should dive conservatively enough to avoid treatment in a recompression chamber, since the pure oxygen used in hyperbaric treatment is known to cause birth defects in infants.

Still another concern to the pregnant diver is a possible adverse reaction to marine animal stings and bites. Severe reactions have occurred and, though it is not certain, the fetus also may suffer harmful effects.

Diving experts have not reached a unanimous decision as to whether a woman should dive during pregnancy. A conservative recommendation by the Undersea Medical Society is to stop diving *entirely*.

SUMMARY

Women, like men, have the opportunity and ability to become certified, competent divers. There is much research still to be done and data to be assembled on the use of oral contraceptives and diving during pregnancy. Women should remain well-informed on these issues and, like all who enjoy the sport, be aware of their mental and physical capabilities.

WATER TEMPERATURE PROTECTION CHART

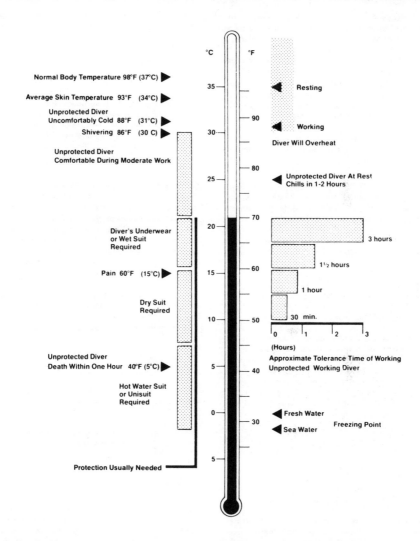

AIR PURITY STANDARDS

STANDARDS FOR AIR 5.2.1.2   Air used in SCUBA operations must meet these standards of purity for the U.S. Navy. This is true no matter what the source of the air or the method used for charging the cylinders. These standards are—

Oxygen concentration	20 - 22% by volume
Carbon dioxide	0.05% (500 ppm)
Carbon monoxide	0.002% (20 ppm)
Oil—mist or vapor	5 mg per cu meter max.
Solid and liquid particles	Not detectable except as noted above under oil—mist or vapor
Odor	Not objectionable

ARCHIMEDES PRINCIPLE AND GAS LAWS

Archimedes Principle: **Any object wholly or partially immersed in a liquid is buoyed up by a force equal to the weight of the liquid displaced.** (a) A negatively buoyant body sinks in a fluid because the weight of the fluid it displaces is less than the weight of the body. (b) A neutrally buoyant submerged body remains in equilibrium, neither rising nor sinking, because the weight of the fluid it displaces is exactly equal to its own weight. (c) A positively buoyant submerged body weighs less than the volume of liquid it displaces. It will rise and float with part of its volume above the surface. A floating body displaces its own weight of a liquid.

Boyle's Law: **If the temperature is kept constant, the volume of a gas will vary inversely as the ABSOLUTE pressure while the density will vary directly as the pressure.** Since the pressure and volume of a gas are inversely related—the higher the pressure, the smaller the volume, and vice-versa. The formula for Boyle's Law is:

PV=C
Where P= absolute pressure
V= volume
C= a constant

Charles' Law: **If the pressure is kept constant, the volume of a gas will vary directly as the ABSOLUTE temperature.** The amount of change in either volume or pressure is directly related to the change in absolute temperature. For example, if absolute temperature is doubled, then either the volume or the pressure also is doubled. The formula for Charles' Law is:

$PV=RT$ or $PV=\dfrac{R}{T}$

Where P= absolute pressure
V= volume
T= absolute temperature
R= a universal constant for all gases

General Gas Law: Boyle's Law illustrates pressure/volume relationships, and Charles' Law basically describes the effect of temperature changes on pressure and/or volume. The General Gas Law is a combination of these two laws. It is used to predict the behavior of a given quantity of gas when changes may be expected in any or all of the variables. The formula for the General Gas Law is:

$$\frac{P_1V_1}{T_1} = \frac{P_2V_2}{T_2}$$

Where P_1 = initial pressure (absolute)
V_1 = initial volume
T_1 = initial temperature (absolute)
P_2 = final pressure (absolute)
V_2 = final volume
T_2 = final temperature (absolute)

Dalton's Law: **The total pressure exerted by a mixture of gases is equal to the sum of the pressures of each of the different gases making up the mixture—each gas acting as if it alone was present and occupied the total volume.** The whole is equal to the sum of its parts and each part is not affected by any of the other parts. The pressure of any gas in the mixture is proportional to the number of molecules of that gas in the total volume. The pressure of each gas is called its partial pressure (pp), meaning its part of the whole. Dalton's Law is sometimes referred to as "the law of partial pressures." The formula for Dalton's Law is:

$$P_{Total} = PP_A + PP_B + PP_C .....$$

and

$$PP_A = P_{Total} \times \frac{\%Vol._A}{100\%}$$

Where P_{Total} = Total absolute pressure of gas mixture
PP_A = Partial pressure of gas A
PP_B = Partial pressure of gas B
PP_C = Partial pressure of gas C

Henry's Law: **The amount of a gas that will dissolve in a liquid at a given temperature is almost directly proportional to the partial pressure of that gas.** If one unit of gas dissolves in a liquid at one atmosphere, then two units will dissolve at two atmospheres, three units at three atmospheres, etc.

AIR CONSUMPTION FORMULA/TABLE

Knowing your air consumption rate is very important. By determining your consumption rate at the surface, it becomes a simple matter to calculate what it will be at any given depth. Since pressure gauges are calibrated in pounds per square inch (PSI), your consumption rate must be in PSI too. The formula is as follows:

$$\frac{PSI \div TIME}{33/33 + DEPTH/33}$$

PSI = PSI consumed in timed swim at a constant depth.

TIME = Duration of timed swim.

DEPTH = Depth of timed swim.

EXAMPLE:

A diver swims at a depth of 10 feet for 10 minutes and consumes 300 PSI of air. You want to determine his surface consumption expressed in PSI.

$$\frac{300 \ (PSI \ used) \div 10 \ (Time) = 30}{33/33 \ + 10 \ (Depth)/33 \ = 43/33} = \frac{30 \times 33}{43} = \frac{990}{43} = 23.02$$

23.02 PSI = PSI CONSUMED PER MINUTE AT SURFACE

NOTE: Consumption rate must be recalculated if tank size is changed.

AIR CONSUMPTION TABLE AT DEPTH

DEPTH IN FEET

Surface	10	15	20	25	30	40	50	60	70	80	90	100	120	140	160
15	19.5	21.8	24.0	27.0	28.5	33.0	37.5	42.0	46.5	51	55.5	60	69	78	87
16	20.8	23.2	25.6	28.8	30.4	35.2	40.0	44.8	49.6	54.4	59.2	64	73.6	83.2	92.8
17	22.1	24.7	27.2	30.6	32.3	37.4	42.5	47.6	52.7	57.8	62.9	68	78.2	88.4	98.6
18	23.4	26.1	28.8	32.4	34.2	39.6	45.0	50.4	55.8	61.2	66.6	72	82.8	93.6	104.4
19	24.7	27.6	30.4	34.2	36.1	41.8	47.5	53.2	58.9	64.6	70.3	76	87.4	98.8	110.2
20	26.	29.0	32.0	36.0	38.0	44.0	50.0	56.0	62.0	68.0	74.0	80	92	104	116
21	27.3	30.5	33.6	37.8	39.9	46.2	52.5	58.8	65.1	71.4	77.7	84	96.6	109.2	121.8
22	28.6	31.9	35.2	39.6	41.8	48.4	55.0	61.6	68.2	74.8	81.4	88	101.2	114.4	127.6
23	29.9	33.4	36.8	41.4	43.7	50.6	57.5	64.4	71.3	78.2	85.1	92	105.8	119.6	133.4
24	31.2	34.8	38.4	43.2	45.6	52.8	60.	67.2	74.4	81.6	88.8	96	110.4	124.8	139.2
25	32.5	36.3	40.0	45.0	47.5	55.0	62.5	70.0	77.5	85.0	92.5	100	115	130	145
26	33.8	37.7	41.6	46.8	49.4	57.2	65.0	72.8	80.6	88.4	96.2	104	119.6	135.2	150.8
27	35.1	39.2	43.2	48.6	51.3	59.4	67.5	75.6	83.7	91.8	99.9	108	124.2	140.4	156.6
28	36.4	40.6	44.8	50.4	53.2	61.6	70.	78.4	86.8	95.2	103.6	112	128.8	145.6	162.4
29	37.7	42.1	46.4	52.2	55.1	63.8	72.5	81.2	89.9	98.6	107.3	116	133.4	150.8	168.2
30	39.	43.5	48.0	54.	57.0	66.0	75.0	84.0	93.0	102.0	111.0	120	138	156	174
31	40.3	45.0	49.6	55.8	58.9	68.2	77.5	86.8	96.1	105.4	114.7	124	142.6	161.2	179.8
32	41.6	46.4	51.2	57.6	60.8	70.4	80.0	89.6	99.2	108.8	118.4	128	147.2	166.4	185.6
33	42.9	47.9	52.8	59.4	62.7	72.6	82.5	92.4	102.3	112.2	122.1	132	151.8	171.6	191.4
34	44.2	49.3	54.4	61.2	64.6	74.8	85.0	95.2	105.4	115.6	125.8	136	156.4	176.8	197.2
35	45.5	50.8	56.0	63.0	66.5	77.0	87.5	98.0	108.5	119.0	129.5	140	161	182	203
36	46.8	52.2	57.6	64.8	68.4	79.2	90.0	100.8	111.6	122.4	133.2	144	165.6	187.2	208.8
37	48.1	53.7	59.2	66.0	69.6	80.6	92.5	103.6	114.7	125.8	136.9	148	170.2	192.4	214.6
38	49.4	55.1	60.8	68.4	72.2	83.6	95.0	106.4	117.8	129.2	140.6	152	174.8	197.6	220.4
39	50.7	56.6	62.4	70.2	74.1	85.8	97.5	109.2	120.9	132.6	144.3	156	179.4	202.8	226.2
40	52	58.	64.0	72.0	76.0	88.0	100.	112.0	124.0	136.	148.0	160	184	208	232

CONSUMPTION RATE AT SURFACE (PSI PER MINUTE)

sport diver open water u.s. navy dive tables

no-decompression limits and repetitive group designation table for no-decompression air dives

Depth (feet)	No-decompression limits (min)	A	B	C	D	E	F	G	H	I	J	K	L	M	N	O
10		60	120	210	300											
15		35	70	110	160	225	350									
20		25	50	75	100	135	180	240	325							
25	(245)	20	35	55	75	100	125	160	195	245	315					
30	(205)	15	30	45	60	75	95	120	145	170	205	250	310			
35	(160) 310	5	15	25	40	50	60	80	100	120	140	160	190	220	270	310
40	(130) 200	5	15	25	30	40	50	70	80	100	110	130	150	170	200	
50	(70) 100		10	15	25	30	40	50	60	70	80	90	100			
60	(50) 60		10	15	20	25	30	40	50	55	60					
70	(40) 50			5	10	15	20	30	35	40	45	50				
80	(30) 40			5	10	15	20	25	30	35	40					
90	(25) 30			5	10	12	15	20	25	30						
100	(20) 25			5		7	10	15	20	22	25					
110	(15) 20				5	10	13	15	20							
120	(10) 15				5	10	12	15								
130	(5) 10				5	8	10									
140	10				5	7	10									

residual nitrogen timetable for repetitive air dives

*Dives following surface intervals of more than 12 hours are not repetitive dives. Use actual bottom times in the Standard Air Decompression Tables to compute decompression for such dives.

The red line and red numbers on the no-decompression limits table above provide recommended limits based on ultrasound studies. The U.S. Navy Dive Table limits are based on extremely physically fit young males. For added safety, stop at 10 feet for one to three minutes at the end of each no-decompression dive. This helps to deplete most or all small nitrogen bubbles.

The black line on the lower table denotes U.S. Navy no-decompression limits. All residual nitrogen times listed to the left of the line will require the use of the Standard Air Decompression Table to compute decompression times and depths.

Repetitive group at the beginning of the surface interval

A	0:10 – 12:00*
B	0:10–2:10 / 2:11–12:00*
C	0:10–1:39 / 1:40–2:49 / 2:50–12:00*
D	0:10–1:09 / 1:10–2:38 / 2:39–5:48 / 5:49–12:00*
E	0:10–0:54 / 0:55–1:57 / 1:58–3:22 / 3:23–6:32 / 6:33–12:00*
F	0:10–0:45 / 0:46–1:29 / 1:30–2:28 / 2:29–3:57 / 3:58–7:05 / 7:06–12:00*
G	0:10–0:40 / 0:41–1:15 / 1:16–1:59 / 2:00–2:58 / 2:59–4:25 / 4:26–7:35 / 7:36–12:00*
H	0:10–0:36 / 0:37–1:06 / 1:07–1:41 / 1:42–2:23 / 2:24–3:20 / 3:21–4:49 / 4:50–7:59 / 8:00–12:00*
I	0:10–0:33 / 0:34–0:59 / 1:00–1:29 / 1:30–2:02 / 2:03–2:44 / 2:45–3:43 / 3:44–5:12 / 5:13–8:21 / 8:22–12:00*
J	0:10–0:31 / 0:32–0:54 / 0:55–1:19 / 1:20–1:47 / 1:48–2:20 / 2:21–3:04 / 3:05–4:02 / 4:03–5:40 / 5:41–8:40 / 8:41–12:00*
K	0:10–0:28 / 0:29–0:49 / 0:50–1:11 / 1:12–1:35 / 1:36–2:03 / 2:04–2:38 / 2:39–3:21 / 3:22–4:19 / 4:20–5:48 / 5:49–8:58 / 8:59–12:00*
L	0:10–0:26 / 0:27–0:45 / 0:46–1:04 / 1:05–1:25 / 1:26–1:49 / 1:50–2:19 / 2:20–2:53 / 2:54–3:36 / 3:37–4:35 / 4:36–6:02 / 6:03–9:12 / 9:13–12:00*
M	0:10–0:25 / 0:26–0:42 / 0:43–0:59 / 1:00–1:18 / 1:19–1:39 / 1:40–2:05 / 2:06–2:34 / 2:35–3:08 / 3:09–3:52 / 3:53–4:49 / 4:50–6:18 / 6:19–9:28 / 9:29–12:00*
N	0:10–0:24 / 0:25–0:39 / 0:40–0:54 / 0:55–1:11 / 1:12–1:30 / 1:31–1:53 / 1:54–2:18 / 2:19–2:47 / 2:48–3:22 / 3:23–4:04 / 4:05–5:03 / 5:04–6:32 / 6:33–9:43 / 9:44–12:00*
O	0:10–0:23 / 0:24–0:36 / 0:37–0:51 / 0:52–1:07 / 1:08–1:24 / 1:25–1:43 / 1:44–2:04 / 2:05–2:29 / 2:30–2:59 / 3:00–3:33 / 3:34–4:17 / 4:18–5:16 / 5:17–6:44 / 6:45–9:54 / 9:55–12:00*
Z	0:10–0:22 / 0:23–0:34 / 0:35–0:48 / 0:49–1:02 / 1:03–1:18 / 1:19–1:36 / 1:37–1:55 / 1:56–2:17 / 2:18–2:42 / 2:43–3:10 / 3:11–3:45 / 3:46–4:29 / 4:30–5:27 / 5:28–6:56 / 6:57–10:05 / 10:06–12:00*

residual nitrogen times (minutes)

NEW GROUP DESIGNATION →	Z	O	N	M	L	K	J	I	H	G	F	E	D	C	B	A
REPETITIVE DIVE DEPTH																
40	257	241	213	187	161	138	116	101	87	73	61	49	37	25	17	7
50	169	160	142	124	111	99	87	76	66	56	47	38	29	21	13	6
60	122	117	107	97	88	79	70	61	52	44	36	30	24	17	11	5
70	100	96	87	80	72	64	57	50	43	37	31	26	20	15	9	4
80	84	80	73	68	61	54	48	43	38	32	28	23	18	13	8	4
90	73	70	64	58	53	47	43	38	33	29	24	20	16	11	7	3
100	64	62	57	52	48	43	38	34	30	26	22	18	14	10	7	3
110	57	55	51	47	42	38	34	31	27	24	20	16	13	10	6	3
120	52	50	46	43	39	35	32	28	25	21	18	15	12	9	6	3
130	46	44	40	38	35	31	28	25	22	19	16	13	11	8	6	3
140	42	40	38	35	32	29	26	23	20	18	15	12	10	7	5	2

JEPPESEN

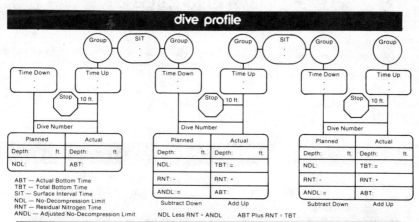

dive profile

ABT — Actual Bottom Time
TBT — Total Bottom Time
SIT — Surface Interval Time
NDL — No-Decompression Limit
RNT — Residual Nitrogen Time
ANDL — Adjusted No-Decompression Limit

Subtract Down   Add Up
NDL Less RNT = ANDL   ABT Plus RNT = TBT

u.s. navy standard air decompression table

Depth (feet)	Bottom time (min)	Time first stop (min:sec)	Decompression stops (feet) 20	Decompression stops (feet) 10	Total ascent (min:sec)	Repetitive group
40	200			0	0:40	*
	210	0:30		2	2:40	N
	230	0:30		7	7:40	N
	250	0:30		11	11:40	O
50	100			0	0:50	*
	110	0:40		3	3:50	L
	120	0:40		5	5:50	M
	140	0:40		10	10:50	M
	160	0:40		21	21:50	N
60	60			0	1:00	*
	70	0:50		2	3:00	K
	80	0:50		7	8:00	L
	100	0:50		14	15:00	M
	120	0:50		26	27:00	N
70	50			0	1:10	*
	60	1:00		8	9:10	K
	70	1:00		14	15:10	L
	80	1:00		18	19:10	M
	90	1:00		23	24:10	N
80	40			0	1:20	*
	50	1:10		10	11:20	K
	60	1:10		17	18:20	L
	70	1:10		23	24:20	M
90	30			0	1:30	*
	40	1:20		7	8:30	J
	50	1:20		18	19:30	L
	60	1:20		25	26:30	M
100	25			0	1:40	*
	30	1:30		3	4:40	I
	40	1:30		15	16:40	K
	50	1:20	2	24	27:40	L
110	20			0	1:50	*
	25	1:40		3	4:50	H
	30	1:40		7	8:50	J
	40	1:30	2	21	24:50	L
120	15			0	2:00	*
	20	1:50		2	4:00	H
	25	1:50		6	8:00	I
	30	1:50		14	16:00	J
130	10			0	2:10	*
	15	2:00		1	3:10	F
	20	2:00		4	6:10	H
	25	2:00		10	12:10	J
140	10			0	2:20	*
	15	2:10		2	4:20	G
	20	2:10		6	8:20	I
	25	2:00	2	14	18:20	J

*See No Decompression Table for Repetitive Groups

LOCATING YOUR NEAREST RECOMPRESSION CHAMBER

The following numbers may be called 24 hours a day, seven days a week. Physicians are on call and consultation can be provided on air embolism or decompression sickness cases. Each maintains a world-wide listing of recompression chambers.

Divers Alert Network
DAN
(919) 684-8111

U.S. Navy Experimental Diving Unit
EDU Duty Phone
(904) 234-4353

EQUIPMENT CHECKLIST

DIVING EQUIPMENT

_____ SWIM SUIT
_____ MASK & ANTI-FOG SOLUTION
_____ SNORKEL & KEEPER
_____ FINS
_____ WET SUIT
  _____ JACKET
  _____ BOOTS
  _____ GLOVES
  _____ PANTS
  _____ VEST
  _____ HOOD
_____ WEIGHT BELT & WEIGHTS
_____ BUOYANCY COMPENSATOR
_____ FULL SCUBA TANK & BACKPACK
_____ REGULATOR
_____ SUBMERSIBLE PRESSURE GAUGE
_____ WATCH
_____ DEPTH GAUGE
_____ COMPASS
_____ DECOMPRESSION TABLES
_____ DIVER'S FLAG/FLOAT & ANCHOR/LINE
_____ WHISTLE
_____ KNIFE
_____ LOGBOOK & PENCIL
_____ GEAR BAG

OTHER ITEMS

_____ DRY CLOTHES
_____ TOWELS
_____ FOOD & DRINKING WATER
_____ SUNGLASSES
_____ SUNTAN LOTION
_____ LOGBOOK
_____ CERTIFICATION CARD
_____ SPORT DIVING MANUAL

SPECIALTY EQUIPMENT

_____ DECOMPRESSION COMPUTER
_____ THERMOMETER
_____ EMERGENCY FLARE
_____ LIGHT & BATTERIES
_____ SLATE & PENCIL
_____ SAFETY LINE (200 FT.)
_____ BUDDY LINE (6 FT.)

_____ LIFT BAG
_____ PHOTOGRAPHY EQUIPMENT
  _____ FLASH
  _____ CAMERA
  _____ FILM
  _____ FLASHBULBS
  _____ BATTERIES
_____ SPEARFISHING GEAR
  _____ SPEAR
  _____ FISHING LICENSE
  _____ GAME BAG

SPARE PARTS & REPAIR KIT

_____ MASK STRAP & BUCKLE
_____ FIN STRAP & BUCKLE
_____ "O" RINGS
_____ CO_2 CARTRIDGES
_____ FIRST STAGE REGULATOR HIGH PRESSURE PLUG
_____ SILICONE SPRAY OR GREASE
_____ WET SUIT CEMENT
_____ NEEDLE & THREAD
_____ EXTRA MASK LENS
_____ WATERPROOF PLASTIC TAPE
_____ PLIERS
_____ WRENCH
_____ SCREWDRIVER
_____ SMALL KNIFE
_____ BUOYANCY VEST PATCHES

FIRST AID KIT

_____ ADHESIVE TAPE
_____ ALCOHOL SOLUTION (70%)
_____ AMMONIA SOLUTION
_____ ANTISEPTIC SPRAY
_____ ADHESIVE STRIPS
_____ BUTTERFLY CLOSURES
_____ COMPRESSES
_____ COTTON SWABS
_____ RAZOR BLADE
_____ SCISSORS
_____ SNAKEBITE KIT
_____ SPLINTS
_____ SOAP
_____ SEASICK PILLS
_____ DIMES & EMERGENCY PHONE NUMBERS
_____ BAKING SODA
_____ NASAL DECONGESTANT

TIDAL CURRENT TABLES

TABLE 1 — DAILY CURRENT PREDICTIONS

Table 1 gives the predicted times of slack water and the predicted times and velocities of maximum current — flood and ebb — for each day of the year at a number of stations. The times are given in hours and minutes and the velocities in knots.

ADMIRALTY INLET (off Bush Pt.), WASHINGTON, 19____

F - Flood, Dir. 180° True   E - Ebb, Dir. 005° True

JANUARY

Day	Slack Water Time (h.m.)	Max Current Time (h.m.)	Vel. (knots)
1 Sa	0028	0345	3.6F
	0721	1017	2.5E
	1347	1536	0.8F
	1718	2139	4.0E
2 Su	0116	0433	3.5F
	0804	1108	2.6E
	1446	1633	0.8F
	1817	2233	3.6E
3 M	0206	0521	3.2F
	0847	1157	2.7E
	1548	1735	0.8F
	1922	2329	3.1E
4 Tu	0257	0610	2.8F
	0928	1251	2.8E
	1652	1845	0.8F
	2038		
5 W		0031	2.5E
	0352	0700	2.3F
	1008	1346	2.9E
	1754	1956	0.9F
	2207		
6 Th		0138	2.0E
	0453	0754	1.9F
	1047	1439	3.0E
	1852	2110	1.1F
	2345		
7 F		0256	1.6E
	0601	0848	1.4F
	1126	1534	3.1E
	1945	2225	1.5F
8 Sa	0120	0414	1.4E
	0717	0950	1.0F
	1203	1627	3.2E
	2032	2322	1.8F
9 Su	0239	0527	1.3E
	0834	1043	0.8F
	1241	1712	3.3E
	2115		
10 M		0016	2.1F
	0342	0629	1.4E
	0945	1135	0.6F
	1319	1758	3.4E
	2155		
11 Tu		0103	2.4F
	0432	0722	1.5E
	1046	1224	0.5F
	1358	1839	3.4E
	2233		
12 W		0144	2.5F
	0514	0807	1.7E
	1138	1308	0.4F
	1435	1919	3.4E
	2308		
13 Th		0221	2.6F
	0551	0846	1.8E
	1224	1348	0.4F
	1513	1954	3.3E
	2341		
14 F		0254	2.7F
	0625	0923	1.9E
	1306	1430	0.4F
	1549	2029	3.2E
15 Sa	0013	0326	2.7F
	0656	0958	2.0E
	1347	1507	0.4F
	1625	2104	3.1E
16 Su	0045	0358	2.6F
	0726	1033	2.0E
	1427	1544	0.3F
	1702	2139	3.0E
17 M	0118	0430	2.5F
	0754	1103	2.1E
	1507	1624	0.3F
	1744	2216	2.7E
18 Tu	0152	0501	2.3F
	0822	1139	2.2E
	1548	1713	0.4F
	1834	2255	2.4E
19 W	0228	0536	2.1F
	0848	1213	2.3E
	1629	1759	0.4F
	1935	2340	2.1E
20 Th	0309	0613	1.8F
	0914	1254	2.4E
	1712	1900	0.6F
	2052		
21 F		0036	1.7E
	0356	0655	1.5F
	0942	1336	2.6E
	1756	2003	0.8F
	2224		
22 Sa		0143	1.4E
	0454	0742	1.2F
	1012	1427	2.8E
	1842	2113	1.2F
23 Su	0004	0300	1.2E
	0607	0833	0.9F
	1047	1518	3.0E
	1930	2222	1.6F
24 M	0137	0425	1.2E
	0729	0936	0.7F
	1131	1615	3.3E
	2018	2323	2.1F
25 Tu	0252	0536	1.4E
	0849	1042	0.6F
	1224	1710	3.6E
	2106		
26 W		0018	2.6F
	0353	0640	1.6E
	0956	1145	0.7F
	1324	1804	3.9E
	2154		
27 Th		0109	3.1F
	0444	0733	2.0E
	1053	1242	0.8F
	1427	1859	4.1E
	2242		
28 F		0157	3.4F
	0530	0822	2.3E
	1144	1340	1.0F
	1530	1948	4.2E
	2329		
29 Sa		0242	3.5F
	0612	0909	2.6E
	1233	1433	1.1F
	1631	2039	4.1E
30 Su	0016	0328	3.5F
	0652	0954	2.8E
	1323	1528	1.3F
	1731	2132	3.9E

FEBRUARY

Day	Slack Water Time (h.m.)	Max Current Time (h.m.)	Vel. (knots)
1 Tu	0150	0455	3.0F
	0806	1125	3.1E
	1506	1719	1.3F
	1935	2314	2.9E
2 W	0238	0540	2.5F
	0841	1212	3.1E
	1602	1819	1.3F
	2043		
3 Th		0012	2.4E
	0330	0625	2.0F
	0915	1301	3.1E
	1700	1926	1.3F
	2200		
4 F		0115	1.8E
	0428	0713	1.5F
	0949	1352	3.0E
	1800	2037	1.3F
	2327		
5 Sa		0226	1.4E
	0537	0809	1.0F
	1023	1446	2.9E
	1859	2146	1.5F
6 Su	0056	0349	1.2E
	0702	0905	0.6F
	1100	1545	2.9E
	1954	2254	1.7F
7 M	0215	0507	1.2E
	0832	1009	0.4F
	1143	1641	2.9E
	2045	2351	1.9F
8 Tu	0317	0610	1.3E
	0948	1110	0.3F
	1234	1732	3.0E
	2129		
9 W		0038	2.1F
	0405	0703	1.5E
	1043	1205	0.3F
	1329	1818	3.0E
	2210		
10 Th		0119	2.3F
	0445	0748	1.7E
	1126	1255	0.4F
	1422	1859	3.1E
	2246		
11 F		0154	2.4F
	0519	0821	1.9E
	1201	1338	0.5F
	1511	1941	3.1E
	2320		
12 Sa		0230	2.5F
	0550	0852	2.1E
	1234	1417	0.6F
	1556	2014	3.1E
	2353		
13 Su		0300	2.5F
	0618	0925	2.2E
	1305	1452	0.7F
	1639	2048	3.0E
14 M	0025	0332	2.5F
	0643	0954	2.3E
	1335	1530	0.8F
	1723	2127	2.9E
15 Tu	0058	0400	2.3F
	0707	1024	2.5E
	1406	1607	0.9F
	1809	2202	2.7E
16 W	0131	0428	2.1F
	0729	1052	2.6E
	1440	1650	1.0F
	1859	2239	2.4E
17 Th	0207	0458	1.9F
	0751	1127	2.7E
	1517	1731	1.1F
	1955	2326	2.1E
18 F	0248	0533	1.6F
	0815	1202	2.7E
	1600	1825	1.2F
	2101		
19 Sa		0015	1.7E
	0336	0614	1.2F
	0840	1245	2.8E
	1650	1924	1.3F
	2219		
20 Su		0120	1.4E
	0437	0657	0.9F
	0911	1336	2.9E
	1746	2033	1.5F
	2348		
21 M		0240	1.2E
	0557	0758	0.6F
	0950	1435	3.0E
	1846	2150	1.8F
22 Tu	0116	0409	1.2E
	0731	0914	0.4F
	1044	1543	3.1E
	1946	2257	2.2F
23 W	0229	0523	1.5E
	0853	1027	0.4F
	1157	1650	3.3E
	2043	2354	2.6F
24 Th	0327	0627	1.8E
	0953	1139	0.6F
	1318	1752	3.6E
	2137		
25 F		0050	2.9F
	0416	0715	2.2E
	1041	1240	0.9F
	1434	1847	3.8E
	2228		
26 Sa		0139	3.1F
	0458	0801	2.6E
	1126	1336	1.3F
	1542	1943	3.8E
	2316		
27 Su		0222	3.2F
	0537	0845	2.9E
	1210	1430	1.6F
	1645	2033	3.8E
28 M	0002	0305	3.1F
	0612	0926	3.2E
	1253	1519	1.8F
	1744	2121	3.5E

TABLE 2 — CURRENT DIFFERENCES AND OTHER CONSTANTS

Table 2 contains mean time differences by which the reader can compile approximate times for the minimum and maximum current phases at the subordinate stations. Time differences for those phases should be applied to the corresponding phases at the reference station. It should be noted that although the speed of a given current phase at a subordinate station is obtained by reference to the corresponding phase at the reference station, the directions of the current at the two places may differ considerably. Table 2 lists the average directions of the various current phases at the subordinate stations.

NO.	PLACE	METER DEPTH (ft)	POSITION Lat. (° ' N)	Long. (° ' W)	TIME DIFFERENCES Min. before Flood (h.m.)	Flood (h.m.)	Min. before Ebb (h.m.)	Ebb (h.m.)	SPEED RATIOS Flood	Ebb	AVG. Minimum before Flood (knots)	(deg.)	Maximum Flood (knots)	(deg.)	Minimum before Ebb (knots)	(deg.)	Maximum Ebb (knots)	(deg.)
	ADMIRALTY INLET Time meridian, 120°W				on ADMIRALTY INLET, p.34 <20>													
	Marrowstone Point																	
985	1.1 miles northwest of <27>		48 07	122 42	-3 31	-2 20	-1 02	-1 42	0.8	0.5	0.0	--	1.3	100	0.0	--	1.3	275
990	0.4 mile northeast of <27>		48 06	122 41	-1 20	-1 03	-0 04	-1 03	1.1	1.1	0.0	--	2.4	122	0.0	--	3.1	338
995	0.3 mile northeast of		48 06	122 41	-0 53	-1 36	-1 13	-0 13	1.2	1.2	0.0	--	2.3	170	0.0	--	2.8	015
1000	1.6 miles northeast of <27>		48 07	122 40	-0 16	+0 07	-0 03	-0 17	1.2	1.2	0.0	--	2.3	152	0.0	--	2.6	344
1005	2.5 miles northeast of <28>		48 08	122 38	--	--	--	--	--	--	--	--	--	--	--	--	--	--
1010	Nodule Point, 0.5 mile southeast of		48 02	122 40	-1 27	-0 47	-0 59	-0 24	1.2	1.0	0.0	--	2.0	160	0.0	--	2.5	339
1015	ADMIRALTY INLET (off Bush Point)		48 02	122 38	Daily Predictions						0.0	--	1.6	179	0.0	--	2.6	003
	HOOD CANAL																	
1040	Foulweather Bluff		47 56	122 38	0 00	-0 24	-0 15	-0 25	0.4	0.4	0.0	--	0.7	140	0.0	--	0.9	325
1045	Port Gamble Bay, 0.5 mile N of entrance.		47 52	122 38	Current weak and variable													
1050	Port Gamble Bay entrance.		47 51	122 35	-1 03	-0 39	+0 04	-0 14	0.6	0.3	0.0	--	0.9	185	0.0	--	0.7	000
1055	Port Gamble Bay.		47 50	122 34	Current weak and variable													
1060	South Point.		47 49	122 41	--	-0 44	--	-0 29	0.4	0.4	0.0	--	0.6	218	0.0	--	1.0	040
	PUGET SOUND																	
1080	Useless Bay.		47 59	122 30	Current weak and variable													
1085	Foulweather Bluff.		47 57	122 35	+0 09	+0 01	+0 14	-0 18	0.9	0.7	0.0	--	1.5	115	0.0	--	1.8	335
1090	Edmonds, 2.7 miles WSW of.		47 48	122 27	+0 44	+0 06	+0 13	+0 19	0.1	0.1	0.0	--	0.2	170	0.0	--	0.5	000
1095	Apple Cove Point, 0.5 mile east of.		47 49	122 28	--	-0 11	--	-0 29	0.3	0.3	0.0	--	0.5	168	0.0	--	0.8	008
1100	President Point, 1.5 miles east of.		47 46	122 26	--	-0 38	--	-0 41	0.2	0.2	0.0	--	0.3	203	0.0	--	0.5	024
1105	Port Madison entrance.		47 43	122 30	Current weak and variable													
1110	Agate Passage, north end.		47 43	122 33	-1 28	-1 00	-0 18	-0 59	0.8	0.7	0.0	--	1.2	230	0.0	--	1.8	032
1115	Agate Passage, south end <27>		47 43	122 34	-1 25	-0 53	0 00	-0 47	2.0	1.4	0.0	--	3.3	216	0.0	--	3.6	037
1120	Port Orchard.		47 38	122 35	Current weak and variable													
1125	Port Orchard, off Keyport.		47 42	122 36	Current weak and variable													
1155	Alki Point, 0.3 mile west of.		47 35	122 26	-0 36	-0 44	-0 13	-0 39	0.3	0.2	0.0	--	0.5	160	0.0	--	0.5	330
1160	Restoration Point, 0.6 mile ESE of.		47 35	122 28	--	-0 38	--	-0 06	0.3	0.3	0.0	--	0.5	135	0.0	--	0.7	034

Endnotes can be found at the end of Table 2.

TABLE 4 — DURATION OF SLACK

The predicted times of slack water given in the Tidal Current Tables indicate the instant of zero velocity, which is only momentary. There is a period each side of slack water, however, during which the current is so weak that, for practical purposes, it may be considered negligible.

The following tables give, for various maximum currents, the approximate period of time during which weak currents not exceeding 0.1 to 0.5 knot will be encountered. This duration includes the last of the flood or ebb and the beginning of the following ebb or flood; that is, half of the duration will be before and half after the time of slack water.

Table A should be used for all places *except* those listed below for Table B.

Table B should be used for **Decepton Pass, Seymour Narrows, Sergius Narrows, Isanotski Strait,** and all stations in Table 2 which are referred to them.

TABLE A

Maximum current	Period with a velocity not more than —				
	0.1 knot	0.2 knot	0.3 knot	0.4 knot	0.5 knot
Knots	Minutes	Minutes	Minutes	Minutes	Minutes
1.0	23	46	70	94	120
1.5	15	31	46	62	78
2.0	11	23	35	46	58
3.0	8	15	23	31	38
4.0	6	11	17	23	29
5.0	5	9	14	18	23
6.0	4	8	11	15	19
7.0	3	7	10	13	16
8.0	3	6	9	11	14
9.0	3	5	8	10	13
10.0	2	5	7	9	11
11.0	2	4	6	8	10
12.0	2	4	6	8	10

TABLE B

Maximum current	Period with a velocity not more than —				
	0.1 knot	0.2 knot	0.3 knot	0.4 knot	0.5 knot
Knots	Minutes	Minutes	Minutes	Minutes	Minutes
1.0	13	28	46	66	89
1.5	8	18	28	39	52
2.0	6	13	20	28	36
3.0	4	8	13	18	22
4.0	3	6	9	13	17
5.0	3	5	8	10	13
6.0	2	4	6	8	11
7.0	2	4	5	7	9
8.0	2	3	5	6	8

When there is a difference between the velocities of the maximum flood and ebb preceding and following the slack for which the duration is desired, it will be sufficiently accurate for practical purposes to find a separate duration for each maximum velocity and take the average of the two as the duration of the weak current.

TIDAL CURRENT WORKSHEET

DIVE DATE	MINIMUM SLACK BEFORE FLOOD	MAXIMUM FLOOD	MINIMUM SLACK BEFORE EBB	MAXIMUM EBB
TIME ESTIMATES Reference Station (Table1)				
Subordinate Station (Table 2) Correction Factor				
Subordinate Station Time				
Duration Correction(Table 4)				
Actual Dive Time (Start)				
CURRENT VELOCITY (Table 2)				
Average Speed	///////		///////	
Direction	///////		///////	

TIDAL CURRENT WORKSHEET

DIVE DATE	MINIMUM SLACK BEFORE FLOOD	MAXIMUM FLOOD	MINIMUM SLACK BEFORE EBB	MAXIMUM EBB
TIME ESTIMATES Reference Station (Table1)				
Subordinate Station (Table 2) Correction Factor				
Subordinate Station Time				
Duration Correction(Table 4)				
Actual Dive Time (Start)				
CURRENT VELOCITY (Table 2)				
Average Speed	///////		///////	
Direction	///////		///////	

METRIC SYSTEM

UNIT	ABBREVIATION	NUMBER OF	APPROXIMATE U.S. EQUIVALENT
LENGTH			
myriameter	mym	10,000 meters	6.2 miles
kilometer	km	1,000 meters	0.62 mile
hectometer	hm	100 meters	109.36 yards
dekameter	dam	10 meters	32.81 feet
meter	m	1 meters	39.37 inches
decimeter	dm	0.1 meters	3.94 inches
centimeter	cm	0.01 meters	0.39 inch
millimeter	mm	0.001 meters	0.04 inch
AREA			
square kilometer	sq km or km^2	1,000,000 sq. meters	0.3861 square mile
hectare	ha	10,000 sq. meters	2.47 acres
arc	a	100 sq. meters	119.60 square yards
centare	ca	1 sq. meters	10.76 square feet
square centimeter	sq cm or cm^2	0.0001 sq. meters	0.155 square inch
VOLUME			
dekastere	das	10 cubic meters	13.10 cubic yards
stere	s	1 cubic meters	1.31 cubic yards
decistere	ds	0.10 cubic meters	3.53 cubic feet
cubic centimeter	cu cm or cm' also cc	0.000001 cubic meters	0.061 cubic inch

CAPACITY

UNIT	ABBREVIATION	NUMBER OF	CUBIC	DRY	LIQUID
kiloliter	kl	1,000 liters	1.31 cubic yards		
hectoliter	hl	100 liters	3.53 cubic feet	2.84 bushels	
dekaliter	dal	10 liters	0.35 cubic foot	1.14 pecks	2.64 gallons
liter	l	1 liters	61.02 cubic inches	0.908 quart	1.057 quarts
deciliter	dl	0.10 liters	6.1 cubic inches	0.18 pint	0.21 pint
centiliter	cl	0.01 liters	0.6 cubic inch		0.338 fluidounce
milliliter	ml	0.001 liters	0.06 cubic inch		0.27 fluidram

TABLE OF CONVERSION FACTORS

TO CONVERT			MULTIPLY BY	TO CONVERT			MULTIPLY BY
LENGTH				**AREA**			
cm	to	inches	0.394	cm^2	to	inches^2	0.155
meters		feet	3.28	meters^2		feet^2	10.76
kilometers		nautical miles	0.540	kilometers^2		miles^2	0.386
inches	to	cm	2.54	inches^2	to	cm^2	6.45
feet		meters	0.3048	feet^2		meters^2	0.093
nautical miles		kilometers	1.853	miles^2		kilometers^2	0.3861
VOLUME AND CAPACITY				**WEIGHT**			
cc or ml	to	cu. inches	0.061	grams	to	ounces	0.035
cu. meters		cu. feet	35.31	kilograms		pounds	2.205
liters		cu. inches	61.02				
liters		cu. feet	0.035	ounces	to	grams	28.35
liters		fluid oz	33.81	pounds		kilograms	0.454
liters		quarts	1.057				
cu. inches	to	cc or ml	16.39	**TEMPERATURE**			
cu. feet		cu. meters	0.0283				
quarts		liters	0.946	°C	to	°F	9/5 then add 32
				°F		°C	5/9 after subtracting 32

TO CONVERT			MULTIPLY BY
PRESSURE			
pounds per sq. in.	to	kg/cm^2	0.0703
pounds per sq. in.		cm of Hg	5.17
pounds per sq. in.		ft. of sea water	2.18
feet of sea water		psi	0.445

U.S. WEIGHTS AND MEASURES

UNIT	ABBREVIATION OR SYMBOL	U.S. EQUIVALENT	APPROXIMATE METRIC EQUIVALENT
LENGTH			
mile	mi	5280 feet, 320 rods, 1760 yards	1,609 kilometers
rod	rd	5.50 yards, 16.5 feet	5.029 meters
yard	yd	3 feet, 36 inches	0.914 meters
foot	ft or '	12 inches, 0.333 yards	30.480 centimeters
inch	in or "	0.083 feet, 0.027 yards	2.540 centimeters
AREA			
square mile	sq mi or m^2	640 acres, 102,400 square rods	2.590 square kilometers
acre		4840 square yards, 43,560 square feet	0.405 hectares, 4047 square meters
square rod	sq rd or rd^2	30.25 square yards, 0.006 acres	25.293 square meters
square yard	sq yd or yd^2	1296 square inches, 9 square feet	0.836 square meters
square foot	sq ft or ft^2	144 square inches, 0.111 square yards	0.093 square meters
square inch	sq in or in^2	0.007 square feet, 0.00077 square yards	6.451 square centimeters
VOLUME			
cubic yard	cu yd or yd^3	27 cubic feet, 46,656 cubic inches	0.765 cubic meters
cubic foot	cu ft or ft^3	1728 cubic inches, 0.0370 cubic yards	0.028 cubic meters
cubic inch	cu in or in^3	0.00058 cubic feet, 0.000021 cubic yards	16.387 cubic centimeters
CAPACITY			
		U.S. liquid measure	
gallon	gal	4 quarts (231 cubic inches)	3.785 liters
quart	qt	2 pints (57.75 cubic inches)	0.946 liters
pint	pt	4 gills (28.875 cubic inches)	0.473 liters
gill	gi	4 fluidounces (7.218 cubic inches)	118.291 milliliters
fluidounce	fl oz	8 fluidrams (1.804 cubic inches)	29.573 milliliters
fluidram	fl dr	60 minims (0.225 cubic inches)	3.696 milliliters
minim	min	1/00 fluidram (0.003759 cubic inches)	0.061610 milliliters
WEIGHT			
		Avoirdupois	
ton			
short ton		20 short hundredweight, 2000 pounds	0.907 metric tons
long ton		20 long hundredweight, 2240 pounds	1.016 metric tons
hundredweight	cwt		
short hundredweight		100 pounds, 0.05 short tons	45.159 kilograms
long hundredweight		112 pounds, 0.05 long tons	50.802 kilograms
pound	lb	16 ounces, 7000 grains	0.453 kilograms
ounce	ox	16 drams, 437.5 grains	28.349 grams
dram	dr	27.343 grains, 0.0625 ounces	1.771 grams
grain	gr	0.036 drams, 0.002285 ounces	0.0648 grams
		Troy	
pound	lb t	12 ounces, 240 pennyweight, 5760 grains	0.373 kilograms
ounce	oz t	20 pennyweight, 480 grains	31.103 grams
pennyweight	dwt also pwt	24 grains, 0.05 ounces	1.555 grams
grain	gr	0.042 pennyweight, 0.002083 ounces	0.0648 grams

index